Rule of Law and Democracy

International Studies in Sociology and Social Anthropology

VOLUME 115

Rule of Law and Democracy

Inquiries into Internal and External Issues

Edited by

Leonardo Morlino and Gianluigi Palombella

BRILL

LEIDEN • BOSTON
2010

Cover illustration: The Windmill at Sanssouci Park, Potsdam, Germany. The windmill's owner was brave enough to oppose the expropriation ordered by Friedrich II of Prussia when the latter wished to build his castle and gardens in mid XVIII century at Sanssouci. The owner received a favorable ruling by a judge in Berlin, and in this way became the first successful champion of the rule of law against absolutism. Photographer: Federico Arnao (iStockphoto).

This book is printed on acid-free paper.

Library of Congress Cataloging-in-Publication Data

Rule of law and democracy : inquiries into internal and external issues / edited by Leonardo Morlino and Gianluigi Palombella.
p. cm. — (International studies in sociology and social anthropology ; v. 115)
Includes bibliographical references and index.
ISBN 978-90-04-18169-4 (hardback : alk. paper) 1. Rule of law. 2. Democracy. I. Morlino, Leonardo, 1947– II. Palombella, Gianluigi. III. Title. IV. Series.

K3171.R8483 2010
340'.11—dc22

2009050330

ISSN 0074-8684
ISBN 978 90 04 18169 4

PRINTED IN THE NETHERLANDS

CONTENTS

PART THREE
THE INTERNATIONAL SPHERE

NOTES ON CONTRIBUTORS

Monica Ciobanu is assistant professor of sociology in the Department of Sociology and Criminal Justice at SUNY Plattsburgh. She has written about democratization in Eastern Europe and her current work is focused on issues of memory, truth, and justice after Communism.

Christian Joerges is Research Professor at the University of Bremen (Germany). Among his last publications, the "Darker Legacies of Law in Europe" belongs in his long-term project about anti-liberal traditions in Germany and Europe.

Poul Kjaer is a Research Fellow at the Cluster of Excellence "The Formation of Normative Orders" at the Goethe University, Frankfurt am Main. Recent key publications include: "Three Forms of Governance and Three Forms of Power", in E.O. Eriksen/Ch. Joerges/F. Rödl (Eds.): *Law, Democracy and Solidarity in a Post-national Union* (Routledge, Oxford, 2008) and "The Under-complexity of Democracy" in G.P. Calliess/A. Fischer-Lescano/D. Wielsch/P. Zumbansen (Hrsg.): *Soziologische Jurisprudenz.* (Gruyter-Verlag, Berlin, 2009).

Friedrich Kratochwil is Chair of International Politics at the European University Institute, Florence, Italy and professorial fellow of Kyung Hee University (Korea). He has published widely in American and European journals on international relations, social theory, international organizations, and international law.

Leonardo Morlino is Professor of Political Science at the Istituto Italiano id Scienze Umane in Florence (Italy) and director of the PhD Program in Political Science in the same Institute. He has widely published on democratizations in Southern and Eastern Europe and on the quality of democracy in the same areas and Latin America.

Gianluigi Palombella is Professor of Legal Philosophy at the University of Parma (Italy), and Inaugural Fellow 2009 at the "Straus Institute for Law and International Justice" at New York University. His last publications include "The Rule of Law, Democracy and International Law" in *Ratio*

Juris (Dec. 2007) and the volume *Relocating the Rule of Law* (Oxford 2009) which he co-edited.

Daniela Piana is Assistant Professor at the University of Bologna. She published extensively on judicial reforms in post communist countries, institutional and constitutional changes, rule of law and democracy. Her main publications include: *Costruire la democrazia* (2007) and *Judicial Accountabilities in New Europe* (2009).

INTRODUCTION

Leonardo Morlino and Gianluigi Palombella

The rule of law is one the most cherished ideals in international debate in the fields of law, politics, sociology and legal theory. In the present book, which develops a special issue of "Comparative Sociology", scholars from different disciplines deal with the import, problems and virtues of the rule of law in our contemporary society.

The works here gathered have asked some of the most crucial and strategic questions concerning the rule of law and its transformations. They show how the nature of the rule of law belongs inherently in law, while at the same time being at the center of political concerns and social science enquiry.

The rule of law generates contestations especially when it has to be squared with democracy, the social or welfare state, fundamental rights, and even when it is appealed to outside the national State. At the same time, however, it is very often considered as a necessary premise for these objectives to be achieved. This has been a reason for collecting new enquiries from more than one perspective and disciplinary field, and for resorting to both legal and political analyses, theoretical and empirical approaches. This choice contributes in widening the present debate and showing the complexities of the rule of law realities in some relevant contexts.

The rule of law is understood firstly by Gianluigi Palombella in a general essay, which draws a theoretical proposal, on conceptual, historical and comparative arguments. It provides, through the notions of liberty, legal non-domination, and the "duality" of law, for a fresh potential, suited to enhance the import of the Rule of law in the present State and the global transformations. Then, starting from the theoretical definition provided in the previous chapter, Leonardo Morlino suggests and elaborates on the two main empirical definitions of the rule of law that are necessary to understand and carry out research in transitional or hybrid cases and in consolidated democracies. Third, adopting a political science approach, Daniela Piana deals with the central institutional pillar of the Rule of law, i.e. independence and impartiality of adjudication. Judicial accountability is offered as the bridge between legal and political control, along the line that connects judicial governance, the rule of law and democratic government.

In part two, themes that are related to the European setting are addressed. Thus, in the fourth chapter Monica Ciobanu further applies the analytic framework of the democratic quality, where the rule of law is set up in connection to other dimensions, of the kind already identified by Morlino's chapter. The analyzed countries are Hungary and Poland, the 'old-new' members of EU as well as Bulgaria and Romania, the 'new-new' members. Her analysis points out virtues and some limits of the framework. In the fifth chapter, coping with the issue of the rule of law non-nationally-based, Poul Kjaer suggests the way through which legal control can develop in highly differentiated hybrid systems, like the EU, by resorting to a constitutionalism based on a conflict of laws three dimensional concept. The latter is capable of dealing with horizontal conflicts (among Member States), vertical conflicts (among the EU and members) and eventually horizontal conflicts on the level of functionally differentiated social wider structures. By addressing substantially similar concerns, in the sixth chapter, Christian Joerges presents one of the most fundamental questions in the debate about the meaning and import of the rule of law, a feature that was also famously emphasized by Friedrich von Hayek in the middle of last century. Is the idea of the Rule of law compatible with a commitment to social justice? At the core of the first great constitutional debate in the newly constituted Federal Republic of Germany, the issue is here also viewed as strategically inherent in the regional developments of the Rule of law in the European Union, and even more so after the enlargement to Eastern Europe.

Finally, part three switches the focus from Europe to the widest international and supranational spheres: the latter prove to be the most recent challenge to the normative interpretation of the rule of law, which is asked to extend itself beyond its familiar "state" dimension. According to Friedrich Kratochwill, in the seventh chapter, the liberal internationalist view of the rule of law can be questioned, from the perspective of the science of international relations, on the basis of the recurrent risk of abstractness and for the detachment of its formal universality from the material basis of political power. Such a problem, unsurprisingly, lies at the core of the ambiguities that the concept of "Rule of law" might evoke.

On the whole, all contributions are aimed at coming to terms with the rule of law from common concerns about its significance and reality, definitional soundness and empirical transformations. Thus, focus on feasibility is never pursued outside of a normative awareness about its theoretical shape. Despite flowing from common concerns, the contributions here presented cover a broad range of thematic enquiries. The book can hopefully do justice to the expectations of diverse interlocutors, whether interested in theoretical construction of a rule of law normative concept or in testing its operational value through the present and most challenging contexts. In so far as it succeeds even in making an interdisciplinary dialogue develop, it should hopefully promote as well the interest for further appraisals, beyond the current uses.

PART ONE

RULES OF LAW

CHAPTER ONE

THE RULE OF LAW AS AN INSTITUTIONAL IDEAL

Gianluigi Palombella

The rule of law is an institutional ideal concerning the law. Owing to its normative nature, in fact it has been held to mean different things at different times and in different contexts. Its complexity and contestability is due to many causes, including the interweaving of conceptual, historical, philosophical meanings. There is also the fact that the concept belongs in multiple domains, from law to political morality.

Thus, a general reconsideration, sensitive to such complexity, can emerge from pursuing historical, comparative, philosophical analyses and their interrelations. The issue can be addressed through various avenues: one of them is semantic, where rule of law is traditionally contrasted with the "rule of men"[1] through its *differentia specifica*. Although it may seem rather abstract, by initially following a similar path taking choices at the crossroads we can set the scene. We can approach the significance and deeper implications of general questions associated with an expression such as "Rule of Law."

However, an investigation on the rule of law aimed at making sense of its potentialities in the twenty-first century needs to move on to a historically oriented recognition, focusing on institutional and comparative analysis. Through the latter the rationale of different conceptions can be more intelligibly recognised. Thus, the normative meaning of the "rule of law" can be identified by tracing it back to its distinctive (English) institutional setting, one that can be better understood by contrasting it with other similar experiences (on the European continent, mainly, the pre-constitutional *Rechtsstaat*).

The normative meaning can be subsequently discussed and elaborated on through some of the theoretical issues that it raises in the

* I am grateful to Christine Chwacsza and Ana Vrdoljak for their precious and generous comments. I owe special thanks to Martin Krygier and Neil Walker for invaluable and ongoing conversations on the rule of law.

[1] Starting with Aristotle 1984:III 16 1287 a–b.

context of political, moral, and legal theoretical analysis. The rule of law confronts questions in turn concerning justice, the problem of liberty and non-domination, the balance between the right and the good, and of course, the validity of law.

The purpose of such reconsideration here is to suggest, carefully going through the stages just described, the meaning that the rule of law bears as: a) consistent with its historical constants, instead of being forged on a purely abstract basis; b) critically extendable to contemporary institutional transformations, even beyond the State; and c) conceptually sustainable on a philosophical and legal theoretical plane.

The rule of law ideal requires institutional settings that actually depend on time and context, but they must have in common coherence with the normative objective the ideal evokes. As I will maintain, this ideal concerns the law, not directly power or social organization. More specifically, it concerns the adequacy of legal institutions to prevent the law from turning itself into a sheer tool of domination, a manageable servant to political monopoly and instrumentalism.

Thus, the rule of law rests on a normative underlying structure, one that is often overlooked by scholarly debates, however concerned they are with the validity or morality of law, or with lists of formal or substantive requirements. This structure can be made to resurface: here it shall be essentially evoked through headings which include the "duality of law", institutional balance, and "non-domination" that I conceive as relevant features on a distinctive legal plane.

Preliminary Semantics: "Rule of Men" and "Rule by Law"

As an ideal, rule of law is not just a set of statements reflecting what is needed for law merely to be law. But the ideal is often conceived as mere compliance with the rules that law prescribes, assuming that some value can be found and cherished precisely within the certainty and predictability that enacted rules are trusted to grant.

Among the possible interpretations, we might understand the point of the contrast between rule of law and of men just by treasuring the very fact that some law does exist. However, this minimalist conclusion does not necessarily promise that the ideal called rule of law is thereby achieved. Yet, making the fact that some law exists a sufficient condition for fulfilment of the ideal happens to run against some simple common sense.

One explanation for this uneasiness lies with the rather unfocused or elusive issue about "who" or what "rules."[2] Should we just submit ourselves to a sovereign's sanctioned commands (Austin 1954)? Is this enough to dissolve the sheer "rule of men" and supersede it with "rule of law"?

According to Hayek (1960:153): "It is because the lawgiver does not know the particular cases to which his rules will apply, and it is because the judge who applies them has no choice in drawing the conclusions that follow from the existing body of rules and the particular facts of the case, that it can be said that laws and not men rule." In principle, if we expect the sheer form of law to generate the rule of law, thereby displacing the substantive issue of "who" rules, this hope is destined to be disappointed. Law as such does not promise that much.[3]

Although Aristotle thought of law in a rather evocative way, as reason without passion,[4] law could be apt to frame and serve both democratic and autocratic regimes. It has often been held that law's indeterminacy itself ultimately leads to opposite results depending on "political winds" (Gordon 1984:125). Even the liberal stance, that law is a limitation on power, is untenable. In fact, so the argument goes, law is ultimately just a product of the will of the most powerful class. The expectations with which law is burdened are bound to suffer such a weakness, if not to hide ideological purposes.

In abstract terms, then, it is hard to cast the revered flag of "rule of law, not men" in an innocent mode. "Rule of men," in the range of its semantics, includes rule which takes place also through law. This opens a path as well to another traditionally alleged adversary of the rule of law: "rule by law." The latter cannot rest implicitly on anything less than the "rule of men." Its distinct meaning evokes the service of law, and narrows it, however, to the role of an instrument.

Of course, in plain words, it would be against the grain to declare that law is not an instrument. But the rule of law conceives of an institutional setting which is held to bear an *inherent* value thanks to a

[2] Stephen Holmes (2003:51) writes that "the degree of justice or injustice depends on who wields power and for what ends."

[3] Martin Krygier (2009) interestingly argues against the primacy of *a priori* formal requirements for establishing the rule of law, and invites to focus instead on the ends to be pursued, i.e. on teleology as the true key to Rule-of-law.

[4] Aristotle 1984:III 16 1287a 30.

specific articulation of law. Nonetheless, bearing an inherent value is also compatible with being a constitutive essential of some other ultimate values (Raz 1984:187 ff., 191 ff.). However, the evocative force of the "rule by law" alternative is properly meant to bring into focus and reflect a narrower case, when law is intended to be *just* an instrument. As Arthur Goodhart (1958:947) wrote: "I am not speaking about rule by law which can be the most efficient instrument in the enforcement of tyrannical rule: I am speaking about rule under the law which is the essential foundation of liberty. The two are totally distinct."

Against this picture, however, one can find remarkable views from the opposite side. For example, drawing on Rousseau, Stephen Holmes (2003:49–51) argues that, the law being just an instrument, it is a matter of distribution of power among social groups whether the law will result as just or unjust. Going further, he maintains implicitly that there is only a degree difference between "rule by law" and rule of law: the difference is due to the social distribution of power, that is, it depends on the development of a full-fledged "polyarchy."

Although this might be acceptable, I doubt it does justice to the qualitative shift which comes about, also on the legal plane, when socio-political distribution of power changes from tyrannical monopoly to polyarchy. It is not to be understated how the passage to the rule of law, to the extent it occurs, would allow for a radical turn, which consists of the emergence of law not just as an instrument of social groups. From the perspective of each social group, law shall start showing an authority which does not coincide with its manageability as their own instrument.

In order for this to be feasible, the law itself will have undertaken transformations, which cannot prevent political power from brushing away some guarantees of, say, polyarchy, but which can prevent it from doing so legally. All in all, if Holmes's argument is that law's instrumentality (rule *by* law) is constant, and the change toward rule of law is a mere matter of power, then it largely avoids what I believe is the point in the rule of law ideal. Although one can admit that the explanation of social and legal change depends on some non-legal factors, one shouldn't fail to see what transformations are to be recorded in the legal realm. Rule of law would no longer rest on an identical instrumentality, but rather would bear an inherent value: it would be upheld by meaning something different from "rule by law," and exceed the spectrum the latter encompasses.

Although it is not possible now to deal at length with the "instrumentality" of law,[5] its differentia vis-à-vis the rule of law calls for at least one more remark. After all, it is to be noted that the scope of "instrumentality" must follow the nature of the instrument itself. As to the law (and its "nature"), some can assume an especially thin neutrality of the instrument, as good for everything. Others, however, might depict law in such a way that it can lead only to some uses and results, for example, by narrowing the definition of law to a thick, morally encumbered concept.

Against the full neutrality thesis, it might be said that however "neutral" the law can be, one can hardly get rid of the canon prescribing the adequacy of means to ends. Since not all instruments can be used to attain whatever ends, it may turn out to be senseless to resort to a knife, however sharp it may be, in order to generate, say, linkages instead of slashes. This is testament both to the resistance of the instrument to uses that would be irrational in respect to it as well as to its amenability to be adopted as an instrument in some more "appropriate" ways.

In his explanation of the Nazi "Doppelstaat," for example, Ernst Fraenkel (1969:56 ff.) showed that the Nazi dictatorship dismissed legal procedures and suspended its jurisdiction on arbitrary grounds, whenever it was convenient in order to pursue its ends. Nonetheless, Thomas Hobbes taught how, although not subject to laws, Leviathan does rule by the law: it sets up rules, public competences, and organised procedures in stable and prospective ways (Hobbes 1946: chaps. 26–28). This excess of ambivalence certainly belongs in the domain of the "rule by law."

However, it begs our attention because its distinctive meaning rests on exploiting law, downplaying inner qualities per se or ideal visions (like the rule of law itself) that might turn out to check arbitrary use or limit flexibility in the pursuit of whatever goals. For sure, by sticking to instrumentality, one denies that the rule of law is that kind of ideal form where law is endowed with primacy and non-instrumental value - that the law can acquire some qualities which would narrow its

[5] Explaining the passage to an instrumentalist view, Horwitz (1977:253) asserts that American judges before 1900 didn't analyse law "functionally or purposively," or as "a creative instrument" directed to "social change." See also, Tamanaha 2006.

indiscriminate capacity. From this view, then, it holds true that "rule by law" emerges at odds with "rule of law."

What is the point instead in rejecting the alleged contrast between rule of law and rule of men? From some angles the claim that rule is inconceivable other than as "rule of men," a claim that would endorse Hobbes's stance rather than Aristotle's,[6] appears understandable. After all, rule of law cannot be automatically interpreted as a passage toward a de-humanised "objectivity" of legal imperatives, nor can it be deprived of its positive (law) aspect. That is, whatever content the law is conceived to be bound to include (unless it is just like laws of gravity and natural causality), it has to be connected with some active role played by men's rule in its plain meaning. This applies to Hobbes as much as to all "modern" contractualist (natural) law doctrines of the seventeenth and eighteenth centuries, to say the least.

Moreover, law is always a rule which men are responsible for, and it is men that govern through law. It is not the law that governs of its own accord. Eventually, the connection between power (a premise for "men" to exercise their rule) and the rule that law is must be recognised as necessary.

Thus, on the one hand, as explained above, "rule of law" suggests some ideal directly concerning the law, which does not dissolve into "rule by law." On the other hand, insisting on some "objective" meaning of rule of law as contrasted with (and independent of) "rule of men" may raise traditional concerns about its ideological function: Rule of law might be reduced to a patina for the legitimization of power; it might just hide the rule by law, far from being an "unqualified human good" in virtue of which rulers end up being inhibited or constrained by the laws they enacted (Thompson 1974:264–66). Focusing instead on rule of law precisely through contrast with "rule by law" helps us to become aware of such hidden ideological potentialities.

Returning to the venerable idea of "the rule of laws, not men," the antithesis can emerge meaningfully if we try to understand whether any law really does exist that gains some autonomous normativity, even *vìs-a-vìs* the will of those who ultimately are responsible for its protection and application. In what follows, I suggest that this contrast

[6] Joseph Raz (1979) endorses the continuity between rule of law and rule of men whereas Hobbes (1946:chap. 46, part 4) considered the opposition an error of Aristotle's "politics."

can make sense only if we presuppose (a) a valid *positive* law (b) which is not under the *purview of the ruling power,* and (c) appears *from the vantage point of the latter* to be irreducible to a sheer instrument. Accordingly, not all the law shall be an available instrument of the will of the rulers or of the sovereign ("rule by law").

Maybe the general question can be evoked through the lines of Dicey himself, when he maintains that the sovereignty of Parliament "favours the supremacy of the law" and it is "erroneous" to think that English solutions are just merely "formal," or "at best only a substitution of the despotism of Parliament for the prerogative of the Crown" (Dicey 1915:268, 273). Although law is always a man-made artefact, the rule of law is held to designate some other law (however problematic it appears to be) which does not reduce itself to the actual ultimate will of Parliament.[7]

To make sense of Dicey's reference we must rule out the alternative of some natural law, whose just content would be self-evident and self-imposing. Within these coordinates, it turns out that following the rule of law is not for Parliament to surrender itself to natural law. In theoretical terms, the puzzle is engendered instead precisely from the quest for legal imperatives (not merely moral ones) to prevail over the will of the sovereign. It would be a weak hypothesis to think that the rule of law ideal, on a legal plane, would be respected *absent any legal reason.* Inasmuch as it would depend on Parliament's will, the rule of law would be imprisoned within a circle.

The assumption that this conception can be entitled to represent the "idea of the rule of laws, not men" would be clearly undermined. It is tantamount to saying that it hardly any law can exist which ultimately enjoys any self-standing status. Even if Parliament will not interfere against some old or traditional norms, contingent non-interference against the latter would not disprove that the law actually is under Parliament's dominating ordinary will.[8] Thus far, the rule of law would

[7] Dicey (1915:273) writes: "Parliament is supreme legislator, but from the moment Parliament has uttered its will as lawgiver, that will becomes subject to the interpretation put upon it by the judges of the land, and the judges, who are influenced by the feelings of magistrates no less than by the general spirit of the common law, are disposed to construe statutory exceptions to common law principles in a mode which would not commend itself either to a body of officials, or to the Houses of Parliament, if the Houses were called upon to interpret their own enactments."

[8] The concept of "non-domination" is central to the wider political theory of Philip Pettit (1997). I return to this later. See also Skinner (1998).

still fail to distinguish itself within the competing areas designated by "rule of men" and "rule by law."

Within this picture, the remaining pretensions of the rule of law would retain only a paradoxical sense, that is, they would boil down simply to asserting that morality must rule (The Rule of Morality). But it would be counter-intuitive to allege that rule of law asks morality to rule directly, and thereby supersede legal control.

The scene of our rule of law ideal must be set differently, and the same is equally true of the interplay between men and laws. Although there may also be a moral ideal which is often recognised within rule of law, as connected to its root of liberty, certainty, non-arbitrariness, or even human dignity, it does not directly prescribe moral objectives. It prescribes only legal features. It does not ask for the law to bear some specific content, the good law, nor does it claim to dictate the internal form of the realm of power (for example, that power be organised democratically). As I will maintain in this chapter, although "rule of men" plainly cannot be replaced, rule of law means respect for a legally desirable situation. According to the latter, dominating law appears to be contestable, as a matter of law, on the basis of *some* independent legal force and institutional structures in the interest of everyone.

Historical reconstruction, providing for institutional traces, can support such a view. The general leitmotiv is that law can satisfy the rule of law ideal when "rule of men" turns out to be legally channelled, up to the point where the ruling power would face some other man-made rule and legal institutions sufficiently stable to prevent a monopoly on legal production and contents. Indeed, rule of law does not raise untenable pretensions, that is, that men are not ruling but that the law itself is ruling by its own fiat. Thus, conflict is not engendered against the rule of men *tout court* (*lato sensu* version) but rather against the (*stricto sensu* version) rule of men as domination. The latter emerges where no positive laws or legal devices are institutionally available, that are suited to cope with this dominating feature.

The rule of law is in contrast to the possibility that under the purview of ruling powers law can be reduced to a sheer instrument of their preferences alone, lacking any other law which falls outside their reach and can be traced back to wider needs or ends within the social whole. Since reference to rule of law appears to have been made constantly in legal history and in contemporary legal documents as well, its status as an ideal cannot be envisaged only from a desk. It must also be reconstructed through its historical recurrence. Thus I will deal with the rule of law by drawing its lines along historical, institutional, and conceptual paths.

The European Legislative State

An overview of the wider European scene, recalling the main characteristics of the *Rechtsstaat* and its continental equivalents, can illuminate some elements of the rule of law as a distinctive historical-institutional concept.[9] "Rule of law" is not really the same thing as *Rechtsstaat* or *l'Etat de Droit*, or *l'Estado de derecho, lo Stato di diritto*, and so forth. But the general idea of a "law-bound" State emerges most clearly through the institutional model of a *Rechtsstaat*, which developed its identity as a new form of State coming to replace the *Polizeistaat*, or *l'Etat de police*. The latter was entitled to apply any discretional decision to the life of citizens in order to define their well-being. By contrast, *l'Etat de droit* related to its subjects only by submitting itself to the law, and to rules (Carré de Malberg 1920:I, 488–9).

As F. J. Stahl (1870:137 ff.) and the German public law doctrine[10] worked out the concept of *Rechtsstaat*, this new State was to act under precise and fixed mechanisms, and pre-defined rules, thereby self-limiting its own power through the law. At the same time, it accomplished the public or welfare tasks of the State while maintaining its abstention from interfering with personal spheres (as regards guaranteeing happiness or religious salvation) (Boeckenfoerde 1991:145 ff.). Beyond enlightened absolutism (and State paternalism) it appeared to move from the law of power to the power of the law.

As an institutional and ideological concept the State still is attributed a metaphysical personality: it is a willing entity, preserving its primacy over society. The *Rechtsstaat* means that law is the structure of the State, not an external limitation to it. Its voice is rationality and strict legality of administrative action, the supremacy of which over ordinary citizens was granted despite the recognition of rights and the autonomy of individuals. Liberty is a consequence not truly a premise

[9] The arguments in this and the next two sections are drawing on my earlier work, esp. Palombella 2009a.

[10] The expression itself was definitely famous after L. von Mohl (1832); cf. Boeckenfoerde (1991:144).

of the law. The authority vested in this conservative aristocratic state protected civil liberties as a service offered through the State.[11]

The idea of *Rechtsstaat* in its overall European meaning includes in its institutional organisation both the separation of powers and the so-called principle of legality, which requires that no authority can exist which is not created and conferred by legislation. In Otto Mayer's definition (1895:64 ff.), it is a State in which the administrative power is created by legislation and submitted to it as a product of (of course, largely elitist) Parliaments.

The priority of legislation can both formally grant individual rights, and subordinate them. The independent role of the judiciary was trusted rigidly to respect the legislative will. Law turns out to be the authentic voice of the State, through which it expresses its own will: it is not the constraint but rather the "form" of the State's will.

The importance and dominance of legislation was also a product of the process of codification of law which took place in continental Europe from the seventeenth through twentieth centuries. Moving beyond feudal privileges, codification overcame the particularities, uncertainty and arbitrariness engendered by the frustrating, multi-layered law of still fragmented European territories, wherein common law, Roman law, natural law and customary law were all valid and competing sources. After the successful process of codification, beyond legislation there was no instance or superior institution. Thus, there was no superior check on the law. Rather, through its clarity and unity, the basis for certainty was built. The price was not only the ultimate sovereignty of the State, but also its self-reference, that is, its being founded solely upon itself.

The poverty of the legislative state is generated by the hierarchical model of law, and mainly by the lack of a plurality of equally relevant protagonists and actors on the (institutional) scene. This was clear enough, if one focuses on the relationship between rights and legislation.

According to Georg Jellinek (1919) citizens hold "public subjective rights" on the ground that the latter result from a self-obligation of the sovereign, of the State. After the Revolution and the Declaration of the Rights of Man and of the Citizen, France's great lawyers and reformers endeavoured to protect positive legislated law from instability, change

[11] See Krieger 1957:14. See also his reference to von Mohl's theory of the *Rechtsstaat* at 1957:259 ff.

and the claims of natural law.[12] The same line has to be drawn throughout the rest of Europe, from Spain to Italy, as well eventually to Germany (in the *Buergerliches Gesetzbuch* of 1900).

The main French concern became that of having an unadulterated "democratic" inspiration of the institutions (rooted in Sièyés and Rousseau), rather than re-opening interpretative liberty on natural rights or granting them a force equal to the sovereign will (i.e. legislation).[13] "*La loi*" is meant to express the final and supreme regulation which has no peers. In the German context, *die Herrschaft des Gesetzes* is the ultimate source of the law, beyond the contrasting dualism of King and Representatives.

The law-based state that came into being in Europe was based neither on "rule of law" nor on the practice of modern constitutionalism, as it developed in 1787 in the American Constitution. Instead of the flag of rights, sovereignty rooted in the French Nation or in the *Volksgeist* was generally prevailing. There is almost nothing which can be real, whether laws or rights, unless it is contained in legislation. The liberal state, of course, protected the "bourgeois" freedoms of the late eighteenth century. Indeed, the Code Napoleon was so lofty and solemn an instrument of private law that it could be called the "Constitution of the Bourgeois." But the tussle between rights and public power could only be "decided" by legislation.

Accordingly, a view of the self-limitation of the State also developed, outside of which nothing autonomous could be recognised, not even "rights" (Jellinek 1919). The latter cannot be intended as showing any external limits against the omnipotence of legislation.

As von Gerber wrote in the middle of the nineteenth century, the concept (and reality) of the rule of law already had spread itself even as far as the United States and its constitutional setting: rights depend on the State leaving "free, outside its circle and influence, that part of the human being that cannot be subjected to the coercive action of the general will in accordance with the ideas of popular German life" (Gerber 1913:64–5). Thus it is true that rights did not consist of any "substance" but only of a form, the legal form of the legislative reserva-

[12] As then was taught by the hegemonic School of Exegesis, the caenaculum of the high priests of the Napoleonic Code, whose objective was to proclaim the priority and untouchable status of the Code itself.

[13] Carré de Malberg (1920:140) was aware that Parliamentary monopoly over State sovereignty was a potential danger to French liberties.

tion (Zagrebelsky 1992:59). This is ultimately the conception according to which "the 'law' is what the state determines it to be" and "individual rights are, and must be, defined by the state and, as a consequence, are necessarily dependent on the state. In this vision of reality the state itself, along with its various arms and agencies, is subject to no rules beyond its internal limits" and there is "no meaningful constitution in this construction."[14]

In the history of the European continent the collective ground of community and mainly the implicit idea of commonweal were the prevailing good that takes priority over ideas of justice. The declaration of independence of rights from State legislation was written only when contemporary Constitutions were written, that is during the twentieth century. It was the constitution - not legislation - which created this autonomy, which long had been awaited on the continent. Constitutional rules and principles granted fundamental rights as high a rank as parliamentary legislation and the democratic principle: through an effective Constitution individual rights came to be placed on the same plane as the public weal of the institutions (*salus publica suprema lex*). Prior to this, it would have been impossible in Europe to follow the logic embedded in the rule of law.

The Rule of Law

Contrary to a *Rechtsstaat* (or a *Stato di diritto*), understood as a peculiar form of the State, the rule of law as an ideal presupposed that, in part, positive law be beyond the disposal or "will" of the King, or the sovereign power. Its ideal can be shown as one based upon a relationship, providing a link between two essential western law domains developed within the medieval tradition and evoked through the couple *jurisdictio* - *gubernaculum*: justice and sovereignty.

The rule of law appears to consist of a history of institutional conventions, customs and social practices where law is interconnected with a particular system of power. Even if the supremacy of the English Parliament is beyond doubt, its inclusion in a wider picture is inherent in the things themselves. The principles inherited (Matteucci

[14] The definition is in James Buchanan (1977:290), appropriate to German legal writing especially between the nineteenth and twentieth centuries even as Buchanan intends it to span "legal positivism" pure and simple.

1993:157–8) in the line which unites Henry de Bracton (cf. the pair *gubernaculum* and *jurisdictio*) with Edward Coke (cf. Bonham's case), the U.S. *Federalist Papers* and ultimately U.S. judicial review are — despite their differences - evidence of a general unitary logic.

There is a plurality of sources which go together to make up the intrinsic diversity of the law of the land. It allows for rights to be retained and emerge with an autonomous aspect.

To be sure, the law also includes Parliamentary sovereignty, that is, the unlimited authority of legislation, the assumption that as a matter of abstract law legislation can even infringe rights (Dicey 1915:4–5). This was the motivation for the "grotesque expression" (as De Lolme put it, cited by Dicey) that the English Parliament "can do everything but make a woman a man, and a man a woman" (1915:5). However, sovereignty is complex, shared between Crown, Lords and Commons, and the law has a wider purpose. As a matter of fact, law includes a main second pillar, the common law and the courts, which are in fact the ultimate interpreters of the legal system as a whole.

The complexity of legal achievements in the diverse denominations of common law, precedents, customary law, conventions and rights, is entirely relevant to the "rule of law." The latter is a "founding" element of itself, to the extent that Dicey recognised in it certain quintessentially English features, namely that: no man can be punished for what is not forbidden by law; legal rights are determined by the ordinary courts; and "each man's individual rights are far less the result of our constitution than the basis on which that constitution is founded" (1915: Introduction, LV). As Dicey wrote (1915:21): "[W]ith us...the rules that in foreign countries naturally form part of a constitutional code, are not the source but the consequence of the rights of the individuals, as defined and enforced by the Courts."

The roots in the common law of the land put some qualified rights at the foundation of the constitution, not on the level of the consequences of the constitution. But this endows the constitution and the rule of law with the historical content of liberties, which is part of positive law, not abstract claims from natural law (or, say, organic) doctrines. This historical content cannot be made equal either with some appeal to nature or to the fundamental and obscure soul of the "Volk." And linking contemporary to the ancient tradition, it can be said that even the reasonable character of law is not due to a sort of simple "natural" reason. The claim made by King James I was precisely that being law based on reason, the King might be entitled to decide.

But according to Lord Coke this point was mistaken, since cases were to be treated according to (an importantly different concept) "the artificial Reason" of law, which the King obviously lacked.[15]

The experience of a law which incorporates the "foundational" individual rights of the English is also testament to the conventional and historical character of law that also has matured through prudential judicial assessment. This feature stands at odds with the self-reference of the formalist idea of legality, the final turn of the *Rechtsstaat*. The latter's emptiness was easily laid bare when Mussolini or Hitler purported to take power "legally" and under the authority of the law.

The institutional premises are substantively different. The rule of law embedded substantive liberties and provided procedural guarantees (such as habeas corpus and due process),[16] and its organisation of powers does not simply correspond to the "law." Rather, it corresponds to the law in a specific setting, that is, to structures, practices, ideas in their institutional concreteness. As a consequence, if we can reduce the law to an instrument, perhaps we cannot depict the rule of law, with its specific institutional historical content, as being reducible to empty means.

Moreover, if we narrow the rule of law to a form re-presenting the State, we would be making a big mistake. As Giovanni Sartori (1964:310) noted, "the Rule of Law does not postulate the State, but an autonomous law, external to the State: the common law, the case law, in sum the judge made and jurists' law. Therefore, there is a 'rule of law' without the State; and more exactly it does not require the State to monopolise the production of law." However, while the reality of a *Stato di diritto* is the self-subordination of the State by its own law, in the case of the "rule of law" the State is subordinated to a law which is not its own (1964:311).

A further note, however, should be dedicated to the glorious victory of the seventeenth century Parliament against absolutism, the restoration of the rights and privileges of the English people against the King's claims. Here the parallel becomes even more instructive: while the *Rechtsstaat* or *l'Etat de droit* defeated the ultimate absolute power of

---

[15] See Charles Fried (1981:57) and his quotation of E. Coke, *Reports* 63, 65 (pt. 12, 4th ed. 1738), reprinted in 77 Eng. Rep. 1342, 1343 (1907).

[16] Article 39 of the Magna Carta (1215)

the King, because it was the King's, the rule of law defeated it because it was absolute.[17]

The root of this difference is normally traced back to the thirteenth century medieval "rule of law," as described by George Haskins (1955:535–6): "[T]here appeared a noticeable reluctance to permit alterations in common law, and we soon hear of cases in which writs brought by the King were quashed by his own judges.... To this extent at least, the rule of law was extended to limit prerogative action and to prevent the king from making further changes in the substantive rights and procedures of his subjects." Haskins continues: "But this was not all. The remarkable feature of the development was that the rights and remedies of the common law came to be identified with the rule of law itself."

Also interestingly on this point, Charles McIlwain elaborated on the pairing of *jurisdictio* and *gubernaculum* (1940:85): "For in *jurisdictio*, as contrasted with *gubernaculum*, there are bounds to the king's discretion established by a law that is positive and coercive, and a royal act beyond these bounds is ultra vires. It is in *jurisdictio*, therefore, and not in "government" that we find the most striking proof that in medieval England the Roman maxim of absolutism was never in force theoretically or actually."

As far as these notes are correct, the rule of law appears to be built on a diversity of sources of law, and can reflect a "tension" within the justice-government coupling. The first term refers to the law of the courts and the common law, that is, it does not present itself as an appeal to some ideal of rational or natural justice through its normative force per se.

Jurisdictio and *Gubernaculum*, the Right and the Good

As long as the "rule of law" is a concept with institutional, historical, and normative meaning, it says more than it might appear to say. It does designate a cultural reference to law, but also a normative sense which might be extended elsewhere. Here, it seems that the meaning of the rule of law depends on an enduring continuity with its own past: it would be very hard to accept its alleged coincidence with the

[17] See Kluxen (1983:50 ff.) and Zagrebelsky (1992:26 and his reconstruction, at 24–29).

exclusive substance of one contemporary ideology.[18] When we refer to the Rule of Law, after all, we take account of many more consistent ancient and modern records, an institutional-historical rationale which promises a potential openness, in particular due to its reference to the rule of law as a peculiar balanced relation.

"The aspect of *jurisdictio* which is most important", according to McIlwain's description, was "the fact that in *jurisdictio*, unlike *gubernaculum*, the law is something more than a mere directive force" (1940:85). This aspect of the law is therefore different from the expression of power or will. Nonetheless, it is not the evocation of morality. According to McIlwain the thirty-ninth chapter of the Magna Carta was not conceived "as the Austinians would say, as a mere maxim of positive morality." A principle was insisted upon and enforced as coercive law, namely the principle that "king must not take the definition of rights into his own hands, but must proceed against none by force for any alleged violation of them until a case has been made out against such a one by 'due process of law'" (1940:86).

The rule of law depends on a distinction. On the one hand, there is that part of the law belonging in the land, protecting its positive idea of justice and giving liberties their due: it is the part formed through judicial decisions, the common law and conventions. On the other hand, there is the *gubernaculum*, the will of the sovereign, which embraces instrumental aims and government policies.

As a matter of fact, on one side we find, so to speak, the concrete achievements of minimal requirements of coexistence, respecting the individuality of human beings; on the other side lies the sphere of "the good" (including the common good), evolving through time. The ultimate power of a polity could avail itself of the law only in part: that which is under its sovereign prerogative. The fundamental law of the land appears, after all, to be a complex and collective construct. What is deemed justice is itself artificial, law made by many hands, through the wisdom of decades or centuries.

Jurisdictio refers to law, but in this domain men have the duty to say it (*jus dicere*), not to choose or decide. There is, then, some part of the law which remains at the disposal of the sovereign. But the other aspect

[18] Such as liberal ideology, in a line proposed by Hayek (1960, 1944).

of law is not at his disposal, and the sovereign is thus bound to be deferential.[19]

As McIlwain wrote (1940:90), "in the Middle Ages... government proper, as distinguished from *jurisdictio*, was 'limited' by no coercive control, but only by the existence beyond it of rights definable by law and not by will." The absence of sanctioning through legally coercive devices does not however necessarily coincide with and does not essentially mean being outside law, not counting as law.

Much of this un-decidable (or not disposable) justice has been clarified as having been present in the medieval tradition. It is from this that the Enlightenment experience broke away, especially through the codification of law.

The relationship mentioned above between sovereignty and – as we also might call it – the realm of rights (as a matter of law), has a definitive development in liberal philosophy, and properly so. As John Rawls noted (1971:234), the rule of law "is obviously closely related to liberty." This relationship on a philosophical ground comes to suggest its affinity with the opposites of justice and ethics. The rule of law, in a sense, entails relying on the conceptual capacities of both the "right" and the "good," which appear suited to explain some common lines of its historical developments.

In fact, when the law destroys this relationship and its vitality, it falls into the trap of the full "ethicization" of the legal system, which is a characteristic feature of totalitarian regimes. Writing in the middle of the twentieth century, McIlwain saw in his times "a constant threat to all the rights of personality we hold dearest — such rights as freedom of thought and expression and immunity for accused persons, from arbitrary detention and from cruel and abusive treatment" (1940:139). He defined these circumstances, saying that "never has *jurisdictio* been in greater jeopardy from *gubernaculum*." His institutional history brings him to conclude: "If *jurisdictio* is essential to liberty, and jurisdictio is a thing of the law, it is the law that must be maintained against arbitrary will" (1940:140).

Again, *jurisdictio* is associated with the preservation of the law, not with the preservation of a sort of external morality. But nonetheless, what essentially qualifies it, beyond any other contents, is that it

[19] This aspect was enhanced also by Habermas (1988:217–79), speaking of *Unverfügbarkeit* ("non-disposability").

incorporates the side of positive law whose merit concerns "the right," not "the good" as a sovereign political choice. Where the rule of law is absent, justice, or the "right," has no shield. It provides no filter against the contingency or absoluteness of ethics, that is, to the "tyranny of values" (to cite the title of Schmitt's famous essay, 1996), which can be, and indeed has been, totalitarian.

As is well known, as a question of moral and political philosophy, this opposition was an important part in the work of Immanuel Kant and, in our times, mainly in that of John Rawls (1971, 1993). As Rawls wrote (1971:31), the "principles of right, and so of justice, put limits on which satisfactions have value; they impose restrictions on what are reasonable conceptions of one's good." Principles of justice "specify the boundaries that men's systems of ends must respect.... Interests requiring the violation of justice have no value."[20] This also holds true of political action, pursuing ethical values of majoritarian groups or interests. In Rawls' construction, justice takes precedence and helps to shape the admissible prospects of action towards the good.

This general view is in fact linked, as Rawls knows, to the *Critique of Practical Reason* where Kant clearly argues that our concept of the "good" should not determine what is just and "make possible the moral law." Rather, "it is on the contrary the moral law that first determines and makes possible the concept of the good" (Kant 1996a:191). Moral legislation requires the universal recognition of human beings as coexisting, under innate equal liberty. It concerns justice, not the good nor happiness: "No one can coerce me to be happy in his way (as he thinks of the welfare of other human beings); instead, each may seek his happiness in the way that seems good to him, provided he does not infringe upon that freedom of others to strive for a like end which can coexist with the freedom of everyone in accordance with a possible universal law (i.e. does not infringe upon this right of another)" (Kant 1996b:291).

These very conditions of coexistence can be coerced through the law. The guarantee of the "negative" external freedom of the private sphere precedes and does not even imply any confusion with ethics.

---

[20] This statement falls within the "particular meaning" of the priority of justice, as distinguished later on by Rawls from the "general meaning." The latter refers for Rawls to the priority of the right as a political conception "so that we need not rely on comprehensive conceptions of the good but only on ideas tailored to fit within the political conception" (1993:209).

So a precept's moral and rational validity does not depend upon its conformity with any particular ethics or any view of goodness and happiness. With Kant therefore, rational legislation "is not mingled with anything ethical" (1996b:291).

Law and justice are resorted to conceptually in order to avoid the ("state of nature") condition in which the abuse of personal liberty is unobjectionable. At the same time, it is true that justice in law here is separated from ethics: whatever value of life or social construction dominates, it has to accommodate itself within the coordinates of this minimal justice to human beings. This conceptual distinction depends on a transcendental ideal of law, which sees law as the condition of coexistence through liberty, before any ethical objective can be actually pursued through the means of existing law.

There is a necessary distinction, and a necessary connection, between justice and ethical and political choices. One of the main risks that law can run (from the rule of law vantage point) is the loss of the institutional settings, social guarantees, and practices which realize this relationship in different legal orders and societies. It can fairly be said that the tension between these two poles can be protected through institutional devices and also by the law when it pursues the ideal of the rule of law, demanding the non-disposability of justice (*jurisdictio*) by the rule of the sovereign.

Balance, Liberty and Non-domination

In the event that the "autonomy" of the "*jurisdictio*" side were to be denied, it would alter the equilibrium between conditions of intersubjective justice, liberties and sovereign prerogatives. As a general notion, then, when some rights, or some relations of justice which are conceptually unrelated to the choice of any sovereign (whether the King in Parliament, or the people, or the Nation, etc.) fall "legally" under the purview of the sovereign, a whole part of the law has virtually faded and has been pushed outside. The effect of this is that its normative claim is left out, as belonging at best to sheer morality. In this case – and we should take the following as a *caveat* – there is no more division between *gubernaculum* and *jurisdictio*, and thus no reliable foundation for the rule of law.

I am not suggesting that there is somewhere a substantive conception of justice, which can be defended on the basis of rational natural law arguments, as is done for example in the outstanding work of John Finnis (1980). Instead, the meaning of the rule of law, as its core emerges especially after being compared with the experience of the *Rechtsstaat*, does not simply incorporate some prerequisites – whether procedural or substantive – into the definition of law. It instead incorporates fidelity to an idea of relation, to a relational notion. It implies respect for and protection of the opposition – to use freely these solemn terms – between *gubernaculum* and *jurisdictio*, two sides of the law, with all of their historical evolutions and equivalents. This very relation in fact eventually disappeared on the Continent, and consistently so, with the institutional subordination of rights and justice under the will of the sovereign, with any competing law being eliminated or sidelined (see above, sections on "The European Legislative State" and "The Rule of law").

For example, this structure of the *Stato di diritto* was typically a legal reason to debase the claims of some to a possible institutional protection and "locus standi." If the law exhausts itself within the (monopoly of) legislative sources, and if the latter does not mention a right, then neither harm nor offence can "legally" occur. And if no harm or offence can be alleged, the lack of "locus standi" prevents any challenges to the law from being heard.

The autonomy of the "*jurisdictio*" side of the law and its connection to "rights" and wider common values has today been broadly positivised in national constitutions as well as international charters and conventions. This side of the law and its corresponding institutional and social practice are a prerequisite for the rule of law to exist as the relationship of the kind here argued.

Focusing on this relationship means that we can characterise the rule of law as it is, as well as remain open to its normative extension beyond its territorial manifestation in any particular instantiation. However, this view of the rule of law, that has been explained already with reference to the heuristic couple of the right and the good, can be better characterised by also enhancing the connection of this requisite balance-relation with the non-domination feature mentioned in the opening of this chapter.

According to Dicey (1915:198) the rule of law precludes "the existence of arbitrariness, of prerogative, or even of wider discretionary authority on the part of government." As we have seen in our comparative reconstruction, non-arbitrariness results from the rule of law. Although respect for laws and procedures, regularity and certainty served the attainment of both non-arbitrariness and the rule of law, it would be short-sighted to assume that the rule of law simply coincides (or exhausts itself) with non-arbitrariness – and even more so should non-arbitrariness be understood like such a rule-regularity as that constructed by the so-called legislative European State. The latter has proved largely amenable to conveying the whim of the Executive or of legislative majorities.

What makes it possible for non-arbitrariness – as the absence of an unbridled discretionary authority – to be appreciated certainly includes this kind of formal requirement. But it hardly depends just upon it. Rather, it also depends on the aforementioned "foundational" balance between sovereign and "*jurisdictio*" law. When the rule of law is embedded in the equilibrium of such relations, non-arbitrariness "on the part of the government" obtains as it develops through such a legal-institutional environment, while it might prove flawed outside of it.

The question of law as restraining power, which became entrenched in eighteenth-century modern liberalism, enjoys a wider completion in the rule of law ideal which was "lived" by lawyers and courts since medieval times. Thus, the idea of liberty as "the negative" of power, and that of law as constraint on it, are subsequent transformations of the rule of law's more ancient roots. John Phillip Reid recalls how Bracton's contribution rests on an idea of law, different from the law as command, which enjoyed a millenary tradition from Roman Law to English and German customary law. "What is of significance of this story of liberty is that this theory of autonomous law was the theory lawyers and officials employed when resolving issues" (Reid 2004:12).

Law as the conviction of the community benefited from an autonomous status, which not even the ruling power could afford to disregard, because no will ought to prevail against it. According to Reid: "In a theoretically attenuated sense, the ideal of medieval law was the rule of law" (2004:13).

When seen in the light of the *jurisdictio-gubernaculum* pair, and with its load of Magna Carta guarantees and rights-creating trends, the illegality of arbitrary interference (by the ruling power) is caused by an "autonomous" law capable of resistance and evolution, which bears procedural and substantive pillars. Thus, a legal reason is available for arbitrariness not to take place, whether through the "forms" of law or by the fiat of the King. It is not just liberty as absence of interference; rather, absence of interference is structurally, not contingently granted, by the positive existence of "another" law.

When this situation applies, it could not be improper to describe the ideal of the rule of law as a non-domination principle, provided that we do not measure its extent and depth through criteria of content, social structure, power organization, individual-centred and autonomy concepts we are so used to in liberal democracies. Moreover, it should be observed, as a matter of rule of law, non-domination can only be used in a weak sense, and only in order to mean a pure legal configuration, pertaining to legal institutions, not directly to political or social ones.

We might draw here on the heuristic strength of the couple non-interference/non-domination by adapting Philip Pettit's analysis of it. He emphasises that law does not necessarily offend (or limit) liberty; this would be true only if liberty should reduce itself to non-interference, but not when liberty is conceived as non-domination (Pettit 1997; and 2008). Domination is the case where reason-independent control of others is always possible, and although interference may be absent control remains present. The abstract possibility of arbitrary (reason-independent) interference is admitted, and while this holds true, someone else remains your "master" even if you may feel you are acting according to your preferences.

Thus, freedom as non-domination does not require non-interference but rather absence of control over one's fundamental choices. According to Pettit this ideal, which he sees as a "property" of the person, has consequences for the structure of power. It implies at its best that control be equally shared as it can be through the model of democracy within a neo-republican tradition (Pettit 1997). Accordingly, Pettit assumes that given the structure of democracy, legislation can and ought to be "non-dominating," and that it will fail to be a constraint on freedom (as non-domination).

Although this assumption, in my view, contains the normative vein of the rule of law ideal, it is not addressed as a peculiar ideal of law, but only as the content of a political ideal, *directly* concerning the distribution of *power*, which is equal among the citizens exercising self government. Thus, it concerns the configuration of the "sovereign" and commends a unique political arrangement (neo-republican democracy).

Rule of law, instead, encompasses a wider spectrum of political regimes, and concerns the configuration *of law*. If we narrow the field within the specifically legal domain of the rule of law, it requires that interference into the life of citizens be possible while reason-independent and arbitrary interference be legally impossible. As we now know, this becomes true when another law is available which makes such a control not viable. On the legal plane this rule of law basis applies whatever political regime is meant to be the best for disparate reasons.

Although I have drawn on Pettit for elaboration of terms like interference, or domination, what may get lost through his political focus on neo-republican democracy is that non-domination can be an ideal of the rule of law. Although, in my view, there is no necessary objection that the rule of law theory needs to raise against the political theory as such, nonetheless it is remarkable that the reason for legislation to be non-dominating is not traced back by Pettit to the existence of some law or legal device which accomplishes its own separate task. On the contrary it is directly derived from the transformation of law into a faithful instrument of societal ruling. Once the ruling power is democratic in the recommended sense, then this turns out to be fortunate and produces good law.

Of course, rule of law is not a logical necessity. Insofar as this ideal is mentioned in our most solemn legal documents, though, we might keep trying to make sense of it. After all, what should be counterproductive about cherishing an ideal directly concerning the rule of law? Yet, if we have such an ideal, certainly it will displace the "rule by law" and the purely instrumental conception of the law itself: precisely because they would open conceptually a path to domination and would proscribe the internal balance that, instead, rule of law needs. The point with the rule of law is that it contains the normative conditions for the (legal) conceivability, and appearance of the non-domination ideal as a matter of law.

In its own right, as we shall remark later as well, this depends on the concurrence of the two flanks of law (justice-sovereign law; customary, judge made and legislative; and equivalents) matured through English customary and judge-made autonomous law. But its normative spectrum finds equivalent incarnations of the same non-domination, balance logic. It was also raised to a more complex institutional form by the Constitutional guarantee in the United States, and found rule of law realization in European twentieth century Constitutions, as I already noted. Tellingly, here as well, where the nature of power is democratic, a positive law is protected even against democratic powers.

This law's side proves to be resistant to the sovereign. Thus, should, say, reason-independent and arbitrary interference into that law be made, this would substantively and formally cross the legal order's boundary, thereby dissolving it. This kind of exercise of power would not be legally supported but indeed legally inhibited. Of course the "domination" attempt, so to speak, can be successful, but it will win against law, as a manifestation of naked power (regardless of whether it is democratic or otherwise). This would be the lesson of the rule of law, and perhaps a reason why solemn contemporary legal documents enumerate it, not democracy alone. Not even the democratic sovereign should be allowed to be the ultimate, and thus discretionary, "master" of laws.

The Law, Valid Law, and Rule of Law

Theoretical discourse concerning the "rule of law" has often focussed on the "concept" and on the "validity" of law. I will therefore dedicate some comments to its relations with these two notions.

Generally, the rule of law has been largely entangled in the definition of law.[21] Such a conceptual overlap with what law essentially is (or should be) ends up underestimating the very fact that the appeal to the rule of law as an ideal cannot be satisfied by the mere existence of law. The normative import of the rule of law indeed demands that legality be structured in such a way as to satisfy some further objectives through some institutional configuration, one that law may- or may not-possess.

What is needed for the law to exist as "law" has been viewed from various angles, but in legal philosophy the contributions of Lon Fuller and Joseph Raz are major reference points of theoretical discussion. According to Fuller the law can function on the condition of being based on general, public, non retroactive, non-contradictory and comprehensible rules –, that are possible to perform and relatively stable. Moreover, rules in force must be followed consistently by officials and

[21] It is from this viewpoint that I agree with Waldron's observation according to which the Rule of law has been construed starting from the concept of law. Waldron refers to the possibility that the converse route be taken (Waldron 2008).

administrators (Fuller 1969:ch. 2). It is reasonable to think of these features as describing some "anatomy" of law (Krygier 2009:47 ff.).

It is often debated whether these features convey an "internal morality" of law, instead of just the "virtues" required for it to efficiently guide behaviour (Raz 1979:214). What I would consider debatable, though, is the (whether latent or explicit) pre-understanding, according to which such anatomic requirements, stating what law needs in order to be law, are at the same time a sufficient definition of what the "rule of law ideal" requires.

One should conceive of the "inner moral" value of such requirements, as a notion to be distinguished from "positive" (or socially current) ethics, which is "external" to the law itself and based on a range of varying choices and values. This inner morality of the law is related to the way in which the law presents itself, is constructed and administered. It is fair enough to admit that Fuller is stressing the service to regularity and non-arbitrariness, to the protection of coexistence, and accordingly the moral importance that these features actually have, even taken in themselves, for those who are subject to the law. In a sense, it recognises the value of being under the law, not at the mercy of something else. We can acknowledge these features of law, regardless of the merit of its further contingent goals or substantive contents. I will return once more to this point later.

It is true as well that, beyond *law's anatomy*, when we turn to the ideal of the rule of law we are engaging in some more demanding, or at least better exposed, *teleology* to which the rule of law is committed. As Krygier observed, we can hardly determine *a priori* a universal list of institutional prescriptions for the rule of law (Krygier 2009:47), applicable to every case.

As I interpret this *caveat* , it leads us to the normative *ends* that the rule of law ideal prescribes, on the legal plane, without fixing permanently the ultimate set of requirements, whether procedural or substantial, to be expected as automatically granting the achievement of those ends. Features and ends are, after all, distinguishable.

When we turn to "ends" and teleology, in the rule of law ideal, we should not mistake them for the pursuit of extraneous goals that typically inspire different spheres as politics, ethics, economy. This is what Joseph Raz might have had in mind when he distinguished the rule of law from the "rule of the good law", as he aptly dubbed the stance taken by Hayek, in conflating his liberal market economy ideal with the very definition of the rule of law (Raz 1979:227; Hayek 1960 and 1944; Scheuermann 1994).

As we know, for Raz the rule of law only corresponds to the requirements needed for law, whatever its content, to accomplish its inherent task (i.e. the efficient guide of behaviours). And thus, it is independent of further good or bad goals to be pursued through the law.

Based on my arguments in the above sections, I doubt that a definition of *law* in itself tells the whole story about the ideal historically developed in our modern civilization, that we call *rule of law*. Moreover, the limits of the "anatomical" conception are to be found in their essential reference to the law in itself. The normative core of the rule of law exceeds the mere definition of what counts as law, as much as for example democracy exceeds the definition of a polity, of political society in general. In order for democracy to be achieved the polity must be structured according to further objectives, bearing a coherent scheme of power allocation, the framing of public discourse, the adjudication of at least political rights. The rule of law similarly requires that on the plane of legal institutions a peculiar scheme of legality be available, that can be implemented, in diverse modes, through different contexts. Thus, the functional requirements for the law, be they attributed or not a further moral value, are both necessary for us to be under the law and in themselves insufficient for us to be under the rule of law.

Accordingly, I can share, although for different reasons, the point related to the unacceptable conflation of the rule of law with the rule of the *good* law. The rule of law ideal has to do with a configuration protecting social normativity from being monopolised by one dominating legal source.[22] It purports to safeguard the tension between *gubernaculum* and *jurisdictio*, depending on the (existence of an) equilibrium between two sides of positive law, that we have learned to develop as related to justice and sovereign deliberation. The continuity of this meaning in the last centuries can be maintained if the law is produced and organised by preserving this duality. The latter would be cancelled should, for example, the law be dictated by an unconstrained choice made by the will of the rulers, and should it be called upon to

[22] We started from the fact that the formula gains its meaning from incorporating an institutional logic, wrongly equated with the experience of the pre-constitutional *Rechtsstaat*.

reflect exclusively one conception of the "good" in the absence of a legally separate and independent defence of the "right". In other words, the full ethicization of law (that I have already recalled as typically occurring in totalitarian or fundamentalist regimes) is at odds with the concerns that have since long inspired the rule of law ideal. And the road we take when confusing the normative ideal of the rule of law with the rule of the *good* law (or better said, of *one* good law), is slippery enough and conceptually comparable. On the contrary, the rule of law asks for protection of the balanced duality of law which, as shown above, bears also an accent of non-domination.

Now, a further question has to be addressed: if the rule of law is an ideal with which existent law is asked to comply, it has been and can be at odds with "valid" rules.

For the rule of law, admittedly, a general conception of law is needed, one which would not turn out to be incompatible with its normative pretensions. I am not maintaining thereby that the rule of law posits a definitive claim as to the essential nature of the law, apart from one regarding the potential capability of law to be framed in a way consistent with the rule of law.

As recalled in the opening of this section, the requirements of law certainly have a functional virtue, to which Fuller (1969:42–79) assigned also a moral value. Others, apart from natural law theorists, have also endorsed some moral connection of law, even in its procedural necessities (MacCormick 2005:16; 2008).

In the foregoing pages, I do not deny that as an ideal, as a matter of fact, rule of law embeds moral values. I have not posited, though, the question whether the *validity* of law may be made dependent on moral arguments. The question of the rule of law can be distinguished from the problem of the (criteria of) validity of law: for the law to be valid maybe we need less demanding criteria than those which are required for the rule of law ideal to be achieved.

However, legal positivism does not deny either that law can embody moral content or that it is capable of endorsing pretensions such as those supported within the rule of law ideal. For what concerns the "nature" of law, the validity problem, and the separation thesis (between morality and law), a strict legal positivist like Andrei Marmor reminds us that the Separation Thesis just "asserts that the conditions of legal validity do not depend on the moral content of the norms in question." And this is held to be consistent both with taking law as "essentially good" and "with Fuller's basic insight that the rule of law, properly understood, promotes certain goods which we have reasons to value regardless of their purely functional merit" (Marmor 2004:43).[23]

One can also test the point from a softer legal positivist stance and allow that even moral criteria can actually become part of those comprised within the fundamental rule, or the rule of recognition of a legal order. Indeed, from my point of view, it is necessary that law be held compatible by its nature with the normative meaning of the rule of law. And to this extent, it may also prove to be theoretically adequate to endorse the "inclusive positivist" view according to which moral standards can become part of the fundamental meta-rules governing legal validity.[24]

It is actually valuable that validity in a legal system can be made to depend ("inclusively") upon structural (procedural) and substantive criteria which are suited to protecting the "rule of law," as it occurs in our constitutional states. Yet there have indeed been opposite cases, an eventuality which may also occur in the future, as it can equally happen that a society might still lack reliable structures in order for the rule of law to be realised. For legal positivism in its general attitude this is conceptually admissible.

Legacy and Prospects of the Rule of Law

When we cherish the "rule of law" as the ideal according to which sovereignty is prevented from being "unlimited" and "unbridled", we are not just relying on the concepts of non arbitrariness and certainty.

---

[23] For Marmor (2004:39), Hart and Raz are "wrong about [this] criticism of Fuller" because "most virtues of the rule of law, though essentially functional, are also moral-political virtues." In fact they also "enhance certain goods which we have reasons to value in addition to their functional merit. If the law fails on these conditions, it would not only fail in guiding its putative subjects' conduct, but it would also fail morally." But in his turn, Raz (2007) remarked that legal positivism can stand some connection between law and morality.

[24] Coleman (2000:175) writes: "whether or not morality is a condition of legality in a particular legal system depends on a social or conventional rule, namely, the rule of recognition.... If the rule of recognition incorporates no moral principles, however, then no such principles figure in the criteria of legality." W. J. Waluchow (1985:194) argues that, if moral principles can be incorporated explicitly in a legal system's rule of recognition, then the validity of a norm X cannot be solely a function of its source, but also of its content, seeing that it must be considered in relation to its potential violation by a principle of justice. Although both the norm X and the "moral" principle depend on having a "pedigree", it "remains, however, that more than X's pedigree is relevant in determining its legal validity."

Although these concepts are often part of the rule of law's achievements, in themselves they might just entail a strict "law of rules" (Scalia 1989:1175; and 1996), and end up serving law as a sheer instrument of power (the "rule by law"). After all, the European State, before its contemporary constitutional transformation, proved to be non arbitrary, rigidly submitted to the principle of legality, and yet unsuited to embody the rationale that we have found in the English "rule of law" root. For the latter to be pursued, "another" positive law should be available, which is located somehow outside the purview of the (legitimate) government, be it granted by the long standing tradition of common law or by the creation of a "constitutional" higher law protection, and so forth.

Rule of law is, therefore, a matter concerning the sources of law, their diversity and two-sided equilibrium, their consequential capacity of reflecting – on a true legal plane – social normativity in a non monolithic voice. As I have said so far, this general scheme can be matched at different times and in different contexts by a variety of institutional arrangements and of course it can call for the general requirements, enumerated by legal theorists, for the law to efficiently guide behavior or meet the condition for its very existence. But – as explained in the foregoing – it is this "duality of law" that has to emerge, for the ideal to be achieved.

Thus, our focus shifts from certainty to equilibrium. Certainty as well as pre-determined rules, stable, knowable to subjects and clearly defining spheres of action legally permitted or prohibited, these are actually an unobjectionable achievement of legal civilization (López de Oñate 1953).[25] Nonetheless, certainty can be easily converted into an end in itself.

Certainty was also be attributed a preeminent role as the essential premise for the modern State to be obeyed: it was celebrated as depending on the formal and rational qualities of legislated law in the Weberian "legal State" of the Nineteenth and Twentieth centuries Europe (Weber 1978:82 and 886; Habermas 1996:124 ff.). But certainty always is to be seen in context, thereby depending on time and space.

---

[25] This holds true despite the inherent indeterminacy of the law, which is a well known challenge to the rule of law – as certainty. A convincing defence of the rule of law on this side is in Neil MacCormick 2005.

In present constitutional states, it must be seen in the light of the supervening patterns of social development, and within the context of contemporary democratic communities. Here, the prevailing language conveys reference to values and consensus, and rules are embedded in wider and higher legal principles, whose openness bears concrete implications. The rule of law tends to preserve a balance between substantive and procedural law, as much as between, say, the strength of democratic decision making, its final authority, and the safeguard of justice among the plurality of forces from which democracy is constructed. It is present where legal concerns related to "the right" cannot be overruled by and are shielded against the ethical commitments of the prevailing majorities.

The unstoppable rise of the well known "proportionality principle" witnesses the development of some evaluative, "discursive", rationality, aimed at balancing and weighing between divergent normativities, both substantively and legally legitimate, whose aims are not only to find a mutual constraint, but must sometimes be justifiably sacrificed. Although its outcomes are possibly exposed to contestation, proportionality is considered a "golden rule" of the rule of law (Beatty 2009); its formalised intellectual construction (Alexy 2002:47–50 *passim)*) bears the feature of a shared legal tool, and it has become a "global" (Mathews and Stone-Sweet 2008) constant of the rule of law. If, on the contrary, sheer compliance with rules is unilaterally celebrated it risks being easily abused and instrumentalised (Sajo 2006; Palombella 2006).

The rule of law has been described as depending, as well, on more substantive requirements, including the protection of fundamental rights, and the necessary conditions for a community of welfare or a full-fledged democracy (Craig 1997; Allan 2001). While the "thin" and formal conception comes close to equating the rule of law with sheer conditions for existence of a functioning law,[26] the thick and substantive conceptions require the rule of law ideal to stretch too far, to match one of its historical incarnations, and to embody within its very definition, a political notion of democratic power, or a socio-economic pattern, whether asking for welfare solidarity or individual market-autonomy. On the contrary, the rule of law, as we have seen, can only

[26] Jeremy Waldron has aptly shown, however, how law would totally fade away, denying its own existence, should it turn into crude violence and brutality (Waldron 2005:1681).

have a meaning related to the institutional legal setting, where it requires non-monopolization of legal sources and the safeguard of the tension between the legitimate "gubernaculum" law and a law otherwise developed (through common law, constitutional law, customary law and so forth), one exceeding the ordinary extension of the other.

At least on the conceptual plane, we cannot conflate rule of law and democracy. Although our western constitutional and democratic states approximate quite well, in our times, the conditions for the ideal to be achieved, the rule of law was invoked and proclaimed at least since Medieval times, as our historical reconstruction shows. And the structures and quality of law are at issue, whether related or not to a democratic constitutional State. Obviously, in our *Weltanschauung*, both democracy and the rule of law deserve appreciation and recognition. However, the rule of law is conceptually independent of democracy, since its rationale is meant to confront power regardless of its shape, any forms of government, regardless of its autocratic or democratic nature. As "democratic" power can be unlimited and unbridled, it would be unreasonable to consider the rule of law as an unnecessary problem in a democratic regime, at least until one acknowledges the distinctive service and the distinctive nature of law and politics, despite their stable interweaving.

In a sense, although as a normative ideal the rule of law is not at all "neutral", it is a politically "crosscutting" concept, precisely because it asks for the law to rule, a claim whose theoretical import and historical meaning have been here addressed at length.

Eventually, the rule of law has gained a relevant role in the debate concerning international and supranational law: in these realms its potential is still to be carefully developed. The extension of the normative ideal beyond the State cannot be analysed here in depth. Nonetheless, it can be readily admitted that the perspective of rule of law as an ideal resting on duality, balance and non domination can have a significant critical impact when applied at the international level, where it is suited to functioning as a (counterfactual) check against an environment in which the "non-domination" problem is the essential one.

It is relevant that the rule of law can maintain its core meaning without the State, in the absence of any democratic device whatsoever, and that it takes as central the point of irreducibility of law within the reach of the ruling powers. These items find their intuitive weight precisely in the problematic International Law concurrence of sources, and in related issues, such as coordination between customary and treaty law, or the relatively recent development, beyond conventional law, of a community or *super partes* law which is the reason for the invalidity of contrary treaties. But while this turn, at least in the last sixty years, has caused the tension between law and power to resurface, the occurrence of further transformations has made the quest for the rule of law even more daunting.

The search for legal constants to be woven in the *global space* is impelled less from the obsolescence of the State than by the multiplication of law-producing entities operating as "global regimes" in functionally separated and often interrelating fields; by the increasing of institutionalised supranational authorities that end up affecting individuals and peoples, often without proportionate guarantees and countervailing legal checks. In a setting where neither democracy nor a State is available, the weaving of the rule of law proves its importance in the face of some newly originating legality whose generators are at best self-controlling. It is still unclear how far its service can reach, although admittedly it appears to be an essential precondition for a decent legal environment.

Its urgency, again, has to do neither with the purposes of a cosmopolitan democracy nor with the systemic aspirations of a world constitutionalism. Prior to these achievements, the rule of law, outside the templates we have so far associated with it, amounts to the claim for legal principles widely practiced, conditioning the viability of legal intercourses, and capable of developing as "positive" law. The rule of law claims to be more than the exercise of power *by law*. The jurisgenerative potential of the most active entities, be they States, supranational organisations, or "economic" actors , is already clear and visible. At stake is instead the mentioned duality of law, the conflict between power and justice (Palombella 2007), the feasibility of "another law" at odds with the superimposition of an unrivalled normativity (Palombella 2009b) conveying dominant conceptions of "the good". It might generate slowly or emerge through institutional practices, where admittedly a primary role might be played by mutual reference, legal canons and reasoning laid down by the multiplicity of courts and tribunals now operating in the global sphere (Cassese 2009).

As a general comment, it should be stressed that in this realm the rule of law, as described above, remains an ideal, whose objectives are still to be achieved, and whose configuration, however, should make its use as an apologetic and ideological concept more difficult.

References

Alexy, Robert. 2002. *A Theory of Constitutional Rights*. Translated by J. Rivers, Oxford: Oxford University Press.

Allan, Trevor R. S. 2001. *Constitutional Justice, A Liberal Theory of the Rule of Law*. Oxford: Oxford University Press.

Aristotle. 1984. *The Politics*. Translated by Carnes Lord. Chicago: Chicago University Press.

Austin, John. 1954. *The Province of Jurisprudence Determined*. London: Weidenfeld & Nicolson.

Beatty, David M. 2009. "Law's Golden Rule." Pp. 99–116 in *Relocating the Rule of Law*, edited by G. Palombella and N. Walker. Oxford: Hart Publishing.

Boeckenfoerde, Ernst-Wolfgang. 1991. *Recht, Staat, Freiheit*. Frankfurt-am-Main: Suhrkamp Verlag.

Buchanan, James. 1977. *Freedom in Constitutional Contract. Perspectives of a Political Economist*. College Station: Texas A&M University Press.

Carré de Malberg, Raymond. 1920. *Contribution à la theorie general de l'Etat*. Paris: Sirey.

Coleman, Jules. 2000. "Constraints on the Criteria of Legality." *Legal Theory* 6-2: 171–83.

Craig, Paul. 1997. "Formal and Substantive Conceptions of the Rule of Law: An Analytical Framework." *Public Law* Autumn: 467–487.

Dicey, Albert Venn. 1915. *Introduction to the Study of the Law of the Constitution*, edited by E. C. S. Wade. VIII edition. London: Macmillan. Reprinted 1982. Indianapolis: Liberty Classics.

Finnis, John. 1980. *Natural Law and Natural Rights*. Oxford: Clarendon Press.

Fraenkel, Ernst. [1941] 1969. *The Dual State. A Contribution to the Theory of Dictatorship*. Translated by E. A. Shils, New York: Octagon Press.

Fried, Charles. 1981. "The Artificial Reason of the Law or: What Lawyers Know." *Texas Law Review* 60:35–58.

Fuller, Lon. [1964] 1969. *The Morality of Law*, II ed. New Haven: Yale University Press.

Gerber, Carl F. W. [1852] 1913. *Über öffentliche Rechte*. Tübingen: Mohr.

Goodhart, Arthur, L. 1958. "The Rule of Law and Absolute Sovereignty." *University of Pennsylvania Law Review* 106:943–963.

Gordon, Robert. 1984. "Critical Legal Histories." *Stanford Law Review* 36:57–125.

Habermas, Juergen. 1988. *Law and Morality* (Tanner Lectures on Human Values.) Salt Lake City: University of Utah Press.

—— 1996. *Between Facts and Norms. Contributions to a Discourse Theory of Law and Democracy*. Translated by W. Rehg. Cambridge: Polity Press.

Haskins, George L. 1955. "Executive Justice and the Rule of Law: Some Reflections on Thirteenth-Century England." *Speculum* 30:529–38.

Hayek, Friedrich. 1944. *The Road to Serfdom* (London: Routledge.

—— 1960. *The Constitution of Liberty*. Chicago: Chicago University Press.

Hobbes, Thomas. [1651] 1946. *Leviathan*, edited by M. Oakeshott. Oxford: Basil Blackwell.

Holmes, Stephen. 2003. "Lineages of the Rule of Law." Pp. 19–61, in *Democracy and the Rule of Law*, edited by J. Maravall and A. Przeworski. Cambridge: Cambridge University Press.

Horwitz, Morton. 1977. *The Transformation of American Law, 1780–1860*, Cambridge, Mass.: Harvard University Press.

Jellinek, Georg. [1892] 19192. *System der subjektiven öffentlichen Rechts*. Tübingen: Mohr.

Kant, Immanuel. [1788]. 1996a. *Critique of Practical Reason,* in Id., *Practical Philosophy.* Translated and edited by M. J. Gregor. Cambridge: Cambridge University Press.

—— [1793]. 1996b. *On the Common Saying: "That may be correct in theory, but it is of no use in practice"* in Id., *Practical Philosophy.* Translated and edited by M. J. Gregor. Cambridge: Cambridge University Press.

Kluxen, Kurt. 1983. *Geschichte und Problematik des Parlamentarismus.* Frankfurt-am-Main: Suhrkamp.

Krieger, Leonard. 1957. *The German Idea of Freedom.* Boston: Beacon Press.

Krygier, Martin. 2009. "The Rule of Law: Legality, Teleology, Sociology." Pp. 45–70 in *Relocating the Rule of Law,* edited by G. Palombella and N. Walker. Oxford: Hart Publishing.

López de Oñate, Flavio. 1953. *La certeza del derecho.* Buenos Aires, Ediciones Juŕidicas Europa-América.

MacCormick, Neil D. 2005. *Rhetoric and the Rule of Law.* Oxford: Oxford University Press.

—— 2008. *Institutions of Law.* Oxford: Oxford University Press.

Marmor, Andrei. 2004. "The Rule of Law and its Limits." *Law and Philosophy* 23: 1–43.

Mathews, Jud and Stone Sweet, Alec. 2008. "Proportionality Balancing and Global Constitutionalism." *Columbia Journal of Transnational Law* 47:73–165.

Matteucci, Nicola. 1993. *Lo Stato moderno.* Bologna: Il Mulino.

Mayer, Otto. 1895. *Deutsche Verwaltungsrecht,* vol. I. Leipzig: Duncker & Humblot.

McIlwain, Charles H. 1940. *Constitutionalism: Ancient and Modern.* Ithaca: Cornell Univeristy Press.

Mohl, Ludwig v.[1832–4] 1832. *Die Polizeiwissenschaft nach den Grundsätzen des Rechtsstaates,* I–III, Tuebingen: Mohr.

Palombella, Gianluigi. 2006a. "The Abuse of Rights and the Rule of Law." Pp. 5–28, in*The Dark Side of Fundamental Rights,* edited by A. Sajo. Utrecht: Eleven Intern. Publisher.

—— 2007. "The Rule of Law, Democracy and International Law. Learning from U.S. Experience." *Ratio Juris.* 20:456–84.

—— 2009a. "The Rule of Law and Its Core." Pp. 17–42, in *Relocating the Rule of Law,* edited by G. Palombella and N. Walker. Oxford: Hart Publishing.

—— 2009b. "The Rule of Law Beyond the State. Failures, Promises and Theory." *International Journal of Constitutional Law.* 7:442–67.

Pettit, Philip. 1997. *Republicanism: A Theory of Freedom and Government.* Oxford: Oxford University Press.

—— 2009. "Law and Liberty." Pp. 39–60, in *Legal Republicanism,* edited by S. Besson and J. L. Marti. Oxford: Oxford University Press.

Rawls, John. 1971. *A Theory of Justice.* Cambridge, Mass.: Harvard University Press.

—— 1993. *Political Liberalism.* New York: Columbia University Press.

Raz, Joseph. 1979. "The Rule of Law and Its Virtue" Pp. 210–29, in Id., *The Authority of Law.* Oxford: Clarendon Press.

—— [1984] 1995. "Right-based Moralities" Pp. 182–200 in *Theories of Rights,* edited by J. Waldron. Oxford: Oxford University Press.

—— 1996. *Ethics in the Public Domain.* Oxford: Oxford University Press.

—— 2007. "The Argument from Justice, or How Not to Reply to Legal Positivism." Pp. 17–35 in *Law, Rights & Discourse: The Legal Philosophy of Robert Alexy,* edited by G. Pavlakos. Oxford: Hart Publishing.

Reid, Philip. 2004. *Rule of Law. The Jurisprudence of Liberty in the Seventeenth and Eighteenth Century.* DeKalb: Northern Illinois University Press.

Sartori, Giovanni. 1964. "Nota sul rapporto tra Stato di diritto e Stato di giustizia." *Rivista internazionale di filosofia del diritto,* 1964:310–6.

Sajo, Andras. 2006. *The Dark Side of Fundamental Rights*. Utrecht: Eleven Intern. Publisher.

Scalia, Antonin. 1989. "The Rule of Law as a Law of Rules." *University of Chicago Law Review* 56:1175–1188.

—— 1996. *A Matter of interpretation. Federal Courts and the Law*. Princeton: Princeton University Press.

Scheuerman, Wilhelm. 1994. "The Rule of Law and the Welfare State. Toward a new Synthesis". *Politics and Society*. 22:195–213.

Schmitt, Carl. [1959] 1996. *The Tyranny of Values*. Translated by Simona Draghici, Washington DC.: Plutarch Press.

Skinner, Quentin. 1998. *Liberty before Liberalism*, Cambridge: Cambridge University Press.

Stahl, Friedrich Julius. 1870. *Philosophie des Rechts, vol. II, Rechts- und Staatslehre auf der Grundlage christlicher Weltanschauung*. Heidelberg: Mohr.

Tamanaha, Brian. 2006. *Law as Means to an End*. Cambridge: Cambridge University Press.

Thompson, Edward P. 1975. *Whigs and Hunters: The Origins of the Black Act*. New York: Pantheon Books.

Waldron, Jeremy. 2005. "Torture and Positive Law. Jurisprudence for the White House." *Columbia Law Review* 105:1681–1750.

——. 2008. "The Concept and the Rule of Law." *Georgia Law Review* 43 (1): 1–62.

Waluchow Wil J. 1985. "Herculean Positivism." *Oxford Journal of Legal Studies* 5(2):187–210.

Weber, Max. 1978. *Economy and Society*, vol 2, edited by G. Roth and C. Wittich. Berkeley, CA: University of California Press.

Zagrebelsky, Gustavo. 1992. *Il diritto mite*. Torino: Einaudi.

CHAPTER TWO

THE TWO 'RULES OF LAW' BETWEEN TRANSITION TO AND QUALITY OF DEMOCRACY

Leonardo Morlino[1]

Although there is a good traditional literature and a growing more recent one on the rule of law and democracy (see Magen and Morlino 2008), a number of key aspects still need to be spelled out when the relationships with democracy are empirically and more closely analyzed. Especially when we consider that the rule of law is a pre-condition for the analysis of democratic change and at the same time can be influenced by other institutional and non institutional aspects in established democracies, the complexity of those relationships becomes more evident, its salience can be immediately understood and some ironic features emerge as well.

This chapter builds on my previous empirical research experiences (Morlino 2003, Diamond and Morlino 2005, Morlino and Magen 2008) and a long, fruitful debate with Gianluigi Palombella, co-editor of this volume. It starts with a preliminary general definition of the notion of the rule of law and links it to other definitions provided in the present volume. In the first and second sections it is shown that empirical research can better be carried out if we provide different definitions of the same concept in relation to the two main contexts where an analysis of the rule of law is mostly salient, that is, the transition to democracy and the quality of consolidated democracies. Such a multiple notion can be useful for a better empirical analysis of the two phenomena just mentioned above. This point will be better clarified in the last section, where the rule of law will be seen in connection with two other democratic dimensions, accountability and responsiveness. A few short concluding remarks will point out the main aspects of theoretical analysis proposed here.

[1] I would like to warmly thank my co-editor Gianluigi Palombella for what I consider a very fruitful interdisciplinary collaboration.

To anyone who has done any research or even just some reading on the topic it will be almost obvious that the expression 'rule of law' is afflicted by an extraordinary divergence of understandings. It is a highly contested term that is at the same time evolving in the use made by practitioners and scholars from different disciplines. I would like to start here from Palombella's contribution to this volume (see ch. by him), where the rule of law is viewed as a credible limitation on arbitrariness and a safeguard of individuals and minorities only when, within legal structures and institutions, a *dual track* is available or gradually developing in existing positive law. Thus, there is some "other" law, which has slowly developed outside of the "gubernaculum" area, whose content and sources on a legal plane are neither under the purview of the ruling powers, nor can they be legally changed at their whim (as holds true, in different settings, from ancient English common law to the present western constitutional orders). Indeed, the latter might prove to have a sound and less ambiguous significance, connoting, *from the legal vantage point*, the principle of the supremacy of law, that is, the Ciceronian *legum servi sumus*, and entails at least the capacity, even if limited or very limited, to make authorities respect the laws.[2]

From a political science perspective, this is the core of a high normative notion of the rule of law that requires a corresponding empirical notion. Such an empirical, general notion cannot be only the actual enforcement of legal norms. As a first, key aspect, the rule of law is fundamental to achieve some sort of civil order, that is, a basic requirement for every democracy (see also Morlino 1998). Additionally, as Kleinfeld (2006) observes, in contemporary use the notion the of rule of law can refer to at least five meanings: (1) government bound by law; (2) equality before the law; (3) law and order; (4) predictable, efficient justice, and (5) public power respectful of fundamental rights.[3] Consequently, it should be immediately clear that some of these meanings, i.e. especially the second, fourth and fifth ones, imply a pre-existing democracy whereas others do not. That is, the necessity to specify

---

[2] For the minimal definition of the rule of law see Maravall (2002) and here at p. 47.

[3] For a more developed discussion of this point see Magen and Morlino (2008, ch. 1), Belton (2005), HiiL (2007), Trebilcock and Daniels (2008, 12ff.).

the political context where research is to be carried out immediately emerges, leading one to accept and to adopt different empirical notions of the rule of law. Thus, in the next two sections we will immediately consider the contexts and which two related notions to choose in connection with the two political contexts for a better empirical research on the topic.

The Salience of the Context: Hybrid Regime and Transition to Democracy

The first context to single out is that of *transition to democracy* or also of hybrid regime (see Morlino 2009). Transitional situations or hybrid regimes are the broadest notions to be preferred in this sort of analysis. Here the relevant context is given by political arrangements that in a temporary or more stable way no longer configure some form of non-democracy and do not yet configure a democracy. But in order to understand better such an ambiguous political context we need to start with a definition of 'minimal' democracy as well as a working definition of non democracy.

A minimal democracy is a set of political institutions that are characterized at the same time by: *a*) universal suffrage, both male and female; *b*) free, competitive, recurrent and fair elections; *c*) more than one party; *d*) different and alternative media sources. To better understand this definition, it is worth stressing that a regime of this kind must provide real guarantees of civil and political rights that enable the actual implementation of those four aspects. That is, such rights are assumed to exist if there is authentic universal suffrage, i.e. the whole adult *demos* has the right to vote; if there are free, fair and recurrent elections as an expression of the effective existence of freedom of speech and thought as well; if there is more than one effectively competing party, demonstrating the existence of genuine and practiced rights of assembly and association; and if there are different media sources belonging to different proprietors, proof of the existence of the liberties of expression and thought. One important aspect of this definition is that in the absence of just one of these requirements, or if at some point one of them is no longer met, there is no longer a democratic regime, but some other political and institutional set-up, possibly an intermediate one marked by varying degrees of uncertainty and ambiguity.

Such a minimal definition focuses on the institutions that characterize democracy: elections, competing parties (at least potentially so) and media pluralism. It can be added that it is also important, according to Schmitter and Karl (1993:45–46), that these institutions and rights should not be subject to, or conditioned by, 'non-elected actors' or exponents of other external regimes. The former refers to the armed forces, religious hierarchies, economic oligarchies, a hegemonic party or even a monarch with pretensions to influencing decision-making processes or at any rate the overall functioning of a democracy; in the second case, a regime might be conditioned by an external power that deprives the democracy in question of its independence and sovereignty by pursuing non-democratic policies.

As regards the definition of non-democratic regimes, reference must be made at least to traditional and authoritarian regimes. The former are 'based on the personal power of the sovereign, who binds his underlings in a relationship of fear and reward; they are typically *legibus soluti* regimes, where the sovereign's arbitrary decisions are not limited by norms and do not need to be justified ideologically. Power is thus used in particularistic forms and for essentially private ends. In these regimes, the armed forces and police play a central role, while there is an evident lack of any form of developed ideology and any structure of mass mobilization, as a single party usually is. Basically, then, the political set-up is dominated by traditional elites and institutions' (Morlino 2003:80).

As for the authoritarian regimes, the definition advanced by Linz (1964:255) is still the most useful one: a 'political system with limited, non-responsible political pluralism; without an elaborated and guiding ideology, but with distinctive mentalities; without either extensive or intense political mobilization, except at some points in their development, and in which a leader, or, occasionally, a small group, exercises power from within formally ill-defined, but actually quite predictable, limits'. However, with respect to such a definition, which identifies five significant dimensions, i.e. limited pluralism, distinctive values,[4]

[4] These values include notions like homeland, nation, order, hierarchy, authority and such like, where both traditional and modernizing positions can, and sometimes have, found common ground. In any case, the regime is not supported by any complex, articulated ideological elaboration. In other regimes, like the traditional ones, the only effective justification of the regime is personal in nature, that is, to serve a certain leader, who may, in the case of a monarch who has acceded to power on a hereditary basis, be backed by tradition.

low political mobilization, a small leading group, ill-defined, but predictable limits to citizens' rights, for our purpose we need to stress the constraints imposed on political pluralism within a society that has no recognized autonomy or independence as well as no effective political participation of the people, with the consequent exercise of various forms of state suppression. A further, neglected, but nonetheless important dimension should also be added – the *institutions* that characterize authoritarian regimes, which are invariably of marked importance in many transitional cases. Once created and having become stabilized over a certain number of years, institutions often leave a significant legacy for a new regime, even when it has become firmly democratic.

In addition to Morlino (2003), other authors stress this aspect. For example, it is worth recalling the whole debate on 'electoral authoritarianisms' (Schedler 2006). With this term Schedler (2006:5) refers to specific models of authoritarianism – not to a hybrid regime – specifically characterized by electoral institutions and practices; in this instance, hybrid regimes are the result of changes that begin within these types of authoritarianism. Moreover, the attention given to authoritarian institutions is relevant for other important reasons. Firstly, the existence of efficient repressive apparatuses capable of implementing the above-mentioned demobilization policies, for instance security services, which may be autonomous or part of the military structure. Secondly, the partial weakness or the absence of mobilization structures, such as the single party or unions which may be vertical ones admitting both workers and employers, or other similar state institutions, that is, structures capable of simultaneously generating and controlling participation. There could be distinct forms of parliamentary assembly, possibly based on the functional and corporative representation of interests; distinctive electoral systems; military juntas; ad hoc constitutional organs; or other specific organs different from those that existed in the previous regime. Obviously, there is also another implicit aspect that it is worth stressing: the absence of real guarantees regarding the various political and civil rights.

Limited, non-responsible pluralism, which may range from monism to a certain number of important and active actors in the regime, is a key aspect deserving of attention. For every non-democratic regime, it is important above all to pinpoint the significant actors, for whom a distinction can be made between institutional actors and politically active social actors. Examples of the former are the army, the bureaucratic system or a part thereof and, where applicable, a single party; the latter include the Church, industrial or financial groups, landowners, and in some cases even unions or trans-national economic structures with major interests in the nation concerned. Such actors are not politically responsible according to the typical mechanism of liberal democracies, that is, through free, competitive and fair elections. If there is 'responsibility', it is exercised at the level of 'invisible politics' in the real relations between, for instance, military leaders and economic groups or landowners. Furthermore, elections or the other forms of electoral participation that may exist, for instance direct consultations through plebiscites, have no democratic significance and, above all, are not the expression of rights, freedom and the genuine competition to be found in democratic regimes. They have a mainly symbolic, legitimating significance, an expression of consensus and support for the regime on the part of a controlled, non-autonomous civil society.

Having proposed definitions for minimal democracy, the traditional regime and authoritarianism, it is now possible to delineate *hybrid regimes.* These are more than just 'mixed regimes', which, as defined by Bunce and Wolchik (2008:6), 'fall in the sprawling middle of a political continuum anchored by democracy on one end……and dictatorship on the other end'. As suggested by Karl (1995:80) in relation to some Latin American countries, they may be characterized by 'uneven acquisition of procedural requisites of democracy', without a 'civilian control over the military', with sectors of the population that 'remain politically and economically disenfranchised' and with a 'weak judiciary'. But again this definition only refers to authoritarianisms that partially lose some of their key characteristics, retain some authoritarian or traditional features and at the same time acquire some of the characteristic institutions and procedures of democracy, but not others.

A hybrid regime, on the other hand, may also have a set of institutions where, going down the inverse path, some key elements of democracy have been lost and authoritarian characteristics acquired. An adequate definition of a hybrid regime should, then, include other features, for instance some of the aspects mentioned by Levitsky and Way (2002:52–58) in their analysis of a specific model of hybrid regime (competitive authoritarianism), such as the existence of 'incumbents (who) routinely abuse state resources, deny the opposition adequate media coverage, harass opposition candidates and their supporters, and in some case manipulate electoral results'.

This discussion, however, prompts reflection about two elements. First, a hybrid regime is always a set of ambiguous institutions that maintain aspects of the past. In other words, and this is the second point, it is a 'corruption' of the preceding regime, lacking as it does one or more essential characteristics of that regime but also failing to acquire other characteristics that would make it fully democratic or authoritarian (see definitions above). Consequently, in order to define hybrid regimes more precisely it seems appropriate to take a different line from the one suggested in the literature and to explicitly include the past of such regimes in the definition itself.

The term 'hybrid' can thus be applied to all those regimes preceded by a period of authoritarian or traditional rule, followed by the beginnings of greater tolerance, liberalization and a partial relaxation of the restrictions on pluralism; or, all those regimes which, following a period of minimal democracy in the sense indicated above, are subject to the intervention of non-elected bodies – the military, above all – that place restrictions on competitive pluralism without, however, creating a more or less stable authoritarian regime. There are, then, three possibilities behind a definition taking account of the context of origin, which can be better explicated as follows: the regime arises out of one of the different types of authoritarianism that have existed in recent decades, or even earlier; the regime arises out of a traditional regime, a monarchy or sultanism;[5] or the regime arises out of the crisis of a previous democracy. To these must be added a fourth, which is an important specification of the second: the regime is the result of decolonialization that has never been followed by either authoritarian or democratic stabilization.

If, to gain a closer empirical understanding of a hybrid regime, one develops at least the first and second of these hypotheses a little further – though the majority of cases in recent decades would seem to fall into the first category – it can be seen that alongside the old actors of the previous authoritarian or traditional regime, a number of opposition groups have clearly taken root, thanks also to some partial, relative respect of civil rights. These groups are allowed to participate in the political process, but have little substantial possibility

[5] For a definition and discussion of these regimes see still the classic volume by Linz (2000).

of governing. There are, then, a number of parties, of which one may remain hegemonic-dominant in semi-competitive elections; at the same time there is already some form of real competition amongst the candidates of that party. The other parties are fairly unorganized, of recent creation or re-creation, and have only a small following. There is some degree of real participation, but it is minimal and usually limited to the election period. Often, a powerfully distorting electoral system allows the hegemonic-dominant party to maintain an enormous advantage in the distribution of seats; in many cases the party in question is a bureaucratic structure rife with patronage favours and intent on surviving the on-going transformation. This means that there is no longer any justification for the regime, not even merely on the basis of all-encompassing and ambiguous values. Other forms of participation during the authoritarian period, if there have ever been any, are just a memory of the past. Evident forms of police repression are also absent, and so the role of the relative apparatuses is not prominent, while the position of the armed forces is even more low-key. Overall, there is little institutionalization and, above all, organization of the 'State', if not a full-blown process of deinstitutionalization. The armed forces may, however, maintain an evident political role, though it is still less explicit and direct.[6]

Moreover, hybrid regimes often stem from the attempt, at least temporarily successful, by moderate governmental actors in the previous authoritarian or traditional regime to resist internal or external pressures on the dominant regime, to continue to maintain order and the previous distributive set-up and to partially satisfy – or at least appear to do so – the demand for greater democratization on the part of other actors, the participation of whom is also contained within limits. Consequently, there are potentially as many different variants of transitional regimes as there are types of authoritarian and traditional models. Many cases could be fitted into this model, which says a good deal about their potential significance.

In disentangling empirical realities that fit the previously formulated definition of the hybrid regime from different transitional situations, we should add that there has been some sort of stabilization or dura-

[6] Despite her empirical focus on Central America the analysis by Karl (1995) is also useful to better understand the conditions and perspectives of hybrid regimes in other areas.

tion, at least – we submit – for a decade, of those ambiguous uncertain institutional set-ups. Consequently, to avoid a misleading analysis of democratization processes we can define a hybrid regime as a set of institutions that have persisted, in a stable or unstable form, for about a decade, have been preceded by an authoritarianism, a traditional regime (possibly with colonial characteristics), or even a minimal democracy and are characterized by the break-up of limited pluralism and forms of independent, autonomous participation, but lack at least one of the four aspects of a minimal democracy.

At this point it is worth emphasizing that there may be an overlap between a hybrid regime and a transitional phase. The key difference lies in the fact that hybrid regimes *stricto sensu* are also characterized by the achievement of some extent of stabilization while a transitional phase is not. At the same time, of course, it is important to grasp the ambiguities and the fuzziness of regimes in which features of both democracy and authoritarianism coexist, and in this vein, to consider the notion of the rule of law – useful for detecting both situations, that of a hybrid regime and a transitional one – in order to understand how the situation can evolve or change.

In a context like these ones we need a minimal definition of the rule of law where the possible developments and trends are envisaged. Such a minimal definition of the rule of law (e.g. Maravall 2002:261) refers to the implementation, even if only partially and in a territorially limited fashion, of laws that (i) were enacted and approved.....; (ii) that are not retroactive..., but general, stable, clear, and hierarchically ordered....; (iii) applied to particular cases by courts free from political influence and accessible to all, the decisions of which follow procedural requirements, and that establish guilt through ordinary means.

The dimensions of this notion that are empirically more relevant are:

1. *Effective protection of civil freedoms and political rights*: the focus is, first of all, on the right to life, to be free of fear and torture, to enjoy personal security and the right, guaranteed and protected throughout the country, to own property, plus a number of other basic rights.
2. *Independent judiciary and a modern justice system*: the focus is on mechanisms establishing an independent, professional and efficient judiciary system that allows equal access to justice, free of the undue pressures and enforcement of decisions.

3. *Institutional and administrative capacity* to formulate, implement and enforce the law: the focus is on the governance system (parliament and government) required to ensure the production of high-quality legislation, and the implementation, throughout the country, of a transparent policy-making process allowing for the participation of civil society, and the presence of a professional, neutral, accountable and efficient state bureaucracy.
4. *Security forces that are respectful of citizens rights and are under civilian control*: the focus is on the mechanisms of civilian control over security forces as well as on efficient, uncorrupted, disciplined police forces.
5. *Effective fight against corruption*, illegality and abuse of power by state agencies: the focus is on the existence and implementation of the comprehensive legislative framework to prevent and fight corruption.

The key guiding questions for each dimension are:

1. *Effective protection of civil freedoms and political rights*: What are the major threats to individual life and to the guaranteeing of basic rights in a country?
2. *Independent judiciary and a modern justice system*: Are there structural guarantees of the independence of the judiciary and are the legal guarantees adequately implemented, ensuring that the judicial system is free from interference by the executive or legislative branches? Does the judiciary work efficiently?
3. *Institutional and administrative capacity*: How well developed are the institutions and the administration, and how well do they actually perform.
4. *Security forces under civilian control*: Are army, police and other security forces under the civilian control of authorities?
5. *Effective fight against corruption, illegality and abuse of power by state agencies*: Does a comprehensive legislative framework exist to prevent and fight corruption, and is it implemented?

To better understand this empirical notion some additional clarifications are necessary. First, the notion of the rule of law proposed here has to be considered as a series of (five) different concentric circles where the first dimension comes first and is related to the other ones. Second, the first dimension, which concerns the effective implementation of rights, has to be monitored, as it is a key element in the very definition of the hybrid regime or the transitional phase, or the achievement of a minimal democracy. Third, the key step and transition from ambiguity and a hybrid situation is carried out only when there is a reasonable independence of the judiciary. Fourth, institutional and administrative capacity (a key requisite for the adoption and the implementation of the law) also has to be seen in connection with its territorial diffusion. Finally, rule adoption and rule implementation are the key moments, whereas rule internalization, which is the acceptance or the legitimation of the rule by citizens, belongs to a subsequent phase of democratic consolidation, when the ambiguities of a hybrid regime or the uncertainties of transition are over.

The Salience of the Context: the Quality of Democracy

Let's see now what characterizes the context defined as 'quality of democracy' and what is the most suitable related empirical notion of the rule of law that should be adopted. First of all, an analysis of the quality of a democracy, that is, an empirical check on how 'good' a democracy is, requires that we establish a clear notion of quality in addition to a well- defined notion of democracy. The definition of democracy has already been suggested above. As for 'quality', a survey of the use of the term in the industrial and marketing sectors suggests three different meanings:

1. quality is defined by the established procedural aspects associated with each product; a 'quality' product is the result of an exact, controlled process carried out according to precise, recurring methods and timing; here the emphasis is on the *procedure*;
2. quality consists in the structural characteristics of a product, be it the design, materials, or functioning of the good, or other details that it features; here, the emphasis is on the *content*;
3. the quality of a product or service is indirectly derived from the satisfaction expressed by the customer, by their requesting the same product or service again, regardless of either how it is produced or what the actual contents are, or how the consumer goes about acquiring the product or service; according to such a meaning, the quality is simply based on *result*.

In summary, the three different notions of quality are grounded either in procedures, contents, or results. Each has different implications for empirical research. Importantly, even with all the adjustments demanded by the complexity of the 'object' under examination – democracy – it is still necessary to keep these conceptualizations of quality in mind as we elaborate definitions and models of democratic quality.

Starting from the definition mentioned above, and from the prevailing notions of quality, I consider a quality or good democracy to be one presenting *a stable institutional structure that realizes the liberty and equality of citizens through the legitimate and correct functioning of its institutions and mechanisms*. A good democracy is thus first and foremost a broadly legitimated regime that completely satisfies citizens (*quality in terms of result*). When institutions have the full backing of civil society, they can pursue the values of the democratic regime. If, by contrast, the institutions must postpone their objectives and expend energy and resources on consolidating and maintaining their legitimacy, crossing even the minimum threshold for democracy becomes a remarkable feat. Second, a good democracy is one in which citizens, associations and the communities of which it is composed enjoy at least a moderate level of liberty and equality (*quality in terms of content*). Third, in a good democracy it is the citizens themselves who have the power to check and evaluate whether the government pursues the objectives of liberty and equality according to the rule of law. They monitor the efficiency of the application of the laws in force, the efficacy of the decisions made by government, and the political responsibility and accountability of elected officials in relation to the demands expressed by civil society (*quality in terms of procedure*).

With the above in mind, I can thus indicate eight possible dimensions on which good democracies might vary, and which should form the core of empirical analysis. The first ones are procedural dimensions. Though also quite relevant to the contents, these dimensions mainly concern the rules. The first procedural dimension is the *rule of law*. The second and the third procedural dimensions are electoral accountability and inter-institutional accountability. The other two dimensions, competition and participation, are what Diamond and Morlino (2005) defined as the 'engines of democratic quality'. The sixth dimension of variation concerns the responsiveness or correspondence of the system to the desires of the citizens and civil society in general. The final two dimensions of variation are substantive in nature. The first is full respect for rights that are expanded through the achievement of a range of freedoms. The second is the progressive implementation of greater political, social and economic equality, complemented by solidarity.

Within such a context of established democracies and with the goal of analyzing how well developed and guaranteed the rule of law is, its virtues are inextricably related to the democratic process, in at least three key respects: the rule of law upholds the political rights of a democratic regime; it protects the civil liberties and rights of the entire population (including minority and other disadvantaged groups); and it establishes networks of responsibility 'which entail that all public and private agents, including the highest state officials, are subject to appropriate, legally established controls on the lawfulness of their acts'. (O'Donnell 2005:7). Actually, the interrelation between the rule of law and democracy permeates institutions and spheres across society: 'The Rule-of-Law makes possible individual rights, which are at the core of democracy. A government's respect for the sovereign authority of the people and a constitution depends on its acceptance of law. Democracy includes institutions and processes that, although beyond the immediate domain of the legal system, are rooted in it.' (Carothers 2006:4–5).

In this perspective and with reference to Eastern Europe, Dietrich (2000:6–7) points out that '...a rule of law... *Operates objectively.* The law is interpreted and enforced by lawyers, judges, prosecutors and other officials in an ethical and fair manner, without special preferences and privileges. *Is administered on knowledge of the law.* Those charged with interpreting and enforcing the legislative framework know what the law is, and understand its underlying principles. *Is accessible.* Individuals have meaningful access to the legal system. This means that they know what their rights are, can obtain representation, and filing fees are affordable. *Is reasonably efficient (and)... is transparent.* Citizens affected by legislation have an opportunity to comment on it as it is drafted. Likewise, judicial decisions are justified and explained and subject to press and academic scrutiny. *Is predictable.* Legislation is drafted in a reasonably clear manner, so that outcomes are predictable and undue discretion is not left in the hands of public officials. *Is enforceable.* Judicial and administrative decisions, rendered fairly, are enforced. *Protects private property rights. Protects individual and human rights. Protects legitimate state interests*, e.g., by prosecuting those charged with clearly defined criminal acts.'

This means that in a 'good democracy' the following characteristics should exist:

- Effective enforcement, applicable to everyone, including all state officials, of the legal system, also at the supra-national level, and the guaranteeing of the rights and equality of citizens;
- Implementation of the principle that no one is above the law;
- Supremacy of the legal state throughout the country, leaving no areas dominated by organized crime, local oligarchs or political bosses who are above the law;
- The complete independence of the judiciary at all levels from any political influence;
- Equal, unhindered access of citizens to the justice system in the eventuality of lawsuits between private citizens or between private citizens and public institutions;
- Reasonably swift resolution of criminal inquiries and of civil and administrative lawsuits;
- The hearing and expeditious solution of criminal cases and civil and administrative lawsuits;
- The respect for and enforcement of rulings of the courts by other agencies of the state;
- The supremacy of a constitution that is interpreted and defended by a Constitutional Court;
- Existence of a local, centralized, civil bureaucracy that competently, efficiently and universally applies the laws and assumes responsibility in the event of an error;
- Existence of a professional and efficient police force that respects the individual's rights and freedoms guaranteed by law;
- Absence of corruption in the political, administrative and judicial branches.

On the whole, when compared with the rule of law that has to be analyzed in a hybrid regime or a transitional phase, the key bottom-line aspects are the same, but the empirical focus is different, because in a consolidated, stable democracies several features can be taken for granted whereas others should receive higher attention.

In the analysis of quality, a closer look at the concrete problems of implementation should be accompanied by an awareness of some opposing forces. First and foremost, a rigorous application of laws, or, in certain cases, the relationship with an only superficially efficient bureaucracy can have particularly negative consequences for the most socially weak and vulnerable members of society (O'Donnell 1999:312–13). Then, there is the possible use of the law as a genuine 'political weapon' (Maravall 2002). Here we see a persistent and widespread e temptation for politicians to use the law against their adversaries if, for example, the opposition is condemned to remain so for a long time and has no chance of electoral victory in the near future. Politicians are also tempted to use judicial acts to reinforce their own positions against the opposition. In other cases, when there is collusion among politicians, the judges themselves, with the support of the media, are tempted to turn to the judiciary in retaliation for certain political decisions that they consider unacceptable.

On a different level, there is also a growing tendency among individual citizens or economic groups to resort to the law to assert their own interests. Some scholars note this phenomenon as a 'juridification' of contemporary democracy (see, for example, Guarnieri and Pederzoli, 1997). Finally, and not altogether differently, there is the popular and widespread cultural attitude that interprets the law as a severe impediment to realizing one's own interests that should be circumvented in any way possible. This attitude, common in various countries throughout the world, from Southern Europe to Latin America and also Eastern Europe, extends from the working class to the entrepreneurial classes. The Italian saying "*fatta la legge, trovato l'inganno*", which suggests that fraud goes hand in hand with law, seems particularly apt in this respect.

In summary, the empirical analysis of the democratic rule of law needs to be conducted carefully, with attention to trends that work against its full realization. It remains an essential factor of democratic quality, and it plays a very important role for the existence and development of the other dimensions. What then, are the fundamental conditions that allow for at least a moderate development of the rule of law? Research into various dimensions of this theme suggests that the spread of liberal and democratic values on the popular and, especially, the elite level, as well as the existence of bureaucratic traditions and legislative and economic means are the necessary conditions for the democratic rule of law.

However, these conditions exist in very few countries, and they are very hard to create. Consequently, it is also difficult to cultivate and develop this dimension of democratic quality. The most reasonable and concrete strategy would be to proceed in short, measured steps that follow the lines and objectives that emerged above. This strategy is inherently critical of Putnam's conclusion (1993) that the institutional contours of a specific democratic regime are fixed in the oldest civic traditions of that country, and that a country's institutions necessarily change extremely slowly.

It should be emphasized, even if only in passing, that the analysis proposed here would be extremely expensive and practically impossible to apply to a high number of cases. The level of detail and thoroughness built into the investigation is meant for a limited number of cases, yielding the best results for a project aimed at examining at most four or five countries.

An Addendum on Quality: Connections Between a Few Dimensions

Another key aspect in the analysis of the rule of law and quality is the one concerning the connection with some of the other dimensions of quality. Here, I will only make reference to accountability and responsiveness. Accountability, the second procedural dimension of democratic quality, is the obligation of elected political leaders to answer for their political decisions when asked to by citizen-electors or other constitutional bodies. Schedler (1999:17) suggests that accountability has three main features: information, justification and punishment/compensation. The first element, information regarding a political act or series of acts by a politician or political organ (the government, parliament, and so on), is indispensable for attributing responsibility. Justification refers to the reasons furnished by the governing leaders for their actions and decisions. The third, punishment/compensation, is the consequence drawn by the elector or some other person or body following an evaluation of the information, justifications, and other aspects and interests behind the political act. All three of these elements require the existence of a public dimension characterized by pluralism and independence and the real participation of a range of individual and collective actors.

Accountability can be either electoral or inter-institutional. Electoral accountability is what electors can demand from their elected official, that the governed can require of the governor in the light of certain acts which he/she has executed. This first type of accountability has a periodic nature, and is dependent on the various national, local, and if they exist, supra-national election dates. The voter decides and either awards the incumbent candidate or slate of candidates with a vote in their favor, or else punishes them by voting for another candidate, abstaining from the vote, or by nullifying the ballot. The actors involved in electoral accountability are the governor and the governed, and are thus politically unequal. This dimension of democratic quality can become less irregular only if one considers the various electoral occasions at the local, national, and for European citizens, supra-national levels. Continuity is also supported when citizens can vote in referendums on issues regarding the activity of the central government.

Inter-institutional accountability is the responsibility governors have to answer to other institutions or collective actors that have the expertise and power to control the behavior of the governors. In contrast to electoral accountability, the actors are for the most part political equals. Inter-institutional accountability is relatively continuous, being formally or substantially formalized by law. In practice, it is usually manifest in the monitoring exercised by the governmental opposition in parliament, by the various judgments and checks emitted by the court system, if activated, and by constitutional courts, state accounting offices, central banks and other bodies of a similar purpose that exist in democracies. Political parties outside of parliament also exercise this kind of control, as do the media and other intermediary associations, such as unions, employers' associations and the like (see O'Donnell 1999; Schmitter 1999).

Certain underlying conditions must exist to ensure that the two forms of accountability can be fully claimed. For electoral accountability, political competition and the distribution of power must at least be fair enough to allow for genuine electoral alternatives at the various levels of government. Altman and Perez-Linan's (2001) focus on competition and on the development of an indicator to measure the 'balanced presence of opposition in parliament' should be mentioned here. This indicator has a negative value when the governing party dominates the legislature in terms of seats or when the opposition is so strong that it poses problems for the decisional efficacy of the government. The absence of alternation and bi-polarism between two parties, or between party lines or coalitions, undermines the importance and force of electoral accountability. If it exists, it is relevant only at the level of individual candidates.

The presence of inter-institutional accountability instead hinges on a legal system that, as mentioned above, provides for the exertion of checks and balances by other public entities that are independent of the government, and not competing as an alternative to it. This form of accountability demands strong and well-established intermediary structures; a responsible, vigilant political opposition; independent media that are conscious of their civil function; and a well-developed network of active, informed organizations and associations that share democratic values.

Given the well-known opacity of political processes and the complexity conveyed about them at the moments of information, justification and evaluation, politicians have ample opportunity to manipulate their contexts in such a way to absolve themselves of any concrete responsibility. Accountability frequently becomes a catch-phrase more connected to the image of a politician than to any decisions he or she may have taken or results he or she might have produced. Negative outcomes are easily justified by making reference to unforeseen events, or by taking advantage of a favorable press to influence public opinion. At the same time, good results, obtained sometimes at the cost of sacrifices by the governed, might result in negative or punitive judgments for the governor at the time of the next elections.

The very action, often ideological and instrumental, of parties or other components of the political opposition, or even of media actors that are in the position to conduct public processes, sometimes on inconsistent grounds, reconfirms the difficulty of implementing genuine accountability. The lack of clear distinctions between incumbent leaders and party leaders – the head of government often also controls the parties – means that parties, be they of the opposition or of the majority, are hindered in carrying out their role as watchdogs for their constituents. At the parliamentary level, party discipline is considered more important than accountability towards the electors and, in practice, the parliamentary majority supports the government without controlling it. Furthermore, there should also be a clear distinction between the responsible leader, either of the government or of the opposition, and the intermediate layers of party actors that range from militants to sympathizers. The latter trigger a bottom-up process that gives direction for how parties should control the government or organize their opposition. Recent studies on party organization in many advanced democracies (Katz and Mair 1995) indicate an opposite trend, however, characterized by strong, oligarchic leaders who act in collusion (instead of in competition) with other parties. The most extreme hypothesis relating to this phenomenon is that parties, supported by public financing, effectively shape 'cartels.'

Citizens in European countries encounter further difficulties in ensuring accountability due to the existence of the supra-national dimension created by the European Union. The most fitting example of how governments in these countries avoid accountability is the well-known tactic of 'blame shifting.' Here, the political responsibility for every unpopular decision taken by the government is shifted from the national to the European level, even if they concern clear-cut issues such as streamlining national administrations or reorganizing state finances to meet large national deficits. Governments or national politicians justify actions that arouse extensive public opposition by claiming that their hands are forced by opposing coalitions in the Council of Ministers of the European Union or in the European Council of prime ministers and chiefs of state, or by votes in the European Parliament.

As Maravall (1997) has already discussed, there are many ways in which government leaders can avoid accountability. At the same time, the absence or extreme weakness of inter-institutional accountability leaves electoral accountability as the only instrument for guaranteeing this dimension of quality democracy. The opportunities to exercise electoral accountability, however, are only periodic and in some cases citizens must wait several years before the next elections. The result is that we obtain a sort of 'delegative democracy' (see O'Donnell 1994) – a democracy of poor quality in which the citizen casts his/her vote and is subsequently ignored until the next election. Citizens are left without any means of controlling corruption and bad government, and there are no other institutions really capable of guaranteeing inter-institutional accountability.

The central conditions for insuring accountability are fairly obvious, and are already more or less clear from the above discussion. A few, however, should be explicitly mentioned. First of all, in addition to genuine electoral alternatives and bi-polarism among political parties, for one form of accountability to exist to any effective degree, the other must be present as well, with each thereby reinforcing the other. Next, a magistracy and other public institutions that are independent of the executive and legislature and capable of concretely exercising the checks provided for by law are also necessary. Third, it is also essential that interested, educated and informed citizens who have internalized the fundamental values of democracy remain involved in the political process. Fourth is the presence of independent sources of information. Finally, electoral and inter-institutional accountabilities are both supported when a range of active intermediary actors of various dimensions, such as parties and associations, are organizationally well-rooted and present in civil society.

In analyzing democratic quality, it is fairly common to refer to the responsiveness of government, that is, the capacity to satisfy the governed by executing its policies in a way that corresponds to their demands. This dimension is analytically related to accountability. Indeed, judgments on responsibility imply that there is some awareness of the actual demands, and that the evaluation of the government's response is related to how its actions either conform to or diverge from the interests of its electors. Responsiveness, therefore, must be treated in connection with accountability, although one should be aware that responsiveness is not always consistent with electoral accountability, and even less with inter-institutional accountability.

This dimension of democratic quality is not particularly difficult to define. Eulau and Karps (1977) have already demonstrated how responsiveness is a way to see representation 'in action'. They also show how this dimension is manifest through four main components in relation to: the policies at the center of public interest; the services that are guaranteed to the individuals and groups represented by the government; the distribution of material goods to their constituents through the public administration and other entities; and the extension of symbolic goods that create, reinforce or reproduce a sense of loyalty and support towards the government.

The empirical study of responsiveness, however, is more complicated. In fact, the idea that even educated, informed and politically engaged citizens always know their own needs and desires is at best an assumption, which is especially tenuous in situations where citizens might need specialized knowledge to accurately identify and evaluate those very needs and desires. Simplified, though still satisfactory, solutions, are still in order, however. Empirical measures of citizen satisfaction are easily found in the many surveys that have been regularly conducted for many years, especially in Western Europe, but also, as of late, in Latin America, Eastern Europe and other countries around the world.[7] Some scholars have also indirectly obtained a second measure

[7] A common question, for example, is 'How satisfied are you with the way in which democracy functions in your country?' See Morlino 1998:ch. 7, for more on this in relation to Southern Europe.

of responsiveness by measuring the distance between the governors and the governed on certain policies, and not just in terms of left/right divisions (see, for example, Lijphart 1999:286–88).

Perhaps the most effective method for measuring the responsiveness dimension is to examine the legitimacy of government, that is, the citizens' perception of responsiveness, rather than the reality. This leads us back to a fundamental process of democratic consolidation (see Morlino 1998), but in a slightly different key. In fact, certain dynamics that opened the door for democratic consolidation in many countries, such as uncritical acceptance of the institutions in place, simple obedience for a lack of better alternatives or negative memories of the past are no longer relevant in terms of measuring legitimacy, and might even be interpreted as de-legitimizing factors. Here, the key element is that the support for democratic institutions, and the belief that these institutions are the only real guarantors of freedom and equality, is diffuse at every social level from the most restricted elite to the general masses. The diffusion of attitudes favorable to the existing democratic institutions and the approval of their activities would suggest satisfaction and, indirectly, that civil society perceives a certain level of responsiveness. In contexts characterized by high legitimacy, one should also see a full range of interests and forms of political participation.

There are at least two orders of objective limits on responsiveness. First of all, elected leaders do not always seek to understand and respond to the perceptions and positions of the citizens. As discussed above, at times they work instead to maximize their own autonomy and influence citizens' perceptions and understandings of what the most important issues are. Politicians take advantage of the complexity of problems, and, evidently, of the shifts in political priority that occur over the course of a single legislature – a period that usually spans four or five years.

The second order of limits is shaped by the resources a government has at its disposition to respond to the needs of its populace. Limited resources and economic constraints on public spending affect the responsiveness of even the wealthiest countries. For example, if a certain population that already enjoys an upward trend in its average life demands better pensions and other improvements, a government burdened with budgetary limitations cannot possibly act on their behalf. Likewise, the persistent problems posed by unemployment and immigration are also illustrative of the near impossibility of finding generally satisfactory, legitimate and responsive solutions in contemporary democracies. Indeed, the situation is more and more characterized by discontent, dissatisfaction, fear of poverty and general democratic malaise. Such conditions contribute to a de-legitimization of democratic systems and encourage the type of populism mentioned at the beginning of the chapter.

The contextual conditions that favor responsiveness are similar to those that support accountability. They include a well-established, independent, informed and engaged civil society, with the concurrent presence of strong and active intermediary structures. It is fairly obvious why these factors are essential. Civil society and intermediary organizations are crucial for explaining at least one facet of responsiveness: the perception of needs. Government output, or the actual response of government to its electors, is the other facet of responsiveness. The potential for this form of responsiveness is only possible – with all of the difficulties mentioned above – in richer and more developed democracies and societies. In conclusion, the economic factor, so central to the explanation of democratic consolidation, also plays an important role in the capacity of governments to respond to the needs of their citizens and general populations.

If the previous analysis of the rule of law is related to the discussion developed in this section about accountability and responsiveness, a few important connections are fairly evident. First, while the various aspects of the rule of law provide the grounds for citizens' and other entities' demands for accountability, the presence of genuine accountability promotes improvements in the legal system and in respect for law. Scanty application of the law also results in an inadequate responsiveness. Moreover, one can see the connection between the rule of law – or rather the absence of its guarantee – and the incapacity of governments to respond to the demands of their citizens, for whom the guarantee of law takes precedence over other needs or preferences. Thus, the rule of law is also an essential premise for responsiveness that, in turn, is an important pre-condition for evaluating accountability. The actions of these three dimensions compose a sort of triangle, with each side bearing different weight and meaning. Fig. 1 illustrates the relationships among these dimensions.

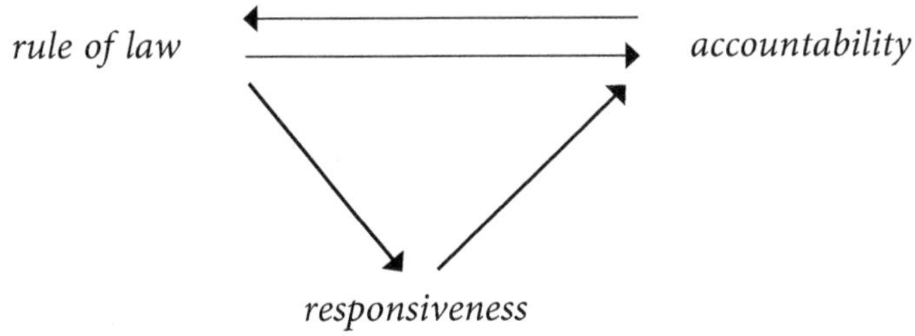

Fig. 1: Democratic Quality: Connections between procedural dimensions and result

Concluding Remarks

To draw together, albeit briefly, the threads of this chapter, we can emphasize how analysis and related empirical research on the rule of law lead to at least two salient conclusions. The first one is that we need another partially different empirical notion of the rule of law if we want to conduct research into hybrid regimes or the transitional phase. Ironically, this research into the rule of law has to pay attention to the effective guarantee of basic rights, and in this vein, to democracy, while in the analysis of the quality of democracy where the rule of law is indistinguishable from democracy – there is only a democratic rule of law – other aspects are relevant when the procedural characteristics of those dimensions support the contents of a stable, fully fledged democracy or the standards of an ideal democracy.

The second conclusion is that the rule of law unfolds with the development of democracy in transitional phases and is closely related to accountability and responsiveness in the analysis of democratic quality. That is, in both perspectives it is by itself a key dimension that cannot be ignored when dealing with these especially relevant topics.

Bibliographical References

Altman, David and Anibal Perez-Liñan (2002), "Assessing the Quality of Democracy: Freedom, Competitiveness and Participation in Eighteen Latin American Countries", in *Democratization*, 9 (2): 85–100.

Belton, Rachel (2005), "*Competing Definitions of the Rule of Law: Implications for Practitioners*, Washington, DC: Carnegie Endowment for International Peace, Carnegie Papers No. 55.

Bunce, Valerie and Stephen Wolchik (2008), 'Mixed Regimes in Postcommunist Eurasia: Tipping Democratic and Tipping Authoritarian', paper delivered at workshop

on *Democratization in European Former Soviet Republics: Limits, Obstacles and Perspectives*, Florence, June 13–15.
Carothers Thomas (2006), ed, *Promoting the Rule-of-Law Abroad: In Search of Knowledge*, Washington, DC: Carnegie Endowment for International Peace.
Diamond Larry and Leonardo Morlino (2005), eds., *Assessing The Quality of Democracy*, Baltimore: Johns Hopkins University Press.
Dietrich, Mark (2000), "Legal and Judicial Reform in Central Europe and the Former Soviet Union. Voices From Five Countries", paper, The International Bank for Reconstruction and Development/The World Bank, Washington.
Eulau, Heinz and Paul Karps (1977), "The Puzzle of Representation: Specifying Components of Responsiveness" in *Legislative Studies Quarterly*, 3: 233–54.
Karl Terry (1995), 'The Hybrid Regimes of Central America', *Journal of Democracy*, 6 (3), 72–86.
HiiL (2007), *Rule of Law: Inventory Report*, in http://www.hiil.org/uploads/File/1-947-Rule_of_Law_Inventory_Report_2007.pdf.
Katz, Richard S. and Peter Mair (1995), "Changing Modes of Party Organization and Party Democracy: The Emergence of the Cartel Party", in *Party Politics*, I (1): 5–28.
Kleinfeld, Rachel (2006) 'Competing Definitions of the Rule-of-Law', in Thomas Carothers (ed.) *Promoting the Rule-of-Law Abroad: in search of knowledge*, Washington, DC: Carnegie Endowment for International Peace, 31–73.
Levitsky Stephen and Lucan A. Way (2002) 'Elections Without Democracy: The Rise of Competitive Authoritarianism', *Journal of Democracy*, 13(2): 51–65.
Lijphart, Arend P. (1999), *Patterns of Democracy. Government Forms and Performance in Thirty-six Countries*, New Haven: Yale University Press.
Linz, Juan J. (1964), 'An Authoritarian Regime: the Case of Spain', in Erik Allardt and Yrjö Littunen (eds.), *Cleavages, Ideologies and Party Systems*, Helsinki: Westermarck Society, 291–342.
—— (2000), *Totalitarian and Authoritarian Regimes*, Boulder: Lynne Rienner.
Magen Amichai and Leonardo Morlino (2008), eds., *International Actors, Democratization and the Rule of Law. Anchoring Democracy*, London: Routledge.
Maravall, José Maria (1997), "Surviving Accountability" in Jean Monnet Chair Papers, European University Institute, Florence.
—— (2002), 'The rule of law as a political weapon', in Maravall and Adam Przeworski, (eds.), *Democracy and the Rule of Law*, Cambridge: Cambridge University Press, pp. 261–301.
Morlino, Leonardo (1998), *Democracy Between Consolidation and Crisis. Parties, Groups and Citizens in Southern Europe*, Oxford: Oxford University Press.
—— (2003), *Democrazie e Democratizzazioni*, Bologna: Il Mulino.
—— (2009), "Are There Hybrid Regimes? Or Are They Just An Optical Illusion?", *European Political Science Review*, 1 (2):273–296.
—— and Amichai Magen (2008), 'Methods of Influence, Layers of Impact, Cycles of Change: A Framework for Analysis', in Magen and Morlino (eds.), *International Actors, Democratization and the Rule of Law. Anchoring Democracy*, London: Routledge.
O'Donnell, Guillermo (1994), "Delegative Democracy", in *Journal of Democracy*, 5(1): 55–69.
—— (1999), "Horizontal Accountability in New Democracies", in Andreas Schedler, Larry J. Diamond e Mark Plattner, (1999), eds., *The Self-restraining State: Power and Accountability in New Democracies*, Boulder: Lynne Rienner, 29–52.
—— (2005), 'Why the Rule-of-Law Matters', in Larry J. Diamond and Leonardo Morlino (eds), *Assessing the Quality of Democracy*, Baltimore: Johns Hopkins University Press, 3–17.

Schedler Andreas (1999), "Conceptualizing Accountability", in Schedler, L.J. Diamond e M. Plattner, (1999), eds., *The Self-restraining State: Power and Accountability in New Democracies*, Boulder: Lynne Rienner, 13–28.

Schedler Andreas (2006), ed., *Electoral Auhtoritarianism: The Dynamics of Unfree Competition*, Boulder: Lynne Rienner.

Schmitter Philippe C. (1999), "The Limits of Horizontal Accountability", in Andreas Schedler, Larry J. Diamond and Marc Plattner, (1999), eds., *The Self-restraining State: Power and Accountability in New Democracies*, Boulder: Lynne Rienner, 59–62.

—— and Terry Karl (1993), 'What Democracy is…and is Not', in Larry Diamond and Marc Plattner (eds.), *The Global Resurgence of Democracy*, Baltimore: Johns Hopkins University Press.

Trebilcock, Michael and Ronald Daniels (2008), *Rule of Law Reform and Development*, Cheltenham: Edward Elgar.

CHAPTER THREE

BEYOND JUDICIAL INDEPENDENCE: RULE OF LAW AND JUDICIAL ACCOUNTABILITIES IN ASSESSING DEMOCRATIC QUALITY

Daniela Piana*

Over the last three decades, the concept of "rule of law" gained spectacular glamour in international political discourse. New democracies emerged under the blessing aura of this principle (Carothers 2006), whereas countries that featured a hybrid and quasi-democratic regime (Morlino 2009) began to show good will in endorsing the principle of the rule of law and in tailoring accordingly their political institutions.[1] Patently beguiled by the fashionable allure of the concept, practitioners involved in the policies of democracy-promotion praised the power of rule of law as an effective prescription for both socio-economic underdevelopment and abuse of political power (Piana 2009).

Maybe a victim of its own success, the concept of rule of law almost erased from both international political and scientific debates other concepts with which it is traditionally associated, such as the concept of "constitutionalism." Even though it might be slippery to say that rule of law refers to constitutionalism *tout court*, it would be easily problematic that any constitutionalism is *ipso facto* an instantiation of rule of law. Yet, the term constitutionalism is associated intimately with the supremacy of law and, in this respect, strictly linked with the meaning of rule of law.[2]

---

* I am indebted to the editors and to an anonymous referee for comments and remarks addressed to previous versions of this chapter.

[1] This does not mean necessarily that the practice of rule of law has been established. Hybrid regimes may exhibit a quite mixed and ambiguous attitude toward its actual implementation. See for instance Brincks 2008 and Hilbink 2008, not to mention the scholars who worked on this double-faced nature of the rule of law as a façade.

[2] A further and slightly different way of giving expression to the constitutional principle is the requirement that social and political conflicts that may surface both among citizens and among political institutions are settled on the base of general, prospective, and impartial norms, which should be applied *erga omnes* (Damaska 1986;

In very general terms, the constitutional principle holds that a political action is legitimate to the extent it emanates from the exercise of a *limited power* (McIlwain 1947).[3] Over the centuries, the development of modern States and the practices of Western liberal institutions gave birth to two different, but related, formal mechanisms to limit the power of the sovereign (and broadly speaking to limit the power of the executive branch): first, its subjection to the law, in an early stage to natural law and then afterward to the parliament; second, the separation of powers, based on the assumption that the three branches of government (legislative, executive and judicial) handle three different kinds of power. It then recommends that these branches perform their functions under the control of mechanisms of inter-institutional (inter-branch) accountability, which ensure that no branch prevaricates and overrules the others.[4]

Independently of the way the power has been bounded, judicial institutions always have been placed in a critical position with respect to implementing the constitutional principle. On the one hand, courts are of paramount importance in keeping public officials accountable to the law. On the other hand, the judicial branch is crucial in implementing the principle of separation of powers (Bellamy 2005).

In arguing favorably on the heuristic value of the concept of "constitutionalism," we extend our hands to those scholars who spoke out against the indiscriminate use of the concept of rule of law (Belton 2005; Panebianco 2004). However, in the following pages we would like to leave this *querelle* and put forth a slightly different thesis.

The concept of "constitutionalism" puts a promising emphasis on the need for holding accountable the exercise of any kind of power, including the judicial power. For this reason, it provides scholars with a fruitful analytical perspective from which to investigate the

---

Hardin 1999). To ensure impartial settlements of disputes, impartial courts are strictly required.

[3] It may be worthwhile to remind readers that this notion stands at a much higher level of abstraction than other notions of constitutionalism, which refer to the protection of individual freedoms, to the participation of sovereign people in the governance of society, and so on. Thus, at a very abstract level, constitutionalism is concerned with the potential abuse of power, which is an intrinsic part of the power *lato sensu*.

[4] The formal design of the State is commonly set in a constitution. However, it would be misleading to say that explicit constitutions are strictly required by the constitutional principle. As many scholars maintain, constitutional norms represent a possible – neither ultimate nor exclusive – mechanism to limit the exercise of power. See on this point, the last work of Ginsburg and Moustafa (2008).

interaction that exists between the dimension of rule of law and the dimension of inter-institutional accountability (both are described by Morlino, in this volume).[5] An impartial adjudication turns out to be of utmost importance for both dimensions. Judges should be protected from undue influences made by external (that is to say non judicial) bodies and authorities. However, the more the judicial power expands and penetrates both politics and society (Tate and Vallinder 1996), the more it needs to be checked and held accountable.

The point is that a better knowledge of the mechanisms by which judges are held accountable may provide an insightful appraisal of the way judicial behaviors and institutions affect the quality of a democracy.[6] Our goal, however, is more analytical and less prescriptive than this. We explore the variety of constitutionalisms and, in turn, the variety of models of judicial governance, by providing a general portrait of European institutional experiences. Then we endeavor to describe the construction of the concept of accountability. We argue in favor of a multi-dimensional concept, whose components are presented in detail. From there, we discuss the levels of analysis required by such a concept.

Finally, we try to apply our analytical grid to the standards issued by European institutions in the judicial field. This will lead us to reconstruct the ideal-type of constitutionalism that seems to be promoted in the EU and, secondly, to assess this ideal-type from the point of view of the functioning of mechanisms of accountability.

Beyond Judicial Independence

As scholars recently reminded us, constitutionalism can be broadly defined as "a method for organizing government that depends on, and adheres to, a set of fundamental guiding principles and laws" (Figueroa 2006; also see Palombella on rule of law in this volume). Judicial independence is in this respect pivotal. A lack of guarantees

[5] A democracy should exhibit effective mechanisms that enact the principle of the constitutionalism (Figueroa 2008) and should hold public officials accountable by mean of these mechanisms.

[6] It should be mentioned here – even though the next section will raise this point in much more specific and detailed terms – that the principle of constitutionalism (and consequently the rule of law) does not entail democratic governance *a priori*. Likewise, conversely, no democracy is even imaginable if the constitutional principle (as we defined it) is not at least entrenched into basic rules of the State.

of judicial independence may be fatal to the effectiveness of limitations of power. Low guarantees of judicial independence may leave judges unprotected from external influences.

Yet, notwithstanding this, the concept of judicial independence is not always well defined and the very relationship between independence and rule of law seems more complex than might be expected. It is certainly dependent on the way it is embodied in the institutional design of the State. This point is also borne out by scholars who are less sanguine about the linearity of the relationship between rule of law and judicial independence. Not only institutions that embody the principle of judicial independence may vary in terms of competence, logics of action, etc. In addition, the way they work in reality depends on a combination of factors that eludes any formal design (Gibson 2006).[7] These factors are cognitive and cultural, as we are going to see.

As a matter of fact, a survey of the models of judicial governance which coexist in Europe would reveal a spectacular variety of institutional solutions. Each solution combines a formal organizational design (identifying who does what in appointing, promoting, evaluating and checking judicial actors) with informal practices and ways of doing, organizational and the legal cultures, which differ from one country to another (Nelken 2004; Cotterrell 2007).

In order to do justice to this irreducible variety and uncover constitutive features of these different systems, we maintain as a promising analytical strategy to refer to *ideal-types of constitutionalism* in which judicial governance has a central place and plays a key role.[8] Ideal-types are but analytical tools from which reality always differs.[9] However, for the sake of our argument, ideal-types prove very helpful in focusing attention on the functions performed by judicial institu-

[7] Scholars point to the multiple semantics of the concept of judicial independence (Russell 2001). Independence may refer to institutional conditions under which judges adjudicate. It also may be associated with the behavioral independence of each judge. In addition, courts can display external and internal independence: the first refers to the degree to which judicial institutions are separated from other political institutions, the second to the degree to which judges are autonomous within the court.

[8] Judicial governance is only one among many other dimensions of an ideal-typical constitutionalism. By focusing exclusively on it, we do not mean to reduce constitutionalism to judicial governance. Rather, we want to frame judicial governance in a broader context, which is the context of a constitutional system.

[9] It is notorious that ideal-types are extensively used in Weberian analyses of sociological phenomena (Weber 1913 and 1922). The methodological choice we are arguing for has been made also by other scholars, such as Langer 2004 and Figueroa 2006.

tions and, as we propose, on the way courts feature different methods of limiting State power.[10]

The first country in which courts played a role as a mechanism of power-constraint was England. By ensuring the impartiality of common law courts, the British system also guaranteed the implementation of rule of law. In the English system legal norms took the form of jurisprudential decisions, through which ordinary judges paved the way for modern English law (Bell 2006).

Over the centuries the English judicial system retained its aristocratic, almost elitist character. Lawyers have been regularly appointed as justices (Thomas 2006; Bell 2007) whereas the promotion of judges has always taken place in relationship with the reputation they gained at the bar. The high moral costs imposed by bad reputation and the elitist culture to which they were socialized were fairly satisfactory in keeping English judges independent and impartial despite the existence of a strong relationship between political institutions (such as the Lord Chancellor) and appointed justices.

Usually the English ideal-type is explained in terms of the persistence of a common law-based legal system. However, a more attentive insight is to appreciate that it is possible to point to other factors, including social pluralism, low fragmentation in the political system, and stability of the institutional framework.

As a matter of fact, despite the adherence to a common law system, the United States developed a slightly different version of constitutionalism. This is bespoken foremost by the introduction of the diffuse judicial control of statutes and regulations and the creation of the Supreme Court as the last resort for the defense of fundamental rights (Pasquino 1994; Slinquist and Cross 2009).

In continental Europe, due to the more straightforward importance of the sovereign State, it is possible to identify two ideal-types of constitutionalism, the French and German. These also correspond to two ideal-types of judicial governance: the Neo-Latin and the continental (Guarnieri and Pederzoli 2002).

French constitutionalism recognizes in the will of a parliamentary majority the first and ultimate source of legal norms. The legitimate law is thus the *lex posita*, that is, the law "made" by the will of the

[10] This design defines the means by which the branches of government perform their functions, whilst the functions they perform are the same in all ideal-types.

people. One can safely say that in this context the judiciary plays a minor role: it enforces legal norms by mean of an application which is a-evaluative and a-interpretative.

Judicial independence is guaranteed in France by ensuring that adjudication is carried out by a strict application of the law (Pasquino 1994).[11] The main mechanism used to ensure that judicial decisions comply with the law is the creation of a bureaucratic model of judicial governance. Judges are selected according to the same model of recruitment used for civil servants, and so are driven to develop an *esprit de corps*. Both socialization and respect of *seniority* guarantee the coherence of judicial decisions.[12] Judicial interpretations should be strictly residual, not creative.

This model, which spread across Southern Europe and Belgium along with the establishment of Napoleonic rule, underwent a process of radical change after the end of the Second World War (Guarnieri and Pederzoli 2002). In France, the constitution issued in 1946 established a Conseil Supérieur de la Magistrature (Renoux 2000), the organ of judicial self-government. Then, a pure model of self-government has been adopted by Southern European countries throughout their democratic transitions. After the fall of pre-war authoritarian regimes, High Judicial Councils have been introduced in Italy, Spain, Portugal and Greece in order to insulate judges from the influence of the executive (Toharia 1975). This is called by scholars a *neo-Latin model of judicial governance* (Di Federico 2005). In this model, the Consiglio Superiore della Magistratura appoints, promotes, evaluates and trains judges (and in the case of Italy also prosecutors).[13]

The second ideal-type of constitutionalism, that of German constitutionalism, relies on the idea of the *Rechtsstaat*. It interprets the legitimacy of the law in terms of procedural correctness, which ultimately depends on the respect legal norms exhibit with the *Gründnorm*, the fundamental rule of the State (Rebuffa 1990). The State, which is the

---

[11] The primacy of the legislative branch has been enhanced during the French Revolution. See Pasquino 1994.

[12] According to the French version of constitutionalism that was developed during the nineteenth century, the judge was considered a *bûche de la loi*. French constitutionalism recognizes a primacy to the Court of Cassation, which represents the highest jurisdiction of the judicial system. Neither discretion nor arbitrariness in the adjudication is admitted by the French conception of the constitutional State.

[13] As a matter of fact, in some cases (such as Italy) the Court of Cassation handles also some competences in the field of training.

depositary of the *Gründnorm*, is endowed with the power to issue the norms of the legal system.[14] The legal accountability of judges functions predominantly as a guarantee of judicial independence.

In this system, undue interference into the judiciary is not expected from the executive, but rather from the legislative. The risk of an overwhelming majority which overrules the fundamental rule of the constitutional State is avoided by adopting a strong constitutional mechanism of judicial review. The review is operated by an *ad hoc* institution, specialized in monitoring the formal and substantial coherence of the statutory law with the *Gründnorm*. This institution is the constitutional court.

The differences between the two ideal types pointed out above disclose the existence of a distinctive variety of ideal-types of constitutionalism and, as a consequence, of models of judicial governance, all them coexisting in Europe. Each of them features a distinctive set of institutional tools; all of them aims at ensuring the judicial independence. In the tradition of French and German constitutionalism, judges are considered a part of the State. The appointment, selection, and promotion of judges are based on 1) general legal knowledge of candidate justices and 2) seniority. This yields a strictly bureaucratic model of judicial governance.

The kinds of constitutionalism described above also differ with regard to the mechanisms of socialization of the judicial elite. Throughout their processes of socialization judges learn to comply with the constitutional principle, which impose a strictly transparent and equal application of legal norms. In each ideal-type, ethical norms and legal ideologies are transmitted and enforced by different institutions that correspond to different social groups (Damaska 1986, Guarnieri 2007). Judicial actors adjudicate according to the norms – interpretative principles and deontological standards – they learn from senior judges, legal actors, and legal scholars (Caenegem 1992).

In the UK model the bar is the source of the behavioural standards with which justices comply. In the continental model, legal scholars and senior justices represent the group of reference for ordinary judges, even if the introduction of the High Judicial Council unbalanced this

[14] It important to emphasize the primacy of the State vis-à-vis fundamental rights. The legal ideology on which this ideal-type relies is favorable to a positivist view of law.

delicate mechanism. Indeed, the organizational innovation represented by the High Judicial Council carries a surreptitious change in the allocation of power within the judicial branch.

Whereas the High Judicial Council maximizes the external independence of justices from the other branches of the State, it challenges and ultimately weakens the internal hierarchy of the judiciary through the introduction of a democratic principle into the judicial governance. Members of the High Judicial Council are elected by ordinary judges. This undermines the cohesiveness of the judicial hierarchy because of the equal status awarded to all judges on the basis of the principle "one man, one vote." In the countries where a self-government model has been adopted ordinary judges who perform their role in neo-Latin settings are placed in a context in which hierarchical ties are released and a more democratic ideology becomes dominant.[15]

The critical remarks developed in this section are designed to clarify the following point. Speaking of rule of law without taking into consideration the organization of the State featured by a given country may lead scholars and practitioners to assess very superficially the way democracy and rule of law are intertwined. Formal institutional designs provide a fairly correct view of how the judicial branch is inserted in the broader context of a constitutional system. But they do not say that much about how in reality courts hold rules and ruled accountable and about the way courts are themselves subjected to mechanisms of control and accountability.

From Independence to Accountability: Beyond Legal Constraints

As noted repetitively in the previous section, constitutionalism is mainly concerned with the need to bound exercises of State power. Because of the failure embedded intrinsically into any human action, constitutionalism is intimately linked with the idea of accountability. But as a concept of "judicial independence," "accountability" is far from being a consensual concept (Mainwaring 2003:15). Descriptive and normative sides are often mixed in such a slippery way that the

[15] This change does not become patent before the 1980s, when the activity of High Judicial Councils and the surge of judicial activism exhibited by Western democracies started to interact (Larkins 1996).

notion of accountability risks becoming almost useless in empirical research, at least if not defined carefully (Lindberg 2009). Unfortunately, the proliferation of meanings attributed to this concept corresponds to a lack of reflection on the elements constitutive of its semantic (Lindberg 2009, Koppell 2005).

At a more superficial observation, the concept of accountability is contested in two respects (Mainwaring 2003): with regard to the agency of accountability and with regard to the scope and instruments by which accountability is enacted. First and principally, scholars debate whether or not accountability is exercised by institutional actors. One position relies on a principle-agent approach and maintains that accountability is intimately related with the existence of a social relationship in which one actor is taking decisions on behalf of a different actor. This second actor, however, is willing to keep the agent's actions under control.

A second view does not deny the insightfulness of principal-agent theory, but it contests its adequacy in shedding light on the complex nature of accountability. Some authors endorse a perspective in which accountability is thought of as a social relationship, which puts an actor in relationship to a forum: "an actor has to explain and justify her conduct" (Bovens 2006:9).

Broad dissent exists also as to whether or not accountability should be associated exclusively with legal mechanisms of answerability (liability). As Mainwaring describes in detail (2003), many comparative political scholars maintained that an actor is accountable if she is held answerable by formal mechanisms of control. If such accountability is thought as a form of legal obligation, few types of social actors are excluded from its semantic field, as for instance civil society organizations and the media. These last two actors have been instead considered as key actors of accountability by researchers such as Smulovitz and Perruzzotti (2003). They put exclusive emphasis on the societal type of accountability, namely the type of control that is exercised by social actors via the structures and the instruments put at their disposal by the press, the new media, etc.

A more abstract view of the "byzantine complexity" featured by scholarship on accountability may touch upon a different and more crucial issue. Whereas the axes of the debate have been made more or less explicit by scholars themselves, not always has this been the case for the logic of the concept and the way the concept is constructed (Lindberg 2009:4–5).

At this point the concept of constitutionalism may be of some help. As pointed out before, the minimal core of the concept of constitutionalism is the need to limit power. At the highest level of abstraction, accountability may be thought as *a method by which the scope of power is limited*. Accordingly, this limitation may be brought about with different institutional and organizational instruments, and at different levels of reality, individual and collective.

If one endorses this analytical solution, the semantic of the concept is then composed in a multi-dimensional way (Lindberg 2009:15). Accountability varies in types as well as in scope and levels of functioning. Individual and collective actors are not subjected to all types of accountability at any moment with the same degree of intensity. Foremost, accountability works in association with different types of norms, legal and extra-legal. It would be misleading to think legal and extra-legal norms as mutually exclusive.

The multi-dimensional structure of the semantic of the concept allows researchers to focus on the different faces of the "method of limiting the scope of power" without undermining the unitary nature of the concept. We maintain, for instance, that accountability may be legal, managerial, societal, institutional, and professional. All of these types of accountability belong to the same semantic field, but they may have a different combination in different stages of the history of a country or at different levels of judicial governance.

Legal accountability is related to the mechanism of legal control. It is guaranteed by judicial review of statutory law, by the mechanism of appeal to higher courts, by procedural guarantees of due process and by the formal relationship that exists among the norms embedded in a legal system.

Managerial accountability refers to the fact that an institution should be accountable to a standard of efficiency. Such administrative accountability ensures that the judiciary allocates resources – in terms of money and time – in an efficient manner, managing case-flow in a way that speeds up judicial proceedings and managing effectively the human resources available to the court (for a comparative view on Europe, see Fabri 2005). Nowadays, the introduction of court management systems represents a way to ensure administrative accountability at the level of judicial offices (courts and prosecution offices).

Institutional accountability refers to the appointment, selection, promotion and disciplinary control of judicial actors. It also refers to the composition of the board of the judicial council, which reveals the political accountability to which the judicial council is subjected during its mandate. These means of control can tackle the problem of providing citizens certainty with regard to the competence and impartiality of the judicial staff, since they formally guarantee the objectivity of the criteria used to govern the judicial staff.

While socio-legal studies emphasised the mutual (and inverse) relationship of judicial independence and judicial accountability, there is weaker tradition stressing the homogeneous nature of these two concepts. Bridging between them is not easy. Our proposal here is that judicial independence is a kind of negative (or forbidden) accountability. Guarantees of judicial independence correspond to a formal mechanism that prevents the other branches of the States and the social actors to exercise any undue influence over judicial behaviour.

Societal accountability spans any kind of control exercised by private actors, in particular by civil society organisations and citizens. Societal accountability is made possible today by using a number of ICT tools provided by court information management systems. As recently pointed out by several scholars (Voermans 2007, Langebroek 2005), these tools allow the public to monitor judicial proceedings, their length and their lawfulness, and decrease enormously the costs faced by the public in finding the information needed in order to appeal to the court. A further, but less diffuse means used to tackle the problem of making the judiciary more sensitive to the demands of the users is an external audit, which creates a process of surveying the citizen trust and satisfaction vis-a-vis the judiciary.

Professional accountability refers to the control exercised by peers on the basis of their knowledge and expertise. Peers also transmit and enforce legal ideologies. Professional accountability is strongly linked with the allocation of moral and cognitive costs. In a way, if a judge wishes to be held in high consideration by her colleagues, she will be encouraged to argue and decide according to the mainstreaming doctrine. This also has an impact on the career paths followed by individual judges.

To uncover the relationship between rule of law and democracy this analytical perspective seems to be promising. Indeed, it may facilitate coming to term with the endless *querelle* regarding the nature of judicial independence, namely by resolutely shifting the focus of analysis from independence to accountability.

Furthermore and foremost, this way of reasoning brings back into the discourse of rule of law and democracy the informal face of constitutionalism, which is related to the way informal mechanisms of accountability work. A dominant view argues that power is limited by the law. However, informal mechanisms of constraint may work as well as the formal ones. This proves to be of paramount significance in the design (and maintenance) of accountability in the public sector. Seminal works in administrative science and sociology of organizations showed to what extent socialization can create internal mechanisms of accountability (informal) that replace and often complement the formal mechanisms of reward and punishment embedded in the structure of an organization (Merton 1949; March and Olsen 1989).

According to these scholars, the life of an organization is therefore nourished with the enforcement of norms throughout mechanisms of *informal and formal accountability*, which connect social actors and the organizational setting. This means that actors act in "a condition in which... who exercise power is constrained by external means and by internal norms" (Koppell 2005).[16]

Let us focus now on the way this concept may be used to inspect the limitations to which judges are subjected when they make decisions. If judges made their decisions on the strict basis of the law, extra-legal mechanisms would be worthless or superfluous at most. Once trained properly to apply the law, any ordinary judge would capable of adjudicating impartially and impersonally. However, this description of judicial behaviour does not correspond to reality.

Research conducted over the last three decades points to the importance of values, attitudes and individual interpretations in the judicial decision-making process. Judges, in particular chief judges or judges appointed to high courts, behave on the basis of a complex, differentiated set of norms and standards (Gibson 2006). They manage resources; they construct the arguments put forth to support their rulings; they interact with the public, the media (more and more), and policy makers. They also communicate with colleagues, exchanging views and information with them, and they set the agenda for the job they are going to do or for the office they are going to lead.

In a word, a judge may be thought of as a social actor, in the broadest sense of the word. She performs her multiple roles on the basis of a complex set of expectations and attitudes. In this respect, the formal

[16] It has something to do with control, which is a way to *bind or to restrain the set of alternative actions* an actor is allowed to consider before deciding what to do or say.

design of institutional guarantees of judicial independence does not have much to say about this complex intertwinement of norms, expectations, interiorized roles.

The reconstruction of the accountabilities (as plural, as we argued) put in motion within judicial governance and between the judicial system and the social system provides a much better description of the configuration of the power of control that is exercised by many different norms, all of them having an impact on the judicial arena. All of these accountabilities work sometimes behind and even possibly against the formal institutional design.

Indeed, the mechanisms of actual control exercised by any of the sources of norms mentioned above – legal coherence, efficiency, institutional aims, societal aims, professional ethics and expertise – correspond to "living institutional orders" (La Torre 1999). To assess the degree of respect of the constitutional principle featured by a system of governance, the accountabilities should be considered as *they work in practice*. Our claim is that the concept of accountability, in the sense of "method of limiting the power," provides us with a powerful analytical perspective with which to assess the way judges and judicial institutions affect the democratic quality of a country. In practice, this means that any empirical research conducted to investigate the quality of democracy should focus on the informal mechanisms of accountability that work within public institutions. Organization theories and sociology of organizations may give a critical contribution to enlightening this point.

Systemic and Middle-Range Judicial Accountabilities

We outlined in the section above some advantages entailed by adopting a multi-dimensional conception of accountability in the study of democratic quality. What is needed now is a connection between this notion and the arguments put forth earlier about the ideal-types of constitutionalism and the quality of democracy. To do this we need to move from a systemic level to a middle-range level of analysis, in order better to grasp the interaction that exists between norms and actors.

In the first place, judges are accountable to legal norms. Therefore, in principle, they should be considered free from any undue influence coming from the social and political systems. Again, in principle, legal norms should set the boundaries within which judicial reasoning is developed (Gibson 2006). But questions about this vision of adjudication are nonetheless somehow legitimate. Can we safely assume judges make only law-determined decisions?

The problem is that the more a judge distances her actual behavior from a strictly law-based model, the more she needs to be held accountable to extra-legal norms. In this respect, legal norms are neither the ultimate nor the exclusive type of normative inputs with which a judge is expected to comply.

Empirical research carried out by socio-legal scholars shows that judges make decisions on the basis of many different norms, some of them being far from strictly formalized or legal in their nature (Stone and Shapiro 2006, Cross and Linquist 2009 are leading sources here).

Extra-legal norms operate in a slightly different way than legal ones. Knowledge of the law is the object of a so-called propositional disposition (for example, I know that "if A, then according to the law B,"). By contrast, the know-how associated with an ability to work within a organizational context – a court, a judicial office, and, at a more systemic level, a judicial system – operates as a source of normative schemata, of behavioural guidelines, as does any kind of tacit knowledge (Polanyi 1960, Baum 2006).

Saying that an actor is accountable to interiorized norms means she is able to exercise a sort of inward-looking control over her own behaviour.[17] In some respects, this inward-looking control can be considered more powerful and effective than the hard controls might be. Indeed, often they are enforced through implicit mechanisms of reputational costs (Baum 2006), which can be reconstructed by a policy maker with many difficulties and therefore changed or reformed.

An important part of the reputational costs faced by a judge is related to the informal evaluation to which she/he is subject by the "group of reference," that is, the group comprised of people to whom a judge feels associated or affiliated (Guarnieri 2007). By arguing in favour of his decision, a judge deploys a legal reasoning on the basis of the arguments he expects might be accepted as reasonable by colleagues and by the public. The cognitive constraints raised by a "dissonant reasoning"

---

[17] Nothing guarantees, however, that the decisions made because of the constraints put on by a public forum is responsive to the public. What we want to say is simply that accountability – in the broader sense we intend here – opens the door to a process of decision-making and reasoning in which public expectations matter.

are very important in the revision of a judicial argument. Thus, even at a cognitive level, judges are subject to a mechanism of accountability by a professional public, a public comprised of peers (Baum 2006).

Accordingly, accountabilities of the societal and professional types are intimately related to the degree of judicial integrity exhibited by particular judges and by the judicial branch as a whole. It is not a simple coincidence, then, that democracy and rule of law promoters insist persistently and restlessly on the importance of re-socializing justices who had not been appointed under democratic rules to a new type of professional ethics and, consequently, to a new form of ethical integrity (ABA 2007; OSCE 2006).

Judges who exhibit a high level of ethical integrity are less inclinef to be subjected to undue influences and therefore to be corrupted or captured by partisan interests. In this respect, policy instruments based on education, socialization and vocational training which ensure a high level of integrity are of paramount importance for the quality of a democratic system: "Without the professional character of persons, however, these institutions become an empty shell. For these institutions to act factually in the public interest, persons who are of integrity are needed, whose intentions are aimed at the public interest and whose deliberations adequately reflect the purposes of the institution... integrity appears as the norm that officials are to be of the right professional character" (Soeharno 2007:17).

The compliance with deontological norms is not always enforced by adopting hard mechanisms of accountability, such as mechanisms of selection and promotion, or mechanisms of disciplinary control (formalized and legalized instruments of accountability). Besides hard accountability (Voermans 2007), judicial actors should be subjected to a wide array of soft accountabilities. These include the obligation of being transparent to the public, being responsive to colleagues (and in particular to senior judges), being morally honest.[18]

Soft and informal accountabilities should then become part of the research agenda. In particular, at a micro level of analysis, scholars should aim to uncover the cognitive mechanisms of self-restraint and self-representation that define, constitute and ultimately govern

[18] We then take distance from both a strictly formalized and legalized view of accountability (Mainwaring 2003)

the roles judicial actors perform.[19] Therefore, we think that judicial accountabilities that take place at the micro level and are associated with expectations of cognitive dissonance, cognitive malaise in legal reasoning and legal decision-making should be included in the picture and accounted for in assessing the quality of justice. Some research already has been conducted on this point (Contini and Mohr 2007, Voermans 2007).

These remarks bear significantly on the way empirical research is carried on. Judges are expected to comply with a manifold set of standards, some of them enacted at a systemic level and others enacted at the level of the action-situation in which judges work each day. When empirical research is carried on a deep insight on the way judicial systems work should both zoom out to the systemic level and zoom in to the level of the action-situation. At both levels, the notion of accountability is salient and pertinent.

For instance, the separation of the judicial branch from the legislative and the executive prevents these last two branches from holding the judicial system accountable. The rule according to which the High Judicial Council should be inspected as for the way it allocates its financial resources (in some countries by the Court of Auditors and in some others by the Parliament) establishes a method to limit the power of the judicial branch at a systemic level.

However, at a middle-range level, judges who perform managerial functions – chief justices – are held responsible for the efficiency and effectiveness of the court. Empirical research aiming at grasping the actual logic of action of judicial actors should then focus on the organizational context in which judges work daily and on the relationship that exists between the judicial offices and the socio-political institutions which govern at the local level. Horizontal patterns of interaction between judicial organizations and social and political organizations (trade unions, entrepreneurial organizations, chambers of commerce, political parties, lobbies and interest groups) should enter into the

[19] Correctly and very pertinently, Merton (1949) and later on March and Olsen (1989) pointed out the following. De-individualization of behaviors and internalization of standards that become guidelines in setting down strategies of behaviors, ways of assessing the acceptability of actions, in a word the grammar of the logic of appropriateness, are steps required in the construction of a formal organization.

scope of an empirical analysis of the quality of democracy (Morlino 2003 and 2008).

Important consequences derive from these remarks also in terms of policymaking. First of all, one-fits-all formulae display clear shortcomings in judicial policy making. If our argument holds, the degree of internalization of norms and the need of socialization (re-socialization in case of nascent democracies) should be assessed empirically before any formal – and sometime superfluous – mechanism of formal accountability is put into motion. Conversely, formal institutions perfectly designed may be fully subverted or captured by judicial elites that did not internalize deontological norms nor exhibit a high level of ethical integrity.

Second, the different faces of accountability, as it has been depicted here, make up a combination of mechanisms of constraint which does not necessarily take the same shape in different contexts. Put differently, legal, managerial, societal, professional and institutional accountabilities interact in different ways and turn out differently under different conditions. This seems to make any intervention in the formal design of a judicial system more as a starting point within an open process of change than a straightforward step toward a specific and given result.

Judicial Accountabilities in Europe: The Still Missed Dimension

Given the previous section one may infer that a good way to assess the contribution of the constitutional principle to the democratic quality is to focus on the accountabilities exhibited by a judicial system and by the organizational texture of judicial institutions (courts, offices, clerk offices, judicial schools, and judicial councils).

Still, the variety of organizational and institutional settings found in different countries sharing this principle has in common the supremacy of the law. In this respect, the constitutional principle is related to the rule of law not as a specific ideal-type of limited government (historically restricted to England). It is instead related as a general ideal (Palombella in this volume, in particular the second and third sections).

This ideal praises the law as the key instrument in limiting power. Rulers are, despite their role, subjected to the law, independently of the way law is legitimately created (*posita lege*, judge case law or, lastly, transnational law, as pointed out by Kratochwil in this volume).

The main thesis of this chapter, however, is that law is necessary but not sufficient condition to holding judges accountable. The thesis has been supported by mostly theoretical arguments. But now we launch a more applicative exercise, by trying to use the concept of accountability we have developed so far to uncover and assess the ideal-type of constitutionalism that is supported by European institutions.

Notoriously, the European Union and Council of Europe do not hold any jurisdiction on the organization of the State. Member States are fully free and sovereign in shaping the organization of the courts' system as long as they respect – and the courts respect as well – articles 5 and 6 of the European Convention of Human Rights, that is, the right to due process of law.

However, beginning in the early 1990s, with the enlargement of the EU toward the ex-communist East, a spectacular variety of standards, recommendations, opinions, peer reviews, have been developed by the EU and Council of Europe. This assemblage of norms, most of them non-binding legally, paved the way for the development of a soft power in the field of judicial governance (based on moral suasion and communicative action, rather than regulation).

From this point forward European institutions represent a laboratory of models and templates of judicial governance. Before the end of the 1990s these normative and cognitive inputs were directly associated with implementing the rule of law and mainly addressing new member States or candidates. From 1999 forward, however, they became the backbone of a new policy field, namely the promotion of the quality of justice, addressed to all members, old and new (Fabri 2005, Frydman 2007).

The goal of this section is not to enter into the details of the process through which standard-setting takes place in Brussels and even more in Strasbourg.[20] Our motivation in dealing with this issue is more analytical than explicative, and it is related to the need to assess the ideal-type of constitutionalism toward which European institutions seem to be evolving. According to the approach adopted here, we reconstruct

[20] These guide-lines are no more an outcome of national processes of rule making, but rather emerge from the interaction of external actors and national institutions, both involved in a new ideal-type of judicial governance.

five types of accountability addressed by European standards, summarized in the table 1.[21]

Table 1. Norms and Standards of Quality of Justice

Mechanisms of accountability	Norms and Standards recommended by the EU and the COE
Legal accountability	Centralised control of constitutionality; judicial review handled by specialised bodies (i.e. constitutional courts). Artt. 5 and 6 of the European Convention of Human Rights. Every citizen should be ensured about the availability of a legal representative in case she can't afford the costs of legal representation. Organisation of systematic and comprehensive programmes of training in law. Introduction of courses of EC law.
Institutional accountability	The Judicial Council's board should be composed by a majority of judges (but not all of the members should be judges). The Judicial Council has representative and administrative functions. The Judicial Council is entitled to handle all the mechanisms of recruitment and promotion. HJC prepares the budget; the court manager is managerially accountable to the HJC. Creation of a judicial school, centralised, providing programmes of initial and in-service training; the State should provide for the budget for training; the School is accountable to the Judicial Council for the programmes and for the management.

[21] We discuss these points in Piana 2009.

Table 1 (*cont.*)

Mechanisms of accountability	Norms and Standards recommended by the EU and the COE
Professional accountability	Legal Training Judges and prosecutors (courses of ICT by experts of public administrations) Adoptions of national and supranational Codes
Managerial accountability	Court manager; system of e-filing Non judicial staff (*Rechtspfleger*) Performance assessment for judges and clerks at the court level ICT tools for judges ICT tools for clerks; data set of case law and doctrine
Societal accountability	Front office; systems of e-filing Web sites of judicial institutions; broad and free availability of information about rights of citizens Information about the development of judicial procedures Statistics and surveys available to public

Sources. Author's elaboration from: CCJE 1994; CCJE 2008; CEPEJ 2004; CEPEJ 2006; CEPEJ 2008.

If some attention is devoted to these standards as a whole one may recognize that they sketch out an ideal-type of constitutionalism. The ideal-type promoted by the EU and COE is the neo-Latin one, which is centred on the exclusive role of the High Judicial Council as for the appointment, promotion, evaluation and disciplinary control of judges and prosecutors. Accordingly, the High Judicial Council should be composed of a fixed number of members, the majority of which are judges elected by colleagues on an equal basis (one man one vote). They sit on the board of the Council together with a minority of members appointed by the Parliament among outstanding legal scholars. The Council should also have full competence in drawing down and delivering programs of training, even if judges and prosecutors should be trained in a separate institution, a Judicial school (CCJE 2008).

Yet, the neo-Latin ideal-type is hybridized with types of accountability more suitable to an English ideal-type. The accountabilities associated with mechanisms of public transparency and of managerial efficiency may be more adequate in a context where judges are supposed to create norms, to make decisions that entail a real use of power. (As noted earlier, where a judicial system is organized as a bureaucracy, judges are expected to apply the law, not create it).

European institutions moved from promoting guarantees of judicial independence toward defining a number of policies of quality of justice (Frydman 2007) aimed at introducing into the judicial branch a number of extra-legal mechanisms of accountability. This makes sense of the emphasis put on managerial accountability. This accountability is strictly and directly related to the idea that judges perform managerial functions, both in their daily work and, in the case of chief justices, at the level of court management. In this respect the focus on time-frame is crucial, since one may argue that justice delayed is unjust.

In sum, from European standards of quality of justice comes an hybridized ideal-type of constitutionalism, in which mechanisms of institutional accountability typically adopted in the neo-Latin ideal-type are mixed with mechanisms of managerial and societal accountability fairly common in the English or American systems, where judges have been always thought of as policy makers (Shapiro 1981).

As for the level of accountability, the standards suggest that both individual judges and judicial systems should be subjected to limits and constraints. Yet, whereas formally enacted accountability may be designed by policy makers and may be curbed or appropriately reshaped, informal accountability – as the one entailed by an inner-looking limitation – is much more difficult to construct or radically change. Primarily, these limits are tied too strictly to the organizational and legal culture to be put into motion artificially.

Above all else, standards seem to be falling short in dealing with the relationship that exists between justice administration, adjudication, and social morality. A so-to-say missed dimension turns out to be critical for the legitimacy of the ideal-type praised by European institutions: the dimension of judicial responsiveness.

Responsiveness and informal mechanisms of accountability are related, though indirectly. The perceived legitimacy of the judicial system depends on many factors, among which stands courts' transparency and efficiency. The more judges are involved in social practices and in policy-making processes, the more they need to be held accountable and to be responsive to the society in which they adjudicate (Cotterrell 2006). Indeed, an *unjust justice* may be correctly rendered but still not acceptable socially. When adjudication is not meant to be only a mechanism of dispute settlement but also a mechanism for pursuing policy aims (Damaska 1986) internal legal culture (the ideas and values that lead adjudicative decisions) and external legal culture (citizen expectations about the function of adjudication in their society) should be considered together, for their coherence and mutual influences (Nelken 2004).

Whereas standards and policies would fail dramatically if they pretended to shape with a one-fits-all solution the cultural contexts in which justice is administered, empirical research might be instead fairly insightful to cast light upon the way justice administration impacts upon democratic quality via judicial accountabilities and responsiveness. The development of an analytical grid in which responsiveness between justice and society is accounted for and assessed goes far beyond the purpose and capacity of this article. To be sure, how justice and democracy are tied together cannot be understood without going beyond considerations of formal guarantees of justice independence. But this still should be taken into account as the background for our inspection of justice administration and, in parallel, for our moving firmly toward appraising how justice is rendered to citizens. It is rendered by mean of actions subjected to a manifold pattern of judicial accountabilities and responsive to expectations of citizens.

Whether it is good or bad that these expectations bypass the conception of passive judicial system and endorse a view of an active judicial system, this is a different question. It remains to be solved case-by-case on the basis of empirical evidence. Theory is in this respect armless, vulnerable to falling victim to prejudicial positions of prescriptive assumptions.

References

ABA. 2007. Judicial Reforms Assessment. Washington.

Abbott, Kenneth and Snidal, Duncal. 2000. "Hard and Soft Law in International Governance." *International Organization* 54: 421–56.

Alasdair, Ian. (2007). "Conclusions and extensions: toward mid-range theorizing and beyond Europe." Pp. 211–240 in *International Institutions and Socialization in Europe* edited by J. Checkel. Cambridge: Cambridge University Press.

Baum, Lawrence. 2006. *Judges and Their Audiences.* Princeton: Princeton University Press.

Bell, John. 2006. *Judiciaries within Europe: a Comparative Review.* Cambridge: Cambridge University Press.

Bellamy, Richard. 2005. *Rule of law and the Separation of Power.* Aldershot: Ashgate.

Belton, Rachel. 2005. "Competing Definitions The Rule of Law. Implications for Practitioners." *Carnegie Papers*, 55.
Bobek, Michal. 2008. "The Fortress of Judicial Independence and the Mental Transition of the Central European Judiciaries." *European Public Law* 14 : 99–123.
Bovens, Mark. 2007. "Analysing and Assessing Accountability. A Conceptual Framework." *European Law Journal* 13: 447–468.
Brincks, Daniel. 2008. *The Judicial Response to Police Killing in Latin America*. Cambridge: Cambridge University Press.
Burbank, Stephen. 2003. "What Do We Mean for Judicial Independence." *Ohio State Law Journal* 64: 323–333.
Caenegem, Raoul. 1992. *Judges, Legislators and Professors*. Cambridge: Cambridge University Press.
Cappelletti, Mauro 1989. *The judicial process in comparative perspective*. Oxford: Oxford University Press.
Carothers, Thomas. 2006. *Promoting the Rule of Law Abroad: In Search of Knowledge*, Washington, Carnegie Endowment Press.
CCJE. 2008. *Opinion 10. Council of the Judiciary in the Service of Society*. Strasbourg: Council of Europe Publications.
Contini, Francesco and Mohr, Richard. 2007. "Reconciling Independence and Accountability in Judicial Systems." *Utrecht Law Review* 3: 26–43.
Cotterrell, Roger. 2006. *Law, Culture, and Society*. Aldershot: Ashgate.
Council of Europe. 2005. *Construire Ensemble l'Europe du Droit*. Strasbourg: Council of Europe Official Publishing.
Damaska, Mirjan R. 1986. *The faces of justice and state authority: a comparative approach to the legal process*. New Haven: Yale University Press.
Di Federico, Giuseppe. 2005. "Recruitment, Professional Evaluation, Career and Discipline of Judges and Prosecutors in Italy." Pp. 203–233 in *Recruitment, Professional Evaluation and Career of Judges and Prosecutors in Europe: Austria, France, Germany, Italy, The Netherlands and Spain*, edited by G. Di Federico. Bologna: Lo Scarabeo.
Fabri, Marco. 2005. "Policies to Enhance the quality of justice in Europe." Pp. 22–45 in *L'administration de la Justice en Europe. L'évaluation de sa qualité*, edited by M. Fabri. Montchrestien: LGDJ.
Figueroa, Juan Rios. 2006. *Judicial Independence: Definition, Measurement and Its Effects on Corruption. An Analysis of Latin America*, Ph.D. Thesis, New York University.
Frydman, Benoit. (2007). « L'evolution des critères et des modes de contrôle de la qualité des décisions de justice ». *Working Papers du Centre Perelmann de Philosophie du droit*, n. 4.
Gibson, James. 2006. *Judicial Institutions*, in R.A.W. Rhodes, S.A. Binder, B.A. Rockman (eds.), *The Oxford Handbook of Political Institutions*, Oxford, Oxford UP, pp. 514–553.
Ginsburg, Tom and Moustafa Tamir. 2008. *Rule by Law. The Politics of Courts in Authoritarian Regimes*, Cambridge, Cambridge University Press.
Guarnieri, Carlo. 2007. "Courts and Marginalized Groups: Perspectives from Continental Europe." *International Journal of Constitutional Law* 5: 187–210.
—— and Pederzoli, Patrizia. 2002. *The Power of Judge: A study of Courts and Democracy*. Oxford: Oxford University Press.
—— and Piana, Daniela. 2009. *Which Independence for the Rule of Law? Lessons from Europe*. paper presented at the Santiago ISPA Conference, July 12th–17th.
Hardin, Russell. 1999. Liberalism, constitutionalism and democracy. Oxford: Oxford University Press.
Hilbink, Lisa. 2007. Judges beyond politics in democracy and dictatorship: lessons from Chile. Cambridge: Cambridge University Press.

Koppell, Jonathan. 2005. "Pathologies of Accountability." *Public Administration Review*, 65: 94–198.
Larkins, Christopher. 1996. "Judicial Independence and Democratization. A Theoretical and Conceptual Analysis." *American Journal of Comparative Law* 44: 605–630.
La Torre, Massimo. 1999. *Norme, istituzioni, valori. Per una teoria istituzionalista del diritto*. Roma-Bari: Laterza.
Langbroek, Philip. 2005. "Quality management concerning judges, judgments and courts services." Pp. 46–52 in *L'administration de la Justice en Europe. L'évaluation de sa qualité*, edited by M. Fabri et al., Montchrestien: LGDJ.
Lindberg, Staffan. 2009. "Byzantine Complexity." *Concepts and Methods*. 28: 1–57.
Slinquist, Stephanie and Cross, Frank. 2009. *Measuring Judicial Activism*. Cambridge: Cambridge University Press.
Mainwaring, Scott and Welna, Christopher. 2003. *Democratic Accountability in Latin America*. Oxford: Oxford University Press.
Malleson, Kate. 1999. *The New Judiciary: the Effects of the Expansionism and Activism*. Aldershot: Ashgate.
March, James and Olsen, Johan. 1989. *Rediscovering Institutions: The Organizational Basis of Politics*. New York: Free Press.
McIlwain, Charlers Howard. 1947. *Constitutionalism: Ancient and Modern*. New York: Ithaca.
Merton, Robert. 1949. *Social Theory and Social Structure*. Glencoe: Free Press.
Morlino, Leonardo. 2003. *Democrazie e democratizzazioni*. Bologna: Il Mulino.
——. 2008. *Assessing the Quality of Democracy in Europe. A Codebook*, Florence, unpublished manuscript.
——. 2009. "Are There Hybrid Regimes? Or Are They Just An Optical Illusion?". *European Political Science Review*, 1: 273–96.
Nelken, David. 2004. "Using the Concept of Legal Culture." *Australian Journal of Legal Philosophy*, 29: 1–28.
Pasquino, Pasquale. (1984). *Uno e Trino*. Milano: Anabasi.
Piana, Daniela. 2007. "Unpacking Policy Transfer, Discovering Actor." *French Politics*, 2: 346–375.
——. 2009a. *Judicial Accountabilities in New Europe*. Aldershot: Ashgate.
Potocki, André. 2006. *Judicial Networks in Europe*. Commmunication at the conference "Transnational Judicial Dialogue: Strengthening Networks and Mechanisms for Judicial Consultation and Cooperation" December 1–2, Harvard Law School, Cambridge, Massachussetts.
Rebuffa, Giorgio. 1990. *Costituzioni e costituzionalismi*. Giappichelli: Torino.
Russell, Peter. 2001, *Toward a General Theory of Judicial Independence*, in Peter Russell and David. O'Brien (eds.), *Judicial Independence in the Age of Democracy*. London: University Press of Virginia, pp. 1–24.
—— and O'Brien, David. 2001. *Judicial Independence in New Democracy*. London: University Press of Virginia.
Shapiro, Martin. 1981. *Courts. A Comparative and Political Analysis*. Chicago: The University of Chicago Press.
Smulovitz Enrique and Peruzzotti, Catalina. 2000. "Societal Accountability in Latin American." *Journal of Democracy*, 11: 147–158.
Soeharno, Jonathan. 2007. "Is judicial integrity a norm? An inquiry into the concept of judicial integrity in England and the Netherlands." *Utrecht Law Review*, 3: 8–23.
Tate, Neil and Vallinder, Torbjorn. 1995. *The Global Expansion of Judicial Power*. New York: New York University Press.
Toharia, Josè. J. 1975. "Judicial Independence in an Authoritarian Regime: the Case of Contemporary Spain." *Law and Society Review* 4: 475–496.
United Nations. 2006. *Access to Justice. The Independence, the Impartiality and Integrity of the Judiciary*. New York: UN Publications.

Voermans, Wim. (2007). "Judicial transparency furthering public accountability for new judiciaries." *Utrecht Law Review* 3: 147–159.

Voigt, Stefan. 2005. "The Economic Effects of Judicial Accountability: Some Preliminary Insights." *ICER Working Papers Series*, n. 19.

Weber, Max. 1913. "Ueber einige Kategorien des verstehenden Sociologie." *Logos*, IV: 427–474.

——. 1922. *Wirtschaft and Gesellschaft*. Tübingen: Mohr.

PART TWO

THE EUROPEAN SETTING

CHAPTER FOUR

THE END OF THE DEMOCRATIC TRANSITION? ANALYZING THE QUALITY OF DEMOCRACY MODEL IN POST-COMMUNISM

Monica Ciobanu

The integration of the former communist countries of East and Central Europe into the European Union (EU) seemed to mark the reunification of Europe and the end of the post-communist transition. This was accomplished as a result of the fourth wave of integration in 2004, which incorporated among fifteen newcomers five Central European countries – the Czech Republic, Hungary, Poland, Slovakia, and Slovenia – and three former Soviet republics from the Baltic region – Estonia, Latvia and Lithuania – together with a fifth wave of integration in 2007, which included Bulgaria and Romania.

Accession came after more than a decade of substantial reforms in the areas of state institutions and economy closely monitored by the EU's mechanisms of integration. This monitoring included the expectation that democracy, the rule of law, human rights and protection of minorities would be institutionalized, as articulated in 1993 at the Copenhagen European Council. The mechanisms of achieving democratic conditionality became more precisely defined and reinforced from 1999 onwards by the introduction of a series of country reports which outline for aspiring countries the necessary steps to meet full EU membership criteria (Pridham 2005:40–41). These criteria of democratic conditionality thus took into consideration both the institutional dimensions and substantive aspects of democracy.

However, a closer look at widespread public dissatisfaction with the performance of democratic institutions, perceived as unaccountable to the needs of citizens, together with recent political developments in some countries in the region, casts some doubt on the successful completion of the democratic transition. Within a global perspective, it is in East and Central Europe that we find the lowest levels of people's experience of rule by "will of the people" and belief that democracy is the best system of government (Transcontinental Books 2006:42).[1] The results of the New Europe Barometer also show that among new members of the EU there is prevailing distrust, weak identification with political parties, and an equally negative evaluation of governance and judicial institutions (Rose 2005:57–64). These democratic deficits in the region are important because they point to problematic ties between governments and governed.

As for recent political developments, we will refer particularly to those in Bulgaria, Hungary, Poland and Romania. The most unexpected result in the 2005 Bulgarian elections was the performance of the xenophobic and anti-Semitic Ataka party, given that until then such political party appeals to ethnic tensions were absent. In Hungary violent riots and mass protests on the streets of Budapest in September 2006 came as a surprise in a country in which the transition to democracy had been dominated by political apathy. These outbursts were triggered by the acknowledgment of the newly elected socialist prime minister, Ferenc Gyurcsany. He had concealed the true state of the economy in order to be re-elected.

The emergence of a religiously and socially conservative coalition government in Poland during the same year generated anxiety among EU officials. In Romania an unstable coalition government resulting from the 2004 elections stalled reforms in the areas of corruption and then in the justice system after the January 2007 accession. Similar concerns were raised in May 2007 by the failed attempt of the legislature to oust incumbent president Traian Basescu, known for strongly supporting the anti-corruption campaign and for his populist instincts.

Across the region, in short, populist electoral gains, weak majorities, political radicalization, factional behaviors and misbehavior of political elites have become main features of political life (Mungiu-Pippidi October 2007:8–16). Yet, despite such setbacks these four countries continue to be classified as consolidated democracies, in accordance with the well-known and widely accepted Freedom House methodology. The only exception is Romania, which remains classified as a

[1] The results of a 2005 Gallup poll on global views of democracy show that unlike North America, Africa and Western Europe, where more than 80 percent of those surveyed agree that democracy is the best available form of government, in East and Central Europe support is only 68 percent. Although the perception that the experience of rule by the will of the people nowhere scored high (the highest score is 37 percent in North America), East and Central Europe have again the lowest score, 22 percent.

semiconsolidated democracy, though not far removed from consolidation (Freedom House 2007).

The methodology used by Freedom House in assessing a country's democracy score is based on the most relevant dimensions of the democratic consolidation model, which include electoral process, civil society, rule of law (the constitutional, legislative, and judicial framework), governance, corruption, and media.[2] Although there are some minor variations, most advocates of this model, such as Juan J. Linz, Alfred Stepan, Guillermo O'Donnell, John Elster, Claus Offe, Ulrich K. Preuss and others, have included these aspects of democratic regimes in their work (see the references). Linz and Stepan's model, for example, includes five specific areas of consolidated democracy, thereby allowing for an empirical operationalization of the framework (1996:3–15). These five areas are:

- Civil society based on freedom of association and communication;
- Political society based on free and inclusive electoral contestation;
- Economic society based on an institutionalized market system.
- Rule of law based on constitutionalism; and
- A state apparatus based on rational-legal and bureaucratic norms.

Although the post-communist democracies noted above are seen as stable and are characterized by the absence of anti-democratic actors threatening to act outside the boundaries of democratic rules or radically to change them, their most important weaknesses lie in the areas of rule of law, quality of state apparatus and extent of citizen participation. Several questions arise here:

- Is the model of democratic consolidation still adequate for analyzing post-communist transitions?
- Is it appropriate to see some end to the process of democratic consolidation and thus to the post-communist transition?
- Are these democracies different from their Western counterparts?

In order to attempt an answer to these questions, we turn to a newly elaborated model of quality of democracy by Larry Diamond and Leonardo Morlino (2005). Before presenting this model, it is

[2] Freedom House classifies the regime type on a scale from 1 to 7, wherein lower scores indicate improvement. This results in the following denominations: consolidated democracy (1–2); semiconsolidated democracy (3); transitional government or hybrid regime (4); semiconsolidated authoritarian regime (5); and consolidated authoritarian regime (6–7).

important to note that prior to its elaboration, students of democratization began to express reservations about the application of the consolidated democracy model and they suggested different conceptual frameworks. Guillermo O'Donnell claimed that the main illusion about consolidation is that institutionalization represents its principal feature, given that so many new democracies remain stable despite being still embedded in particularism and clientelism (O'Donnell 1997:40–57). Others described these new democracies as electoral or delegative, and even went so far as to suggest that the democratization model has exhausted its utility ("the end of the transition paradigm") (O'Donnell 1999; Rose & Shin 2001; Carothers 2002).

These theoretical and empirical ambiguities are addressed by Diamond and Morlino's quality of democracy model. Its starting point is the conceptual distinction between the durability of democratic institutions, as previously examined in studies of democratic consolidation, and the depth of the democratization process. The innovative aspect of this model is that although it is elaborated as an extension of the democratic consolidation model, it is also applicable to established democracies. This is a crucial departure from the previous paradigm, which was based on a normative conception of a liberal western democracy.

Proponents of the quality of democracy model argue that a good democracy requires a legitimate regime that satisfies citizen expectations and provides them with the opportunity to hold democratic actors and institutions accountable. There are eight dimensions of the model that overlap and reinforce each other, of which five are procedural and three are substantive (Diamond & Morlino 2005:ix–xliii). In procedural terms:

- Rule of law, as supported by an independent judiciary which ensures fair treatment of citizens and prevents any abuses by the state;
- Citizen participation, understood in a broader sense as exercising democratic citizenship; not just voting, but also involvement in the life of civil society;
- Competition, which involves strong political pluralism;
- Vertical accountability, which requires elected officials to justify their decisions to citizens and constitutional bodies; and
- Horizontal accountability, which also ensures the accountability of decisions by elected officials through the activity of independent agencies and various judicial bodies.

This last dimension is supported by vertical accountability and, in turn, the two types of accountability are essential pillars of the rule of law.

The substantive dimensions of the Diamond and Morlino model of democratic quality are:

- Freedom, referring to political, civil, and socioeconomic rights;
- Equality; and
- Responsiveness.

Diamond and Morlino see responsiveness as the culminating dimension, "closely related to vertical accountability, and hence to participation and competition. In turn, it also influences how well citizens will be satisfied with the performance of democracy, and to what extent they will view it as the best form of government for their country" (2005:xxx–xxxi).

Diamond and Morlino acknowledge that their model has a cultural dimension in that each democracy values certain dimensions over others. But their point is that, ultimately, all eight dimensions are present in a democracy even if some are less evident than others. According to the them, the flexibility of the model accepts the possibility of different types of sequences or causal relationships and also allows theorists and policy-makers to address both normative and practical aspects of democracy. In particular, given the unique context of post-communist democracies characterized by weak institutionalization of law, the model can be useful insofar as it allows us to examine the rule of law in itself. As Leonardo Morlino points out in the second chapter of this volume, there is an important difference between analyzing the rule of law in relationship to the earlier stage of democratic transition and the subsequent phase of democratic quality. He states that while in the former case the rule of law is indistinguishable from the process of democratization and the guarantee of basic rights, in the latter the rule of law is closely inter-connected with accountability and responsiveness.

Ultimately, Diamond and Morlino say, democracy could achieve legitimacy as a result of reforms that are geared towards enhancing democratic quality. This point – that enhancing democratic legitimacy represents the final step towards consolidation – reflects an important development and departure from the democratic consolidation model. Theorists of democratic consolidation differ in their views regarding what sustains democratic legitimacy and how to assess this empirically.

Linz and Stepan (1996:1–83) discuss the compliance of political actors with the rules of the democratic game. Their argument is that the issue of democratic legitimacy is relatively autonomous from the question of the perception of democracy by the electorate, as merely effective or not in providing for economic and social needs. Other authors, including Andrew Arato (2000), Andras Bozoki (1994) and Gerd Meyer (1994), emphasize the relationship between civil society and democratic legitimacy. They see this supporting a population's internalization of democratic norms and procedures and also providing a means of coping with the challenges of introducing market reforms that often involve high social costs.

John Elster, Clauss Offe, and Ulrich Press (1998) address the crucial importance of legality for the institutionalization of democracy, which they define in Weberian terms as rational-legal authority. They suggest that democratic institutions continue to function as they had in the past, namely in a legally established manner through the agency of political actors. Following the same line of argument, Seymour Martin Lipset (1994:1–22) points to an important distinction, between "the agent of authority and the rulers" (the agents themselves) or, simply put, between democratic institutions and the political actors representing them.

An important advantage of Diamond and Morlino's quality of democracy model, however, is that in showing the complex dynamic among its eight dimensions it helps to increase understanding of the relationship between the performance of democratic institutions and a population's collective perceptions, attitudes and behaviors in respect to democracy. Moreover, the model allows for the possibility of identifying regionally specific determinants that also and equally affect the procedural and substantive dimensions of democratic quality. In a study of Poland and Romania, Alina Mungiu-Pippidi suggests (2005:229) that the quality of democracy in post-communist societies is explained by three contributing factors: the size of the rural population, the degree of collectivism under communism, and the characteristics of political actors (such as communist successor parties and opposition movements).

The intention of the present analysis is to test in a more systematic manner the quality of democracy model and its applicability to the present state of post-communist democracies. By utilizing the procedural and substantive dimensions listed above, the article attempts to answer several questions in light of the political developments in Bulgaria, Hungary, Poland and Romania presented briefly at the outset.

- Can current deficiencies in these democracies, such as the rise in populism, polarization and unstable governance, be interpreted as a decline in their overall performance, or, alternatively, as an indication of ongoing movement towards deepening democracy?
- Does the model help us understand the significance of different aspects of popular legitimacy from the perspective of democratic deepening?
- Can the model recommend ways of improving or correcting the deficiencies in these democracies?

The four cases were chosen based on their currently similar path of reform as mandated by the European Union, which is geared towards modernization of the state and enhancement of rule of law. The fact that Hungary and Poland are at a more advanced stage in their reform agendas, given their admission to the EU in 2004, while Bulgaria and Romania progressed at a slower pace, leading up to EU integration in 2007, provides some important methodological advantages. It provides an opportunity for a fuller account of the dynamic character of deepening democracy. In addition, the choice of these four countries allows for an understanding of how the particular historical and cultural legacies of each impact upon the quality of democracy.

Together with the democracy scores as calculated by Freedom House, which spans the most relevant aspects in the quality of democracy model of Diamond and Morlino, as specified earlier, the analysis here will also use the results of the 2004 New Europe Barometer gathered and examined by Richard Rose. The new Europe Barometer provides insight into significant aspects of democratic legitimacy, such as support for undemocratic alternatives and/or for democratic options, rule of law, governmental responsiveness, participation in politics, and social efficacy (the popular perception that the views of ordinary people are seriously considered by their governments). In addition, I will also refer to specific historical and cultural characteristics of each of the four countries, and to their most recent electoral processes.

However, before pursuing the analysis of the substantive and procedural aspects of democratic quality, I provide below the trend of overall democracy scores since 1997 and for the past two years. These data are not only helpful in laying out the ground for the subsequent

Democracy score	Bulgaria	Hungary	Poland	Romania
1997	3.90	1.50	1.50	3.95
2006	2.93	1.96	2.14	3.39
2007	2.89	2.14	2.36	3.29

* Freedom House, Nations in Transit (2007).
(In all categories in the NIT study, lower scores indicate improvement. See footnote 2 above).

analysis of democratic quality. They also show two successive stages of the democratic transition in the four countries, namely the early post-communist phase and the subsequent phase of post-EU accession.

Looking at these scores, Hungary and Poland followed much earlier paths towards democratic consolidation and then subsequently suffered declines in quality of democracy. This contrasts sharply with the trajectories in Romania and even more so Bulgaria, where they both show significant progress from the status of almost semiconsolidated authoritarian regimes towards consolidation. The two questions that arise from these scores are: Are there serious reasons for concern by an apparent decline in Hungarian and Polish democracy? How uncertain or precarious is the future direction of democratic deepening in Bulgaria and Romania? In seeking some answers to these questions, I examine in the four countries aspects of participation and competition, accountability, governance and rule of law, corruption and responsiveness.

Participation and Competition: Electoral Process and Civil Society Involvement

Participation and competition represent fundamental procedural aspects of any democratic regime. Both the quality of democracy model and Freedom House measure them beyond terms of the simple act of voting by taking into account participation within the context of civil society's capacity to monitor the activities of those elected to office. It is competition especially that ensures there is no one political party that is financially privileged during the electoral campaign, or privileged in other ways, and ensures electoral fairness and accountability. Competition is sustained by legal institutions of horizontal accountability, such as an independent electoral commission, and by independent groups acting on behalf of civil society.

The evolution in the scores of electoral process and civil society, two dimensions of the overall democracy score assigned by Freedom House since 1997 which span aspects of participation and competition, indicate the following. After a period of almost ten years during which Bulgaria and Romania slowly advanced towards consolidation, the gap between these countries and Hungary and Poland has narrowed since 2005. This difference is not simply a reflection of improvement in the performance of electoral process and civil society in Bulgaria and Romania. It is also a result of downward movement in the same scores in Hungary and Poland.

In 2007 Bulgaria and Romania scored respectively 1.75 and 2.75 in electoral process and 2.50 and 2.25 in the area of civil society. Given that in 1997 Bulgaria's and Romania's electoral process scored 3.25 and civil society 4.00 and 3.75, the progress made by the two countries towards consolidation seems evident. In 2007 Hungary's electoral process and civil society scores slid in just one year, to 1.75 and 1.50 from 1.25. Electoral process and civil society in Poland also experienced a decline. Both measures lost 0.25 points during this last year, falling to 1.75 and 1.50. Yet in 1997 the Hungarian and Polish scores in both areas of electoral process, 1.25 and 1.50, and civil society, 1.25, were still significantly ahead of those for Bulgaria and Romania.

It can be argued that this present state of affairs is an indicator that all countries have completed their post-communist transitions. Any initial differences between Bulgaria and Romania on the one hand, and Hungary and Poland on the other, can be attributed to their specific circumstances and paths of revolutionary change since 1989. These initial differences, that is, are no longer significant or relevant after accession to the EU.

The liberal consensus between former communists and opposition groups in Hungary and Poland, achieved as a result of roundtable negotiations between them, led to a relatively well-defined political spectrum. It consisted of a left wing represented by the successors to the communist parties and a liberal center consisting of a coalition of groups and parties previously engaged in anti-communist opposition. A regular alternation in power between these two wings, which for the most part represented a change in government and not in policies, ensured a relatively smooth process of democratization. It prevented attempts at illegal or violent appropriation of power by other political actors.

In this way, Hungary and Poland achieved more rapidly stable conditions of political party participation, what Anna Grzymala-Busse describes (2007:81–132) as the circumstances of "robust party competition." This acted as an incentive for the early introduction of formal state institutions, designed to constrain governing party exploitation of the state during the period of otherwise opportunistic post-communist state-building.

In contrast, the illiberal tendencies of former communists in Bulgaria and Romania inhibited political competition, thereby delaying the democratic process and integration into the EU.[3] That is, former communists captured state institutions and the media, and frequently resorted to ethnic nationalism (at least in Romania).

Even if the anti-communist opposition came to power in Bulgaria five years earlier than in Romania – in 1991 the Union of Democratic Forces (UDF) assumed power whereas the Democratic Convention in Romania (CDR) won elections only in 1997 – in both cases the opposition was immature. Opposition parties had few scruples in engaging in non-democratic behavior in order to challenge the political domination of their opponents. This had the effect of stalling both countries in an uncertain area of the democratization process until the late 1990's. This is when the EU's accession mechanisms required more systematic reforms in the areas of vertical and horizontal accountability. As a result, both the Bulgarian Socialist Party (BSP) and the Social Democratic Party in Romania (PSD) transformed themselves into modern socialist parties, and began to pursue more liberal economic and administrative policies.

However, as Ivan Krastev points out (2007:58–59), "the successes of postcommunist liberalism" across the region were achieved by elites at the expense of mass political participation while these same "liberal elites left their societies with no acceptable ways to protest or express dissatisfaction." The claims advanced by Diamond and Morlino that intensive participation of civil society in the electoral process is conducive to democratic deepening are not confirmed, therefore, by post-communist experience. Yet despite a low interest in politics and low party identification, democratic quality in Hungary and Poland was

[3] For a comprehensive analysis of the quality of successors to the communist parties and their relationship with accession into the European Union see Milada Anna Vachudova (2005).

nonetheless maintained. At the same time, the improvement in the quality of democracy in Bulgaria and Romania also does not reveal any intensification of political participation.[4]

To the contrary, as recent elections and democracy scores in Hungary and Poland show, more intensive mass political mobilization resulted in lower democratic quality. As for Bulgaria and Romania, there is concrete evidence that they, too, are moving in a similar direction. The rhetoric used by winning parties and coalitions in Hungary and Poland during the electoral campaign and afterwards was populist. It emphasized the need for a new political era in which political actors would no longer simply pursue the requirements of transition or EU accession but instead the interests of ordinary citizens.

This means we are no longer in a situation characterized by former communists versus anti-communists, that is by a cleavage that became more and more irrelevant under the circumstances of EU enlargement, but rather in a situation characterized by a more general movement towards responsive and accountable governance. However, the April 2006 Hungarian parliamentary elections nonetheless resulted in a polarized legislature. The previous incumbent Hungarian Socialist Party (MSZP) gained 43.3 percent of the electoral vote but this was only one percentage point ahead of the center-right opposition party, the Alliance of Young Democrats-Hungarian Civic Party (FIDESZ).

These two main actors of Hungarian politics appealed to voters not by advancing specific policies and ideologies, but rather by promoting leaders who engaged in highly personalized politics. This turn of events reflected less voter interest in accountable government then voter fatigue with issues of transitional politics and European integration. Thus, Viktor Orban, FIDESZ's charismatic leader, faced Ferenc Gyurcsany as his opponent, who became leader of the MSZP in 2004. Orban began his political career as a radical liberal but later became a neo-conservative, with a chauvinist and populist message attracting new supporters. Gyurcsany is a young leftist billionaire and believer in the now partially discarded ideology of the "third way" of New Labor in Britain.

[4] The results of the 2004 New Europe Barometer collected by Richard Rose show that the combined percentage of those who have little or very little interest in politics is 60% in Bulgaria, 70% in Hungary, 63% in Poland and 72% in Romania. As for party identification, even if this is higher in Bulgaria and Hungary (38% and 36%) overall it still remains low.

The confrontation between Orban and Gyurcsany took a dramatic turn after the elections when a leaked tape showed Gyurcsany admitting to lying about the state of the economy in order to be re-elected. His refusal to provide an explanation or to apologize, coupled with Orban's confrontational rhetoric, led to civil unrest and forms of violent protest during September and October on the streets of Budapest (Transitions Online April 18, 2005; Kovacks and Molnar October 6, 2006; Higginson October 2006). These events were also aggravated by the politicization of civil society and the participation of extremist groups such as, for example, the 64 Counties Youth Movement that demanded "system change" (Kovacs and Villany 2007).

If elections in Hungary produced the type of polarization that encourages instability (as proved to be the case), Polish elections in September of the same year led to a similarly volatile outcome. The result was a dramatic decline in the power of the former incumbent leftist party, the Democratic Left Alliance (SLD) which had ensured the country's entry into the EU. The SLD lost 162 seats, reduced from 217 to 55. Moreover, a narrow victory by the religiously and socially conservative Law and Justice Party (PiS) brought into a new governing coalition two outsider groups, represented by the League of Polish Families (LPR) and the Self-Defense League (Samoobrona).

It is important to stress that both the LPR and Samoobrona represented the views of those Poles perceiving themselves as excluded from an increasingly capitalist and European Poland. LPR embraces a right-wing ideology, and its leader, Andresz Lepper, had virulently attacked Balcerowicz' market reforms in the past and instigated farmers' protests in the 1990's. Samoobrona entered parliament for the first time in 2001, promoting a populist and anti-EU message.

Likewise, the rhetoric that attracted supporters of the PiS, led by Lech Kaczynsky, the current president, and his prime minister and twin brother Jaroslaw, very much resembled the Hungarian case. The two brothers also represent the right wing of the previous governing factions of the Solidarity movement. Their message went beyond the divisions between legatees of the communist party and Solidarity's successors, for they presented an outline for a "Fourth Republic."

The Fourth Republic represents a break with the post-1989 Third Republic, which had failed to deal with the communist past because it had been shaped exclusively by an agreement between Solidarity and ex-communists. The new republic was to be characterized by a moral revolution that would address especially the corruption of state institutions and then also promote national interests and family values as well as pursue the much delayed purification of the political class through lustration or formal ceremony (see Millard 2006:1007–1031; Ash November 2006:22–25). However, the government's attempts to implement this agenda led to controversial initiatives and actions that negatively affected the quality of political participation and competition.

Among the most criticized government actions were the amendment of lustration laws in a way that infringed upon constitutionally guaranteed civil rights. Krzystof Jasievicz (2007:31–32) lists some of the elements of the new lustration law that were overturned by the constitutional tribunal. These include the retroactive lustration of elected officials, the subjection to lustration of individuals working in private institutions, and forcing the self-incrimination of individuals by applying penalties for non-filing. Other controversial legislative initiatives included changes in electoral legislation, in preparation for local elections that would allow minority parties in electoral coalitions to transfer seats to stronger partners, as well as efforts aimed at undermining civil society (Krajewski 2007).

Likewise, the most recent elections conducted in Bulgaria, in June 2005, and in Romania, in November/December 2004, took place in both cases under volatile circumstances, which resulted in unstable and fragile coalitions and also introduced newcomers to the political scene. The results of both elections posed serious difficulties in forming coalition governments.

After lengthy negotiations finalized in June, the Bulgarian coalition government brought together awkward bedfellows with incompatible ideologies: the Socialist Party (BSP) that had become a member of the Socialist International in 2003, and the former incumbent party, the National Movement Simeon II (NMSS), that had affiliated with the Liberal International.

At the same time, elections in Romania produced a fragile coalition government consisting of the two parties comprising the Alliance for Truth and Justice (DA) that had found themselves on opposite sides during the 1990's: the Liberal Party (PNL) and the Democratic Party (PD). The PD was a splinter group of the successor to the communist party led by Ion Iliescu. Two smaller parties whose loyalty was doubtful from the beginning, the party of ethnic Hungarians (DAHR) and the Humanist Party (PUR), also joined the coalition.

A novel anti-corruption and populist message was employed during both elections. One surprise of the Bulgarian election was the vote gained by the Ataka coalition (nine percent), formed by Volen Siderov shortly before the election. Siderov is a journalist and author of anti-Semitic and anti-Roma articles, calling, for instance, for assimilating the Turkish minority by weakening their distinctive ethnic identity. He was also a virulent critic of earlier governments that had opened the country to foreign investment. Yet local political analysts interpreted the electoral success of the Ataka coalition as evidence of popular dissatisfaction with other political parties, not as a threat to produce an anti-system agenda. Indeed, a significant portion of those who ran on Ataka's lists did so opportunistically, simply to win safe seats in the legislature (Alexandrova July 27, 2005; Brown July 28, 2005; Ganev 2006:75–90).

In respect to elections in Romania, it is important to emphasize the aggressive anti-corruption message promoted by the Alliance for Truth and Justice led by Traian Basescu, the mayor of Bucharest who became the ATJ's presidential candidate. Likewise, the involvement of civil society groups, represented by the efforts of the Coalition for a Clean Parliament and the Pro-Democracy Movement, was also significant in promoting fairness, accountability and transparency in the electoral process.

During the runoff of the presidential elections, Basescu gave a quite spectacular performance. He attracted a wide range of supporters from different political parties with his virulent anti-corruption rhetoric, his populist instincts, and his ability to interact with crowds easily. Ultimately, this performance gave him a margin of 250,000 over his opponent, Adrian Nastase of the Social Democratic Party (PSD), who had led in the first round with more than 700,000 votes. It should also be noted that as late as 2007 Romanian authorities still had not investigated irregularities in the 2004 elections, the most important of which was the "disappearance" of 160,000 annulled votes (Gross, Tismaneanu & Mungiu-Pippidi 2005; Ciobanu & Shafir 2005).

Since the goal and priority of the two new governments in Bulgaria and Romania was to complete EU accession by 2007, by introducing rapid reforms in the areas of the justice system and focusing on issues of corruption, both coalition governments managed to hold together until European integration was finalized. However, immediately afterwards new right-wing populist leaders and parties began to emerge in both Bulgarian and Romanian politics. The European Development of

Bulgaria (GERB), established in December 2006, and the New Generation Party (PNG), dating in Romania since 2000, are led by leaders, Boyko Borissov and George Becali, who constructed their reputations as self-made men. They began drawing support from dissatisfied segments of the population.[5]

One result in Romania was the break-up of the coalition government in March 2007. This was followed in May by an unsuccessful attempt by a sizable coalition in the legislature in a referendum to suspend Basescu from office and impeach him.

This detailed excursion into the latest elections and their consequences in the four countries points towards a new shift in focus, away from an emphasis on a liberal elite-driven, post-communist political transition. Such a transition did produce a relatively free and fair electoral process, with some differences rooted in specific historical circumstances. But it also succeeded, whether purposefully or, most likely, not, in conveniently avoiding significant mass mobilization towards a new type of "catchall" populist politics. The significance and implications of this new, still developing set of conditions for the quality of democracy is further examined in an analysis of accountability, governance and the rule of law.

Accountability, Governance and the Rule of Law

According to Diamond and Morlino, a free and fair electoral process by itself does not represent a sufficient condition for democracy to be sustained in its substantive dimensions. These additional dimensions include: political, civil and socioeconomic rights, equality, and citizen responsiveness – understood as a perception that democratic government is "the best form of government for their country" (2005:xxix). Such a perception by a population can only be accomplished when democratic participation continues to engage both the electorate and officials *between* elections. Citizens should be informed by elected officials of decisions that affect them, or, in other words, officials should be held accountable.

[5] For the rise of populism in Bulgaria and Romania see Rasho Dorosiev and Georgy Ganev (2007) and Michael Shafir (2007) "Vox Populi, Vox Dei and the [Head-] Master's Voice: Mass and Intellectual Neo-Populism in Contemporary Romania" (unpublished, courtesy of the author).

However, as Philippe Schmitter points out (2005:18–31), accountability can be effective only when electoral or vertical accountability is sustained by horizontal accountability, as represented in and through judicial institutions and independent agencies. While constitutional bodies embody judicial institutions, independent agencies act as "guardian agencies;" their role is to scrutinize government. One example of such "guardian agencies" are offices of ombudsman.

More generally, horizontal accountability ensures that the interactions "between arms and branches of the regime and state" conform to "present constitutional or legal rules." At the same time, both types of accountability, horizontal and vertical, simultaneously sustain and are mutually interdependent in respect to one important procedural dimension of democratic quality: the rule of law.

Schmitter emphasizes that in the context of democratic theory the rule of law represents "the legally based rule of a democratic state." Along with the support of an independent judiciary, the rule of law ensures fair treatment of citizens and prevents abuses of state power. Therefore, it can be argued that both strong accountability and rule of law promote universalistic principles as well as the substantive practices of democratically elected institutions. These in turn buttress positive citizen perceptions of government responsiveness and their own effectiveness or ability in influencing government decision making.

In contrast to this, an undifferentiated legal and institutional structure combined with endemic corrupt practice undermines the basic equality of citizens in respect to political institutions. It thereby compromises the concept of citizenship as well as democratic legitimacy. One consequence of this is that certain segments of the electorate may come to support undemocratic alternatives.

The scores assigned by Freedom House on both dimensions of accountability – vertical or ongoing governance and horizontal or constitutional, legislative and judicial framework – reflect a pattern of performance similar to that in the areas of competition and participation. Moreover, this pattern holds true at both an earlier stage of the democratic transition and then during pre- and post-accession into the EU.

It can be argued that the development of a much stronger parliamentary, constitutional and judicial system in Hungary and Poland resulted in a more liberal form of political competition. As a result, given the specific circumstances of the post-socialist transition, during which state assets were privatized, the temptations of institutional capture and the monopolization of decision-making by specific governing parties were to some extent limited.

That is, unlike their Bulgarian counterparts, both the Hungarian and Polish successors to the communist parties – the Hungarian Socialist Party (MSZP) and the Polish Democratic Left Alliance (SLD) – entered the democratic transition from the beginning as committed proponents of liberal political and economic reforms. As a result, both parties were instrumental in organizing the stability and consolidation of democracy in their countries. However, once this liberal consensus among political elites ended, as described in the previous section, mechanisms of horizontal accountability became weaker in Hungary and Poland after 2004.

In Bulgaria and Romania the early transition period came closer to resemble a "hybrid regime" in which the continuing dominance of past institutions and practices left the future direction of the democratization process uncertain and ambiguous.[6] It was characterized by the domination of unreformed successors to the communist parties and weak opposition coalitions. This gave former communists an opportunity to undermine mechanisms of institutional or horizontal accountability. Furthermore, by monopolizing the state media and by manipulating and intimidating independent television stations and newspapers, they inhibited citizen access to a plurality of sources of information.

In more recent years, in contrast, as a result of the process of EU accession, institutions ensuring horizontal accountability were put in place, such as anticorruption strategies and reforms of the judicial system, which demanded more efficient, transparent and stable governance. Yet, given the continuing, strong opposition from segments of the political and economic oligarchy in Bulgaria and Romania during this process, the accession treaty contains a safeguard clause in the area of judicial affairs. This could block EU recognition of the two countries.

These scores reflect not only differences between Hungary and Poland, on the one hand, and Bulgaria and Romania, on the other, but also some differences between leaders and laggards. More particularly,

[6] Morlino defines a hybrid regime as "a set of institutions that maintain aspects of the past" and "is a 'corruption' of the preceding regime, lacking as it does one or more essential characteristics of that regime but also failing to acquire other characteristics that would make it fully democratic or authoritarian."

Governance	Bulgaria	Hungary	Poland	Romania
1999	3.75	2.50	1.75	3.50
2005	3.50	2.00	2.50	3.50
2006	3.00	2.00	2.75	3.50
2007	3.00	2.25	3.25	3.50

* Freedom House, Nations in Transit (2007). It is important to note here that in 2004 Romania's score was 3.75, so EU accession led to some (even if minor) improvement in governance.

Judicial Framework and Independence	Bulgaria	Hungary	Poland	Romania
1999	3.50	1.75	1.50	4.25
2005	3.25	1.75	2.00	4.00
2006	3.00	1.75	2.25	4.00
2007	2.75	1.75	2.25	3.75

* Freedom House, Nations in Transit (2007).

the constitutional arrangements resulting from the specific circumstances of the 1989 anti-communist revolutions explain the superior performances of Hungary and Bulgaria in the areas of governance and judicial framework compared to those of Poland and Romania.

Hungary's polity is organized as a parliamentary democracy. From the state its constitution allowed an effective separation of legislative, executive and judicial powers. This ensured a fairly balanced sharing of influence and power between branches of government and also between the main political parties and coalitions. The parliament and its special committees monitor the government's activities through regular interpellations and questions. In addition it possesses the right to pass a no-confidence vote in respect to the prime minister (but not without prior nomination and endorsement of a new chief of government) which ensures stable governance between elections.

Equally, both the constitutional court and the institution of ombudsman are organized as representative and accountable bodies, which supports the independence of the judiciary. The current Hungarian president, Solyom, is an energetic promoter of a strong judicial system. During his tenure as chief justice of the constitutional court, between 1990 and 1998, he promoted principles of individual rights under the concept of an "invisible constitution." Under his leadership this court abolished laws limiting freedom of speech. He also lobbied for the creation of a fifth public ombudsman, covering environmental issues, and he supported extending civil rights, minority rights, educational rights and protections of information.

The introduction of a four-tier court system in 2003 also contributed to a more efficient justice system. This is particularly notable since most post-communist legal systems, including those of Poland, Bulgaria and Romania, are overburdened by high numbers of unresolved cases – which they are extremely slow in finalizing. It is also remarkable that even under the difficult circumstances of the violent riots of September and October 2007, which both the Hungarian government and opposition were criticized for mishandling, the NIT assessment of the judicial framework and its independence remained unchanged even as the governance score declined to 2.25 (Kovacs & Villany 2007).

Compared to Hungary, Poland's weaker performance in the area of its constitutional, legislative and judicial framework, and its even weaker governance structure, is a consequence of the different legacies of its communist regime. This influenced the constitutional arrangements of the 1989 roundtable and the subsequent type of political participation and competition that emerged from it. What constituted the strength of a diverse mass movement became a source of instability and fragmentation. That is, it had originally unified the anti-communist opposition movement Solidarity, both before 1989. Then, during the immediate aftermath of the negotiated transition, it also unified the extremely diverse composition of contributors, which included labor unions, conservative and religious groups, liberal factions, and intellectuals.

As a result of roundtable negotiations between former communists and Solidarity, the latter successfully won all the negotiated parliamentary seats in the partially free elections of June 1989. However, Solidarity as a political movement was short-lived. Because of its fragmentation and dissolution the first completely free elections, in 1991, resulted in as many as eighteen different political groups forming in the legislature.

Predictably, in the following two years Poland experienced unstable governance. After a shift in power, from the Democratic Left Alliance (1993–1997) to a center-right coalition made up of Solidarity elements (1997–2001), the new government failed in the September

2001 elections to reach the required electoral threshold of eight percent needed simply for parliamentary representation. This not only opened the door for a return to a strong SLD, but also facilitated the entry of newcomers to politics. Some of these newcomers were guided by conservative and nationalist ideologies, including the agrarian and conservative Self-Defense Party (SRP) and the Christian-Nationalist League of Polish Families (LPR).

After 2001 the governance rating of Poland began to decline, from 1.75 to 3.25 in 2007. A significant deterioration occurred in the last year under the right-wing conservative Kaczynski government, as it engaged in activities geared towards concentrating power in the executive. For example, by replacing the existing civil service corps with new staff appointed by the executive, it politicized the civil service (Krajewski 2007). In addition, the Kaczynski government attempted to destroy its political opponents, represented by members of the two major actors in Poland's political transition, the ex-communists and left-wing liberals of the post-Solidarity movement. It did so by passing in July 2006 a new and highly controversial lustration bill, intended to replace the legislation of 1997.

This bill was controversial because it defined so broadly the subjects of lustration (including all public officials, members of the legal profession, journalists, academics). If implemented, it could have affected as many as 700,000 people. Failure to submit an affidavit of collaboration with the communist secret services, or providing inaccurate information, could lead to severe punishment: from losing a job, to a ten-year ban from public office, to possible criminal prosecution (Jasiewicz 2007:31–32).

Turning to the constitutional framework, it took almost eight years after the roundtable for a constitution to be enacted. Prior to this, the framework functioned under the old 1952 communist constitution, to which some amendments had been added in 1992 (known as "the small Constitution"). This apparent legal continuity, and relative delay in drafting a new constitution, did not actually jeopardize newly acquired freedoms, due to the existence of consensus by civil society groups and political elites on democratic principles. Even after 2005, when the performance of the judiciary began to decline, the constitutional court still continued to fulfill its role as a supreme, independent judicial body. In May 2007 it reversed several provisions of the lustration bill, for being in violation of constitutionally guaranteed civil rights.

Freedom House ratings for Bulgaria and Romania in the area of governance reflect each country's much slower progress since 1997 from "transitional government or hybrid regimes" towards semi-consolidated democracy," a version closer to liberal democracy. In Romania's case, these governance ratings also reflect an inability to break away from its early transition path, established through a violent popular uprising that led to the execution of former president Nicolae Ceausescu. Unlike the other three cases, power was immediately transferred to the National Salvation Front (NSF), which had emerged spontaneously, absent any negotiations between former communists and opposition movements.

It is important here to specify that the Romanian and Bulgarian polities exhibit significant differences: while Bulgaria is a purely parliamentary democracy, Romania is a semi-presidential parliamentary democracy. In the context of the Romanian transition, this type of polity, to a far greater extent than the Bulgarian one, inhibited both the development of the separation of powers and the independence of the judiciary. Constitutional provisions granting the president the right to appoint judges and to place magistrates under the minister of justice gave former communists the upper hand in the judicial system.

However, in both countries mechanisms of horizontal accountability during the early transition were weak. This was reflected in significant interference by the political class in the independence of the judicial system, in weak legislatures, and in cronyism and corruption at the level of state administration. Low-level political competition favored state capture as well as the monopolization of power in the hands of a new political and economic oligarchy, which had originated in the former communist nomenklatura. Post-communists elites succeeded not only in significantly designing new democratic institutions but also in shaping themselves as predatory elites.

To the mid-1990's, both the Bulgarian Socialist Party, from 1994 to 1996 under the premiership of Zhan Videnov, and the various successors to the Romanian National Salvation Front, from 1990 to 1996 under the presidency of Ion Iliescu, presided over the privatization of state assets and redistribution of national wealth. The beneficiaries of these economic reforms were former members of the nomenklatura and old communist security services.

One impact of this predatory behavior was an undermining and compromising of the administrative apparatus of the state, and another was a severe curtailing of the independence of the judiciary.

By granting preferential treatment to a new oligarchy, both in securing capital and loans and in shielding them from the law, the financial systems of the both Bulgaria and Romania were effectively bankrupted. Political instability and social turmoil were the result.

The collapse of the banking system in Bulgaria in 1996 triggered major popular dissatisfaction, which led eventually in January 1997 to the fall of the Videnov government and return to power of the UDF. Similarly in Romania, thousands lost their savings following the collapses, in 1996 and 2000 respectively, of the heavily indebted Dacia Felix bank and National Investment Fund. The latter represented a state-run unit trust company founded in 1996. After an embezzlement scandal involving its executives the NIF closed its branches in May 2000 and suspended trading with investors.

In this case in particular the judiciary was slow and inconsistent in settling compensation claims. This led to considerable discontent with a party that had, on a populist-nationalist platform, committed itself to defending against the predations of emergent capitalists and foreign investors.[7] It thereby contributed significantly to the electoral victory of the center-right opposition coalition Democratic Convention (CDR) in 1996, the first alternation of power in Romania. But the sheer heterogeneity of the CDR led to inter- and intra-party conflicts among its members, which resulted in weak and unstable governance (no less than three governments were formed between 1996 and 2000) and the persistence of clientelistic practices (Tismaneanu & Kligman 2001:25–34).

It was only after 2000, under the governance of a new modernized successor to NSF, the Social Democratic Party (PSD), that a party consensus on EU integration was reached and accountability mechanisms began being put into place. However, the activity of the legislature continued to be hindered between 2000 and 2004 by the endemic practice of passing executive emergency ordinances, which undermine the basic constitutional principle of separation of powers.

In respect to Bulgaria, corruption under the UDF (1996–2000) persisted, but now primarily focused on misusing EU funds (Ganev 2006:75–90). Moreover, the Bulgarian legislature operated throughout

[7] For the inefficiency of the justice system in Bulgaria and Romania see Ganev (2001:34) and Alina Mungiu-Pippidi (1997:4, 57–69).

the transition period in a more open and professional manner, unlike the Romanian parliament.

Given continuing lackluster political participation and competition, mechanisms of vertical accountability were not put into place in Bulgaria and Romania until later. In both countries the civil service had been heavily politicized as well as staffed with poorly trained employees. It was not until after 1998 that reforms were introduced to improve the performance of public administration.

In Bulgaria the Administration Act of 1998 so clearly failed to improve the quality of the civil service that in 2004 the Civil Service Law was amended to upgrade the recruitment and performance of civil servants. Only in 2005 was a national ombudsman appointed. Likewise, Romania introduced its legislation to reform its public administration in 1999 and 2002.

Thus, in both cases these reforms were regarded by the EU and civil society organizations as insufficient to introduce real changes in professionalizing the state apparatus. They were more akin to cosmetic reforms. But, in contrast to Romania, the Bulgarian constitutional court and the institution of ombudsman retained considerable independence from the executive. The Bulgarian court, set up during the first UDF government, opposed the reform plan of the Videnov government in 1994–1996. Later, in 2002, it opposed attempts to reform the judicial system that had originated in Simeon Sax-Coburg-Gotha's cabinet.

In comparison, the Romanian supreme court experienced continuous executive interference, in particular from former president Iliescu. In 2005 the court was still dominated by the former ruling PSD party: no less than five of its nine judges once belonged to the party. Even after 2004, when judges were granted tenure, and after a new minister of justice launched a determined campaign to reform the justice system and support its independence – a campaign stimulated in part by impending EU accession – the supreme court was still hesitant to act independently of its former political patrons.

Ultimately, it can be argued that Romania's weaker mechanisms of horizontal accountability, especially in relation to the constitutional and legislative framework, can be attributed to a deficit in political competition during the first decade of its political transition. The latter, in turn, resulted from the circumstances of the December 1989 uprising.

This legacy continued to handicap Romania's governance and judicial framework during the two years preceding EU accession, when it commenced its fast track of judicial reform. Since 2005 this was led by Monica Macovei, a newly appointed and highly popular minister of justice backed by President Basescu. It was in fact external pressure from the EU that managed to ensure the stability of the coalition government between 2005 and the January 2007 accession. This external pressure tempered the opposition of domestic anti-reformist forces to Macovei's "Strategy and Action Plan to Reform the Justice System," the Plan which ultimately increased the professionalism and independence of the judiciary. The same Plan also promulgated several decisive anti-corruption measures (Ciobanu 2007:1446–1447).

In comparison to Romania, Bulgaria's NIT ratings in the area of governance and the judicial system ranked it with Hungary and Poland among the consolidated democracies of post-communist countries. Despite the volatile and unstable political situation resulting from the 2005 election, the coalition government, consisting of the Bulgarian Socialist Party (BSP) and National Movement Simeon II (NMSS) set up in August 2005, introduced reforms that enhanced the transparency, efficiency and accountability of the judiciary. The most important reform was a constitutional amendment, introduced in March 2006, requiring the prosecutor general and chairpersons of the supreme administrative court and supreme court of cassation be accountable to the legislature. It also contains a provision that allows the ombudsman to petition the constitutional court (Dorosiev and Ganev 2007).

The analysis above of the four cases has shown a linkage in post-communist democracies between constitutional frameworks and democratic political participation and competition. This linkage suggests that constitutionally designed arrangements, achieved through negotiation and consensus, can lead in turn to a more mature political pluralism, one that facilitates competition within the framework of democratic norms and procedures.

However, it can also be argued that the choice of these four cases does not offer sufficient variation for comparative analysis, given that all four ultimately followed a similar path of democratization triggered by mechanisms of EU conditionality. As a result, broader generalizations cannot be supported.

Our counterargument is that the advantage of having less variation is that it provides us with much greater in-depth understanding of the interaction between competition, participation and accountability, and then also of the way in which an external dimension influences this dynamic. Since these dimensions, internal and external, represent the major variables of post-communist transition, our comparison becomes preferable within the conceptual framework of the quality of democracy model noted earlier.

At the same time, we examined, in the Romanian case, the incentives and limitations of the externally required dimensions of democratic quality. More important, we also emphasized the weaknesses of elite-driven institutional reforms. We did this by tracing the disturbing direction Hungarian and Polish democracies took following the liberal reforms symbolized by their successful EU accession. Although these short-term political shifts could not be explained easily in terms of the quality of democracy model, their detailed presentation confirms once again an important point made by proponents of this model and by students of democratization more generally. Consolidated or institutionalized democracies are simultaneously stable and yet imperfect. Given, therefore, that democracy always is an ongoing, perfectible project, which goes beyond its institutionalization at any given time, political upheavals are not uncommon events even in consolidated democracies.

What still remains to be clarified is a uniformity across the four cases, regardless of country differences in level of democratic deepening: Low citizen political participation and a widespread perception that democratic governance by no means expresses any semblance of rule by the will of the people. The next section focuses on mechanisms of horizontal accountability and issues of corruption. It also pursues further an analysis of the question of citizen participation. We present evidence of public attitudes and perceptions of democratic institutions and the latter's performance - or, in the vocabulary of the quality of democracy model, evidence of political responsiveness.

Corruption/Horizontal Accountability Mechanisms and Responsiveness

Having discussed how political and constitutional bodies in the four post-communist countries have been designed and how they fulfill their functions, it is necessary in assessing the quality of democracy to analyze the extent to which design and function complement and reinforce each other. This issue gets us specifically to mechanisms of horizontal accountability, which are "usually manifest in the monitoring, investigating, and enforcement activities of a number of independent government agencies... and other bodies that scrutinize and limit the power of those who govern" (Diamond and Morlino 2005:xxi).

Given the specific circumstances of post-communist transitions and the legacies inherited from communist rule, horizontal accountability seems to be particularly problematic. After all, communist regimes created particularistic societies in which people learned to distrust state institutions. They relied on networks of family and friends to provide for their needs, and they accepted and engaged in corrupt practices and behaviors when interacting with public officials and state institutions. The author of one of the most comprehensive studies of corruption in post-communism, Rasma Karklins (2005), demonstrates that these societies share the most permissive attitudes towards corruption. These attitudes were then exacerbated during the transition stage, and particularly by the privatization of state enterprises.

This state of affairs was aggravated by the behavior of post-1989 predatory political elites, who continued to exert power in a personalized manner by engaging in informal practices such as clientelism and patronage. These practices led to a considerable weakening of post-socialist states, particularly in Bulgaria and Romania where low political competition and continuing domination by one political party facilitated a deeper insertion of the new oligarchy into public administration.

The expansion of the state through new agencies charged with privatizing state assets occurred to a greater extent in Bulgaria than Hungary or Poland (Anna Grzymala-Busse 2007:160–163). However, Nicolae Belli (2001) documents a similar over-expansion in Romania. The new Romanian oligarchy was represented by an association of interests spanning networks of: former members of the nomenklatura, with deep ties in the former socialist economy, former communist secret police, and new political elites drawn from middle and higher echelons of pre-existing communist parties. By taking full advantage of inside knowledge of the system and of ties with the financial and law enforcement systems, these groups became the main beneficiaries of state privatization.

This route to private wealth accumulation resulted by the mid-1990s in changing popular perceptions of the socialist past. A more positive (even nostalgic) view of socialism emerged as well as a stronger sense

Corruption score	Bulgaria	Hungary	Poland	Romania*
1999	4.75	2.50	2.25	4.25
2005	4.00	2.75	3.00	4.25
2006	3.75	3.00	3.25	4.25
2007	3.75	3.00	3.00	4.00

* Freedom House, Nations in Transit, 2007. Lower scores for Romania should not be interpreted as lack of progress under the circumstances of accession because in 2002 the corruption score was 4.75 and for the next two years 4.50.

of the direct relation between social justice and evaluations of political systems.[8]

With EU assistance and advice, anti-corruption agencies and other mechanisms of horizontal accountability began forcefully to be implemented after 2000, aimed at enhancing the rule of law. However, the decline in corruption scores of Hungary and Poland and the ongoing political attempts to undermine anti-corruption institutions in Bulgaria and Romania (despite an increase in NIT corruption scores before and after accession) indicate that these reforms were pursued not as a goal in itself but as means for achieving EU accession. These ratings also reveal that there is an evident hiatus between levels of corruption and the accountability mechanisms discussed earlier (governance and the rule of law), despite differences in the quality of democracy between leaders and laggards.

Karklin's analysis shows that among the most successful strategies used by the political class to limit the power of accountability agencies have been: institutional capture, monopolization of decision-making, discretion, and resistance to accountability. In the case of anti-corruption agencies whose role is to monitor public officials, verify private assets, and fight corruption in public procurement, these strategies are easily identifiable. Members of parliament and other public officials avoid declaring their assets or conceal them with family members. One spectacular example involved Adrian Nastase, former Romanian prime minister and speaker of the lower house at the time, whose legal disclosure in 2005 revealed that his wife inherited assets worth one

[8] See David Mason and James K. Kluegel (2000) for the results of two surveys known as the International Social Justice Project, initiated in 1991 and replicated in 1996.

million euros from a deceased octogenarian aunt, allegedly active in real estate.

Quite often criminal activities link the political class with law enforcement agencies. In 2003 the Polish political establishment was shaken when the media revealed that police leaked information to members of the governing party, the SLD. Sometimes extreme acts are perpetrated, such as assassinations of state officials, as was the case in Bulgaria when officials attempted to dismantle the complicated network of corruption linked with the economic conglomerate Multigroup.

There is, in addition, extremely weak transparency within political parties. Regardless of political orientation, parties routinely engage in illegal campaign funding. The intention here is not simply to list such incidents, but to indicate the extent to which widespread deficiencies exist in promoting institutional mechanisms ensuring accountability among elected officials. Studies conducted by international agencies, such as Transparency International, the World Bank, the Council of Europe, or by individual researchers illustrate that corruption in public agencies (health, education, state administration) is not only widespread throughout the region. It is also accepted and encouraged by a cynical public. This state of affairs illustrates a common tension experienced in the area of rule of law rooted in a necessary but difficult coexistence between its legalistic and normative dimensions. Describing the relationship between power and the rule of law as well as its dual characteristic, Gianluigi Palombella argues in the first chapter that "the rule of law appears to consist of a history of institutional conventions, custom and social practice where law is interconnected with a particular system of power." The four cases show that in post-communism the institutional mechanisms of accountability developed by the EU continue to clash with cultural and social practices appropriated by citizens both before and after 1989.

As the table above shows, corruption ratings in Hungary and Poland began to deteriorate after 1999, when scores were respectively 2.50 and 2.25. The international community, particularly the Organization for European Cooperation and Development (OECD) and the EU, viewed this with concern because its impact on international business transactions could be negative.

This is the case in Hungary where, although there are some state institutions empowered to fight corruption, such as the Central Investigation Department of the National Office of the Prosecutor and the

State Audit Office, there are problems in implementing anti-corruption legislation. Among these, Kovacs and Villanyi (2007) mention: the difficulty of following the use or application of public and EU funds, bribery leading to an increase in the costs of public procurements, and a lack of transparency in the financing of political parties as a result of the latter's dubious associations with business.

Poland's corruption ratings also began to reflect a decline since 2003, when the corruption score went from 2.25 to 2.50, and then reached 3.25 in 2006. A series of corruption scandals involving the left-wing governing party, the SLD, contributed to this despite the government's success in integrating the country into the EU and president Alexander Kwasniewski's high profile in foreign affairs. A former top member of the communist party and former president of Poland for two terms, Kwasniewski effectively made Poland an active player in the international arena as a strong ally of the United States in Iraq and as an active supporter of the Orange Revolution in Ukraine.

One of the best examples of how the Polish political class nonetheless undermines various mechanisms of vertical accountability is the "Rywingate" media bribery scandal of 2003. Top members of SLD were alleged to have attempted to extort money from the media holding company Agora in exchange for legislative favors. After a string of reduced sentences, Lew Rywin (considered the best film producer in Poland) served only half of his sentence and was released from jail in November 2006. Another example is that accusations against Kwasniewsky's alleged ties with the oligarchy ultimately led to the resignation of the prime minister Leszek Miller, paving the way for the "fourth republic of Poland" noted earlier.

Consistent with electoral promises and an anti-corruption platform, the new government led by Jaroslaw Kaczynski of the conservative PiS established in June 2006 the Central Anticorruption Agency (CAA), with the authority to investigate high-level corruption by reviewing asset statements of senior officials. So far the CAA's activity has resulted in arrests of several prominent officials as well as extradition of a U.S. businessman involved in a 2001 murder of a Polish police officer (Krajewski 2007). As a consequence of this anti-corruption campaign Poland's corruption score improved to 3.00 in 2007.

However, it still remains to be seen how effective the campaign will be, or whether it will become part of a witch-hunt similar to the lustration law discussed earlier. Thus far, both the president and the prime minister have engaged in gross violations relating to freedom of the state media and other acts of censorship. It is worrisome that the score for the independent media (an important accountability mechanism) dropped to 2.25 in 2007 from 1.75 the previous year.

In respect to Romania and Bulgaria, weaker political competition characterized by the domination of successors to the old communist parties, and weaker democratic opposition during early stages of democratic transition, facilitated state capture and inhibited development of mechanisms of horizontal accountability. Corruption scores in 1999 placed both countries, unlike Hungary and Poland, in the category of semiconsolidated authoritarian regimes. Former members of communist secret services and the political and economic nomenklatura joined forces with post-communist governments in weakening the state apparatus. They did so largely by using state agencies to dispense favors and privileges to members and allies of the new oligarchy.

In both Romania and Bulgaria, members of the communist elite had the opportunity in the 1980's to learn something about mechanisms of the market economy in the West and to establish foreign contacts, which they effectively exploited after 1989. Ilia Pavlov, for example, a former wrestler married in the 1980's to the daughter of the former Director of Military Counterintelligence and well connected to an international network of arm dealers that included Russians, became president of the Bulgarian Multigroup. The vice-presidents and general directors, in turn, were either connected to the new power structure or former ministers and directors of state socialist enterprises (Ganev 2001).

In Romania relatives of former nomenklatura (including some members of the Ceausescu family) also made their fortunes with the assistance of family capital and connections. A notorious case is that of Dan Voiculescu, currently owner of an important media trust with substantial political influence. His wealth dates back to the communist period when, as an agent of the secret police, he was involved with a Cypriot company, Crescent, which Ceausescu used for import-export operations and money laundering (Gabanyi 2004:353–372).

After 2000 the EU became directly and actively involved in designing and implementing anti-corruption legislation and institutions capable of operating without political interference. In Bulgaria two anti-corruption government bodies were created in late 2002 and became operative in 2003: the Commission for Coordinating Actions Against Corruption and the Parliamentary Commission on Fighting

Corruption. In addition, a Private Judicial Enforcement Law was passed in 2005 with the purpose of speeding up enforcement of judicial decisions.

Likewise, institutions and legal mechanisms were also put into place in Romania to address high-level corruption and to ensure accountability and transparency by the political class. These include the National Anticorruption Prosecutor Office, the National Anti-Corruption Department, and the National Agency of Integrity (Noutcheva and Becheve 2008:114–144).

Bulgarian and Romanian governments both undertook even more concrete anti-corruption measures in 2005 and 2006, amidst pressures to comply with the 2005 accession deadline, including a threatened delay of accession for one year if satisfactory progress was not achieved in this area. In Bulgaria, the mayor of Sofia was prosecuted in 2005 and a year later several mid-level government officials were dismissed following corruption allegations (Dorosiev and Ganev 2007). In Romania, thanks to the perseverance of justice minister Macovei and the support of President Basescu, corruption charges were filed against members of the political class. Among those charged were representatives of the political opposition, including former prime minister Adrian Nastase. But also charged were a deputy prime minister and two ministers of the current government, several members of parliament, magistrates, and dozens of law enforcement employees (Mungiu-Pippidi 2007b). These measures were positively received and acknowledged in the last comprehensive report of the European Commission in September 2006.[9]

However, after January 2007 it became questionable whether the anti-corruption campaign in these countries would genuinely and consistently continue. The Bulgarian judicial system failed to address the numerous contract killings (around 150) that took place between 2001 and 2006 as well as more recent killings of local politicians, after January 2007. In Romania, after Macovei's dismissal, the new Minister of Justice, Tudor Chiuariu, with the active involvement of a number of politicians, made serious attempts to undermine the independence and limit the legal powers of the principal mechanism of horizontal

[9] See *Monitoring Report on the State of Preparedness for EU Membership of Bulgaria and Romania* (Commission of the European Communities, Brussels, September 26, 2006).

accountability created with EU assistance, the National Anti-Corruption Department (DNA) (Mungiu-Pippidi 2008).

These recent developments seemed to confirm EU suspicions, and led to its insistence that after accession both countries must report every six months on progress in reforms to curb corruption and streamline their judiciaries. The first follow-up report, issued in June 2007, was partly ambivalent but stated that in both countries "progress in the judicial treatment of high-level corruption is insufficient." Although there were no sanctions at the time, the safeguard clauses could still be imposed in June 2008. Meanwhile, in a February report the EU raised serious concerns about the course of DNA criminal investigations (initiated by the DNA) that involved eight former and serving ministries in Romania. Some of these files had been referred back by judges to the prosecution on procedural grounds.

There are several conclusions to be drawn from this analysis of the significance of horizontal accountability mechanisms for the quality of democracy in post-communist societies. The first conclusion is that neither elite-driven constitutional arrangements, nor relatively stable and fair political competition and participation, could entirely overcome the legacies of communist regimes, that is, weak civil society groups and poor popular conceptions of citizenship.

To a certain extent, an earlier alternation in power between former communists and anti-communist opposition as well as a stronger judicial framework in Hungary and Poland prevented the degree of institutional capture and patronage-driven state-building found in Bulgaria and Romania. But, as the ideological differences between these two major political actors became increasingly irrelevant, it also became clearer to the public that behind their liberal policies both benefited equally from the spoils of transition. Current political polarization and instability in Hungary as well as preference for right-wing populism in Poland both indicate that electorates in these two countries are no longer seeking mere governmental change. They are seeking a change in their relationship to the government based on some measure of trust and accountability.

On the other hand, the cases of Bulgaria and Romania clearly show that when an external actor, the EU, becomes actively instrumental in implementing mechanisms of transparency and accountability there is some tendency of domestic political actors to resist. This resistance then weakens and destabilizes national governance. Ultimately, electoral preferences in Bulgaria and Romania suggest that a path similar to that in Hungary and Poland is now being pursued. It can be argued that this apparent crisis should not be interpreted as a rejection of democracy by East and Central European citizenry. It should instead be seen as some evidence of democratic deepening, in which electorates attempt to become more active participants in the democratic process.

In support of this claim, we turn finally to the last dimension of the quality of democracy model – responsiveness – understood as citizen confidence and satisfaction with the performance of democratic institutions. The results of the 2004 New Europe Barometer (NEB) survey and of the 2006 Barometer of the New Democracies (BND) offer an important insight into some of the essential aspects of democratic legitimacy in this sense.

The 2004 survey illustrates that a significant majority of the populations in each country (close to 80 percent or more) perceive government as unresponsive to their needs. An even greater majority (close to 90 percent or more) perceive themselves as powerless in respect to their ability to influence government policy (Rose 2005). The BND survey shows that the level of trust in political parties is nearly as low in the four countries (66 percent). In Hungary, Bulgaria and Romania more than 50 percent of respondents mistrust parliament.

But even if democracy remains remote and distant for most citizens, and even if they express disillusionment with the performance of democratic institutions, democracy still represents for them the most – perhaps only – viable form of government. According to the BND survey, anti-democratic alternatives such as suspension of parliament or reliance on a strong leader represent the option of less than a third of respondents.[10] If one compares these data with the results of a 1991 early transition survey, when general but probably uncritical support for democracy was shared by an absolute majority of public opinion (with even higher support in Bulgaria and Romania where communist regimes were most repressive), it is fairly evident that citizens of East and Central Europe have become much more informed, rational and critical of democracy (see Rose and Mishler 1994). Moreover, experience with democracy leads to higher and more precise expectations about what democracy can accomplish. Such experience

[10] Some of the results of the BND 2006 are presented by Alina Mungiu-Pippidi in "Romania: Annual Report 2007," accessed at www.sar.org.ro.

is also conducive to greater awareness and understanding of an important existing gap between democratic ideals and principles and actual government performance.

Conclusions Regarding the State of Democratization in Post-Communism and the Quality of Democracy Model

We conclude by addressing two types of empirical and theoretical questions regarding the state of democracy in Bulgaria, Hungary, Poland and Romania. First, the extent to which the transition to democracy in these countries has been achieved or whether future challenges lie ahead. Second, the utility of the quality of democracy model in understanding the post-communist case.

Given the durability of democratic institutions and the support of majority electorates for democracy as the preferred form of governance, the institutionalization of democracy has essentially been achieved. But from the perspective of the early paradigm of democratic consolidation, other trends cannot easily be explained, namely current high levels of mistrust and dissatisfaction with the political class and democratic institutions, unstable governance, and political polarization. By employing some of the procedural and substantive aspects of the quality of democracy model, we reached some conclusions regarding how the convergence of some of these dimensions has led to institutionalizing democracy. It is important to note at the same time that this same convergence has been at the expense of stalling or retarding democratic deepening.

During their early stage of democratic transition, democratic consolidation in Hungary and Poland was accomplished as a result of fair and balanced political party participation and competition facilitating good governance, a solid constitutional framework, and a relatively independent judiciary. However, this participation effectively failed to involve the citizenry. It instead remained the exclusive territory of incumbent governments, which decided the course of liberal political reforms and socio-economic policies. Eventually, after the late 1990s, the Bulgarian and Romanian governments followed the same path.

Under the circumstances of weak mass participation, the mechanisms of horizontal accountability put into place amidst EU accession have had little impact in stemming corruption by political elites. When these mechanisms did make some difference in promoting governmental accountability, it was short-lived, triggered strictly by external pressures, particularly in Bulgaria and Romania. Finally, when electoral politics in Hungary and Poland did begin to appeal to and involve mass participation the overall quality of democracy tended to decrease. Greater participation was accompanied by setbacks in the areas of governance and corruption. Despite the EU's threat to invoke the safeguard clause these tendencies also remain strong in Bulgaria and Romania.

These tensions suggest that the interaction between the proposed dimensions of the quality of democracy model is not necessarily conducive to the achievement of democratic quality on the ground. Diamond and Morlino themselves acknowledge that there are trade-offs and incompatibilities between some of the dimensions.

In the case of post-communist democracies some of the legacies of communist regimes – particularistic societies, weak states prone to cronyism, patrimonialism and corruption – pose to varying degrees the biggest challenges to democratic deepening. What still remains unclear and unanswered is how the hoped-for outcome of democratic quality, that is, responsiveness or democratic legitimacy, can be effectively institutionalized? Thus, it can be argued that although the model proves its ability in providing us with more precise empirical tools in assessing the specificity of the various dynamics and peculiarities of the cases we considered, it is less successful in clarifying this crucial question.

Perhaps the answer lies in the weaknesses of the liberal democratic model itself. The fact that the process of democratization became so intertwined with the liberal project of Europeanisation, and perhaps unintentionally led to the current state of political affairs in our four cases, indicates substantial imperfections in this western liberal model. It might also be the case that the built-in expectations of the model are set so high as to almost guarantee failure among countries newly embarking on such a difficult course of political transformation. Conceptual models deriving from the western liberal model, therefore, may include criteria of consolidation, deepening or quality which ultimately prove incapable of realizing, however valuable in many respects they may be. The most recent populist rhetoric and electoral gains of populist parties in Bulgaria, Hungary, Poland and Romania seem in this regard to illustrate one of the old dilemmas in democratic theory and practice: the disparity between government effectiveness and government popular legitimacy.

References

Alexandra, Polia. 2005. "Bulgaria: Keeping Attack at Bay." Transitions Online, July 27. Retrieved February 5, 2008 (www.tol.cz).

Arato, Andrew. 2000. *Civil Society, Constitutionalism and Legitimacy.* New York: Rowman and Littlefield.

Ash, Garton T. 2006. "The Twins' New Poland". *The New York Review*, February 9, pp. 22–25.

——. 2007. "Poland has made a humiliating farce out of dealing with its ghosts". *The Guardian, May 9.* Retrieved, March 5, 2008 (www.guardian.co.uk).

Belli, Nicolae. 2001. *Tranzitia mai Grea Decit un Razboi [Transition more Difficult than War].* Bucharest: Expert.

Bozoki, Andras. 1994. "Confrontation and Consensus: On the Forms of Political Integration." Pp. 3–14 in *Democratic Legitimacy in Post-Communist Societies: Concepts and Problems*, edited by A. Bozoki. Budapest: T-Twins Publishers.

Brown, Duncan. 2005. "Bulgaria: The Least Desirable Result." *Transitions Online*, July 28. Retrieved February 5, 2008 (www.tol.cz).

Carothers, Thomas. 2002. "The End of the Transition Paradigm." *Journal of Democracy*, 13:5–21.

Commission of the European Communities. 2006. "Monitoring Report on the State of Preparedness for EU Membership of Bulgaria and Romania", September 26. Retrieved January 10, 2008 (http://ec.europa.eu/enlargement/pdf/key_documents/2006).

Ciobanu, Monica. 2007. "Romania's Travails with Democracy and Accession to the European Union." *Europe-Asia Studies*, 59:1429–1450.

——. and Michael Shafir. 2005. "2004 Romanian Elections: A Test for Democratic Consolidation?." *RFE/RL East European Perspectives*, Vol. 7, No. 3. Retrieved April 15, 2005 (www.rferl.org/reports/asafiles).

Diamond, Larry and Leonardo, Morlino. 2005. "Introduction." Pp. ix–xliii in *Assessing the Quality of Democracy*, edited by L. Diamond and L. Morlino. Baltimore: John Hopkins University Press.

Dorosiev, Rashko and Georgy Ganev. 2007. "Bulgaria". In *Nations in Transit 2007: Democratization from Central Europe to Eurasia*, edited by Freedom House. New York: Rowman and Littlefield Publishers, Inc.

Elster, Jon, Claus, Offe and Ulrich, Preuss, K. 1998. *Institutional Design in Post-Communist Societies: Rebuilding the Ship at Sea.* Cambridge: Cambridge University Press.

Freedom House (ed.) 2007. *Nations in Transit 2007: Democratization from Central Europe to Eurasia.* New York: Rowman and Littlefield Publishers, Inc.

Gabanyi, Ute Anneli. 2004. "The New Business Elite: From Nomenklatura to Oligarchy." Pp. 353–372 in *Romania since 1989: Politics, Economics, and Society*, Maryland, edited by H. F. Carey. Boulder, New York: Lexington Books.

Ganev, Venelin. 2001. "The Dorian Gray Effect: Winners as State Breakers in Communism." *Communist and Postcommunist Studies*, 34:1–24.

——. 2006. "Ballots, Bribes, and State Building in Bulgaria." *Journal of Democracy*, 17:75–90.

Gross, Jan, Vladimir, Tismaneanu and Alina, Mungiu-Pippidi. 2005. "The End of Postcommunism in Romania." *Journal of Democracy*, 16:146–161.

Grzymala-Busse, Anna. 2007. *Rebuilding Leviathan: Party Competition and State Expansion in Post-Communist Democracies.* Cambridge: Cambridge University Press.

Higinson, Matthew. 2006. "A good lie badly told and the likely consequences." *Budapest Business Journal*, October, p. 12. Retrieved January 10, 2008 (www.bb.hu).

Jasiewicz, Krzsztof. 2007. "The Political Party Landscape." *Journal of Democracy*, 18:26–34.
Karklins, Rasma. 2005. *The System Made Me Do It: Corruption in Post-Communist Societies*. New York: M. E. Sharpe, Inc.
Kovats, Roland and Balint Molanr. 2006. "The Political Fallout: Patriot Gambles." *Transitions Online*, October 6. Retrieved February 5, 2008 (www.tol.cz).
Kovacs, Balasz and Viktoria Villanyi. 2007. "Hungary." In *Nations in Transit 2007: Democratization form Central Europe to Eurasia*, edited by Freedom House. New York: Littlefield Publishers, Inc.
Krajewski, Andrzej. 2007. "Poland". In *Nations in Transit 2007: Democratization from Central Europe to Eurasia*, edited by Freedom House. New York: Littlefield Publishers, Inc.
Krastev, Ivan. 2007. "The Strange Death of the Liberal Consensus." *Journal of Democracy*, 18:56–64.
Linz, Juan and Alfred, Stepan. 1996. *Problems of Democratic Transition and Consolidation*. Baltimore: John Hopkins University Press.
Lipset, Seymour Martin. 1994. "The Social Prerequisites of Democracy Revisited." *American Sociological Review*, 59:1–22.
Mason, David. and James, Kluegel, R. (eds.). 2000. *Marketing Democracy: Changing Opinion about Inequality and Politics in East Central Europe*. New York: Rowman and Littlefield Publishers.
Meyer, Gerd. 1994. "Democratic Legitimacy in Post-Communist Societies: Concepts and Problems." Pp. 13–55 in *Democratic Legitimacy in Post-Communist Societies*, edited by A. Bozoki. Budapest: T-Twin Publishers.
Millard, Frances. 2006. "Poland's Politics and the Travails of Transition after 2001: The 2005 Elections." *Europe-Asia Studies*, 58:1007–10031.
Mungiu-Pippidi, Alina. 1997. "Crime and Corruption after Communism Breaking Free at Last: Tales of Corruption from the Postcommunist Balkans." *East European Constitutional Review*, 6:57–69.
——. 2005 "Poland and Romania." Pp. 213–237, in *Assessing the Quality of Democracy*, edited by L. Diamond and L. Morlino. Baltimore: John Hopkins University Press.
——. 2007a. "EU Accession is No End of History." *Journal of Democracy*, 18:8–16.
——. 2007b. "Romania". *In Nations in Transit 2007: Democratization from Central Europe to Eurasia*, edited by Freedom House. New York: Littlefield Publishers, Inc.
——. 2008. "Romania: Annual Report 2007." *Romanian Academic Society*, January 13. Retrieved March 10, 2008 (www.sar.org.ro).
Noutcheva, Gergana and Dimitar Becheve. 2008. "The Successful Laggards: Bulgaria and Romania's Accession to the EU." *East European Politics and Societies*, 22:114–144.
O'Donnell, Guillermo. 1997. "Illusions about Consolidation." Pp. 40–57 in *Consolidating the Third Wave Democracies: Themes and Perspectives*, edited by L. Diamond, L. Platner, M. F. Chu. Baltimore: John Hopkins University Press.
——. 1999. "On the State, Democratization, and Some Conceptual Problems: A Latin American View with Glances at Some Postcommunist Countries." Pp. 142–156 in *Counterpoints: Selected Essays on Authoritarianism and Democratization*, edited by G. O'Donnell. Notre Dame, IN: University of Notre Dame Press.
Pridham, Geoffrey. 2005. *Designing Democracy: EU Enlargement and Regime Change in Post-Communist Europe*. New York: Palgrave MacMillan.
Rose, Richard. 2005. *Insiders and Outsiders: New Europe Barometer 2004*. Glasgow, University of Strathclyde: Studies in Public Policy 404.
——. and William Mishler. 1994. "Mass Reaction to Regime Change in Eastern Europe: Polarization or Leaders and Laggards?." *British Journal of Political Science*, 24:159–182.

——. and Doh Chull Shin. 2001. "Democratization Backwards: The Problems of Third Wave Democracies." *British Journal of Political Science*, 31:331–354.

Shafir, Michael. 2007. "Vox Populi, Vox Dei and the [Head-]Master's Voice: Mass and Intellectual Neo-Populism in Contemporary Romania." Paper presented at the conference "Populism in East Central Europe" organized by the Czech Association for International Affairs (AMO) on November 22, 2007 (unpublished manuscript).

Tismaneanu, Vladimir and Gail, Kligman. 2001. "Romania's First Post-Communist Decade: from Iliescu to Iliescu." *East European Constitutional Review*, 10:25–34.

Transcontinental Books. 2006. *Voice of the People 2006*. Montreal, Quebec: Leger Marketing.

Transitions Online. 2005. "Hungary: Situation Vacant", April 18, Retrieved January 10, 2008 (www.tol.cz).

Schmitter, Philippe. 2005. "The Ambiguous Virtues of Accountability." Pp. 18–31 in *Assessing the Quality of Democracy*, edited by L. Diamond and L. Morlino. Baltimore: John Hopkins University Press.

Vachudova, Anna Milada. 2005. *Europe Undivided: Democracy, Leverage and Integration after Communism.* New York: Oxford University Press.

CHAPTER FIVE

CONSTITUTIONALIZING GOVERNING AND GOVERNANCE IN EUROPE

Poul F. Kjaer*

The European Union (EU)[1] operates "in-between" its member states (MS) and global trans-national structures (Kjaer 2007b). Thus, the EU's legal order is neither characterized by hierarchy in the nation-state sense nor is it characterized by the kind of radical heterarchy which is a key feature of global legal structures (Fischer-Lescano and Teubner 2004; Fischer-Lescano and Teubner 2006; Fischer-Lescano and Teubner 2007). Rather the EU is a hybrid which combines hierarchy and heterarchy in a particular manner. This hybridity is also apparent in the organizational form of the EU. The EU is an organizational conglomerate which consists of an entire range of institutional structures. From an overall perspective, the EU can nonetheless be understood as resting on a two-dimensional organizational structure in the sense that it, on the one hand, contains a hierarchical governing dimension, consisting of the triangular relationship between the Council of the European Union (the Council), the Commission of the European Communities (the Commission) and the European Parliament (EP) and a heterarchical dimension consisting of a multitude of governance structures (GS), such as the Open Method of Co-ordination (OMC),[2]

* I am grateful to Christian Joerges and Gunther Teubner as well as to Leonardo Morlino and Gianluigi Palombella, the editors of this volume, for comments on earlier drafts. Full responsibility remains with the author.

[1] Unless otherwise indicated the term 'European Union' (EU) refers to the EU as well as its predecessors in the form of the European Communities (EC), the European Economic Community (EEC), the European Coal and Steel Community (ECSC) and Euratom.

[2] The OMC was officially launched in 2000 within the realm of the so-called Lisbon process as a mode aimed at ensuring systematic mutual observation between the Member States (MS) through benchmarking and systematic comparisons. De facto this "new" mode is however to a large extent only formalising already existing informal structures of mutual observation, which has existed since the beginning of the integration process (Kjaer 2009b). For an overview over the various forms of OMC processes see Borrás and Jacobsson (2004).

Comitology[3] and (regulatory) agencies.[4] The first dimension constitutes the core political system of the EU. The latter dimension, on the other hand, represents forms through which the political system of the EU ensures its embeddedness in its social environment.[5] This dimension therefore reflects the functionally differentiated basic structures (*Tiefenstrukturen*) of the wider society just as it is directly aimed at overcoming the distinction between the public and the private spheres of society (Kjaer 2009a). Accordingly, it can be argued that the distinction between governing and governance constitutes the central distinction (*Leitdifferenz*) on which the EU is founded, in the sense that this distinction represents a functional equivalent of the "old-European" (*alteuropäische*) state/society distinction originally introduced by Hegel.

Thus, this contribution picks of where the contribution of Morlino ends insofar as the kind of transitional hybrids between authoritarian and democratic rule he refers to are situated within the nation-state universe. In contrast, the current state of the decision-making structure in the EU cannot be understood as a mere transitional regime which is on the way to become democratic. Instead the hybridism of the EU must be understood as a permanent feature. The question how to describe the constitutional form of the EU must therefore be transformed into the question of how the relationship between the governing and the governance dimensions, as well as how the relations between the different forms of GS is being constitutionalized? The

[3] Comitology dates back to the beginning of the 1960s. In a narrow sense comitology committees only deal with the implementation of Community legislation. Different committees exist for the preparation and negotiation of legislation. Hence, the exact number of comitology committees remains disputed. Estimations differ from 300 to around 1000 committees depending on the criteria's used. The committees consist of Commission officials, MS officials and – to a lesser extent – private actors (Haibach 2000).

[4] The first two agencies were established in the 1970s. From the mid 1990s the number of agencies has however expanded rapidly. Currently 32 agencies exist and several more has been planned. Although the agencies in an organizational sense have a hierarchical nucleus, a common feature is however that they mainly serve as coordinators and secretariats of heterarchical networks which are occupied with the gathering, processing and re-dissemination of information (Kjaer 2010).

[5] To the three main forms of governance structures mentioned above one could also add mutual recognition, the partnership concept, originally developed within the context of Community structural founding, the so-called social dialogue as developed under the framework of the Maastricht Treaty, and the concept of Environmental Policy Integration (Scott and Trubek 2002).

argument presented here is that this question can only be answered through the development of a third category of constitutionalism which extends beyond traditional nation-state constitutionalism whilst taking into consideration the differences between the EU and the kind of radically functionally differentiated and heterarchical global structures described by Fischer-Lescano and Teubner (2004; 2006; 2007). Accordingly, it is suggested that a coherent concept for the description of how legal conflicts in the European context are being stabilized should be based on a three-dimensional concept of conflict of laws capable of describing horizontal conflicts between territorially delineated entities in the form of the Member States (MS), vertical conflicts between the EU and its MS, as well as horizontal conflicts between the functionally differentiated basic structures of the wider society. In relation to the latter dimension, which is concerned specifically with GS, it is moreover suggested that a constitutional principle of functional separation, more extensive than the classical concept of a functional separation of powers, could provide a basis for legal stabilization of norm production.

The Transformation of Constitutionalism

Although the MS provide substantial limitations to its level of self-determination, the EU must be understood as an autonomous social structure which possesses the freedom to select between various possible operations. The autonomy is also expressed in the understanding that the EU's legal order is converging with the legal orders of the MS but nonetheless remains a separate and independent legal order (Amstutz 2006). The autonomy implies that the EU needs to justify its selections (Neyer 2008). Firstly, this is the case because all autonomous social structures are faced with a continual demand to ensure their own coherency through the reproduction of narratives that connect their selection of specific operations with their overall structure. But in addition, autonomous social structures are reflexive to the extent that they are conscious that they fulfill specific functions towards society as a whole, as well as towards other partial social structures (Hellmann 2002:99). Hence, they are continuously faced with the demand to substantiate their operations towards their environments.

Such justifications are however paradoxical in nature, as they always are *self*-justifications. They are internal operations which are based on the structure's own understanding of the expectations emerging in their environments. A common feature of social structures, including a hybrid such as the EU, is therefore that they develop strategies intended to "cover up" the paradoxical nature of such justifications. They construct semantic artifacts internally which they can claim are external in nature. The religious system refers to a concept of God, the economic system to the market, the (democratic) political system to the people and the legal system to systems of (natural) rights. Hence, these systems can claim that their operations merely reflect the will of God, market demand, the will of the people or self-evident universal rights. These metaphors are assigned a foundational quality, but they also serve as mirrors which the respective functional systems use in order to scrutinize themselves, thereby potentially increasing their level of reflexivity. Hence, these concepts provide the functional systems in question with the possibility of internally evaluating and substantiating their operations.

Within the political system, such practices are also described by the concept of legitimacy. As indicated, democratic political systems derive their claim for legitimacy through reference to the will of the people, who the rulers claim to represent. But in addition, the political system has engaged in a specific strategy of reflexive "self-binding" through a carefully developed "partnership" with the legal system. This strategy falls under the name constitutionalization. In a narrow sense, constitutions serve as structural couplings between the legal and the political systems, thereby allowing the former to rely on legislation enacted in the political system as a basis for its rights-based jurisprudence (Luhmann 1990). In the same way, the political system accepts limitations to its autonomy through a legal framing of its activities. The legal framing diminishes the contingent character of political operations, thereby serving as a tool which facilitates a stabilization of the expectations arising in the environment vis-à-vis the political system. This is vital since the continued functioning of social structures is conditioned by generally stable expectations concerning the environment within which they operate. It is exactly this kind of stability which the "rule of law" ensures for the political system (as well as for other social systems) since the central function of law is the stabilization of normative expectations. The political system can therefore claim legitimacy by referring to the legal framing of its operations as this, in principle, guarantees that its impact on the remaining parts of society is reflected in the selection of its operations.

As previously indicated, constitutionalism was largely oriented towards the relationship between law and politics in the era of classical modernity.[6] The radicalization of modernity in the latter half of the 20th century has however placed the nation states, and thereby the nation-state model of constitutionalism, under increased pressure. As a consequence, it is possible to observe two interrelated developments: Firstly, a move towards societal constitutionalism, in that the legal system increasingly engages in couplings that possess a constitutional quality, with social structures falling outside the realm of the political system (Sciulli 1992; Teubner 2004). Secondly, within the emerging post-modern paradigm of trans-national law, it is argued that new types of law (such as Lex Mercatoria and Lex Digitalis) have emerged and that these forms of law operate within a context of "extreme self-reference". This arises because the functional synthesis (*Funktionssynthese*) between the legal and political systems, which was made possible in the nation-state realm through structural couplings between the legal and the political systems via constitutions and legislative acts, is not or at least only partially in place, at the trans-national level. Hence, trans-national law is not capable of relying on legislation enacted by the political system to provide external reference points for its jurisprudence. Instead trans-national law is forced to rely on itself to a degree which is even more radical than has traditionally been the case at the nation-state level (Amstutz and Karavas 2006). In contrast to classical international law, new forms of trans-national law therefore, increasingly rely on self-defined principles.[7] Global and regional political-administrative GS are confronted with a similar situation since they increasingly expand their operations without being subject to a formal legal framing. If law is activated at all, this tends to take place ex-post (Ladeur 2002:32). Scholars who celebrate the intrinsic link between the rule of law and democracy as a key accomplishment of modernity have observed this with some concern (Habermas 1992:167f.; Habermas 1998). Positive interpretations of this development have, on the other hand, emphasized that "hard" legal norms are merely being replaced or complemented by "soft" legal norms, acting

[6] As illustrated by Koselleck (2006) the limitation of constitutions to the relationship between law and politics is however a specifically modern phenomenon. In the Middle Ages constitutions occurred in multiple forms.

[7] For international and trans-national economic law see Panezi (2007).

as functional equivalents of hard norms, at the trans-national level (Trubek, Cottrell and Nance 2006). Whatever interpretation is chosen, the emergence of a dense net of trans-national structures does however imply a break with, or at least a transformation of, traditional concepts of constitutionalism, since the legal framing of non-nation state political-administrative structures assumes a different form compared to the classical modern forms which emerged in the nation-state context (Walker 2007).

Partial Statehood

When "applying" the above post-modern perspective to the EU, certain "misfits" are however apparent. The EU fulfils Luhmann's minimalist definition of a state (Luhmann 2000:390f.), as it consists of a political and a legal system structurally coupled through a constitutional framework. Hence, although imperfect, a functional synthesis between law and politics can actually be observed in the EU context. In addition, the EU's political system is capable of relying on a hierarchically organized bureaucratic machinery of considerable magnitude. The EU is moreover, structurally coupled to a territory and has (tentatively) developed a concept of citizenship. Within the governing dimension, it relies on a distinction between the public and private spheres of society and has adopted traditional state symbols (flag, hymn etc.). These state-like features are moreover, reinforced by the understanding that the EU must be regarded as an autonomous phenomenon since its political system has developed its own policy programs and, with considerable success, has also been able to ensure implementation of these programs, just as the EU legal system, as already indicated, has established its own legal order and independent sources of authority. If we consider that the 19th- and 20th-century nation states, defined by their monopoly on political and legal authority within a given territory, are anomalies whose reign lasted for only a relatively short time span (MacCormick 1993), it is therefore possible to regard nation states as one possible variant among other forms of state, thereby making it possible to argue that the EU also falls within the state category (Stichweh 2007:26ff.).

Such a "traditionalist" view does not however sufficiently emphasize the differences between the EU and the nation states. Only a faint distinction can be made between policy programs and polity structure in EU. Instead, the evolution of the constitutional structure and specific policy programs such as the establishment of the customs union, the common agricultural policy, the internal market and the economic and monetary union have gone hand in hand, in the sense that the launch of all these policy programs implied new treaties altering the EU's constitutional structure. Moreover, no distinction exists between government and opposition in the EU setting. The EU relies on collective binding decisions but has no means of ensuring compliance through negative sanctions and hence no *Weberian* territorial control exists.[8] Although the distinctions between the political and administrative levels are also blurred at the nation state level (Jarass 1975:125–37) the EU embodies the perfect dissolution of this distinction through its special form of "political administration" (Bücker and Schlacke 2000). This is not only the case within the realm of GS, but also within the Commission, where the Commissioners' roles fall between those of politicians and civil servants, just as the personal cabinets of the Commissioners continue to assume a dual political and administrative role (Riekmann 1998).[9] Consequently, the EU has also been characterized as a *Weberian* instrument of rule (*Herrschaftsinstrument*) without a master (Luhmann 1994b:6).

Thus, the EU is a hybrid structure which oscillates between the structure of a state and that of trans-national governance, in the sense that it contains elements of both forms at the same time. It consists of a complex bundle of heterogeneous and partly contradictory juridical, political and administrative processes (Sand 1998). This is also reflected in its reliance on the key distinction between governing and governance and its position "in-between" the nation states and the global realm.

The Integration Overlay

The heterogenity of the European conglomerate is countered through the establishment of certain unity insofar as the different processes, although to different degrees, are subordinated to an integrationist

[8] The EU does not fulfill Pierre Bourdieu's revised *Weberian* definition of the state either, as he defines the state as the institution which "successfully claims the monopoly of the legitimate use of physical and *symbolic* violence over a definite territory and over the totality of the corresponding population" (Bourdieu 1994; 3).

[9] For a historical account of the function of the Commissioners' office see also Hintze (1981).

logic, which is expressed in the Union's regulatory idea of creating an "ever closer union" and which tends to make integration an objective in itself (*Selbstzweck*).

Subordination to the objective of integration helps explain why the political system in the nation-state form continuously encounter disappointments whenever it attempts to control the operations of the EU. Even when their priorities appear to be fully accepted, as was the case with the United Kingdom (UK) during the negotiations of the Single European Act (SEA) in the mid 1980s, such political priorities are merely "translated" and they consequently assume a completely different connotation and purpose when transferred from the sphere of the MS to the EU sphere. In the specific case of the SEA, and to the surprise of the UK government, the move towards negative integration through the abolishment of barriers to trade was intrinsically linked to a move towards positive integration through re-regulation at the European level. Hence, the Thatcher government quite clearly shared the naivety of the intergovernmentalist brand of EU researchers in believing that the process could be controlled on the basis of nation-state priorities even though the integration process is guided by a logic which is substantially different compared to the kind of logic guiding MS politics.[10]

In other words, it is possible to observe a deeply-rooted division between the forms of policy making in the EU context compared to the MS contexts. There have been countless attempts to explain that the EU is a "normal" power-based political system (e.g. Hix 1999). However, power politics is based on the ability to ensure subordination on the basis of a distinction between superiority and inferiority (*Machtüberlegenheit/Machtunterlegenheit*) through the possible deployment of negative sanctions (Borch 2005; Luhmann 1989; Luhmann 2000:88 and 97). But the EU does not possess such power and has therefore been compelled to resort to other means than force in order to achieve its objectives (Joerges and Zürn 2005). Moreover, in established democracies the traditional distinction between superiority and inferiority has increasingly been replaced with the distinction between government and opposition. As already indicated, this distinction has not materialized at the EU level. As opposed to the

[10] For an intergovernmentalist view on the emergence of the SEA see Moravcsik (1991).

political system in its nation-state form, the measure of success within the EU is not therefore related to the government/opposition distinction, but instead, concerns whether integration is progressing or at a standstill.[11]

Moreover, the key element of power, namely its exercise, necessitates knowledge of who is exercising power, or at least the existence of a *symbolic* structure which one can assume, constitutes the centre of power. The absence of the government/opposition distinction means, however, that there is no clearly identifiable centre of power within the EU. Whether governing (*Regieren*) takes place at all within the EU therefore remains a relevant question (Jachtenfuchs and Knodt 2002) since the kind of Schmittian decisionism, which is an inherent part of the self-understanding of the political system in the MS form, does not exist within the EU. Instead, as embodied in the "Monnet Method", the EU has identified integration as a "technical task", where traditional power politics is regarded as an obstacle to integration rather than a tool of integration. Indeed, every time the EU has pursued integration within areas which have been conceived of as politically crucial by the MS, and which they have been strong enough to reproduce within their respective national settings, it has encountered a wall of resistance. It is therefore not surprising that the "technical tools" with which integration has been pursued have been legal instruments, which dominated the 1960s and 1970s, market instruments, mainly during the 1980s and early 1990s, and governance instruments from the mid-1990s onwards. In contrast, genuine political acts in the nation-state sense have largely been avoided and when tried have led to disappointment. Obvious examples of such disappointments include the failure of the European Defense Community in the 1950s and the Constitutional Treaty (CT) in the first decade of the new millennium. The transformation of the CT into a mere "technical exercise" through the Lisbon Reform Treaty moreover, represents a classic circumvention strategy. One of the strongest features of the integration process is in fact, the tendency to transform political issues into technical issues in order to allow integration to proceed (Bach 1999). For example, the transfer of monetary policy from the national to the European level after Maastricht implied that the majority of the national central

[11] Verhofstadt (2006) arrived at similar conclusions in that he compares the integration process with riding a bike. One needs to keep pedalling in order not to fall off.

banks, which had not been politically independent before the launch of the Maastricht process, gained such independence. Moreover, the independence granted to the European Central Bank, as evidenced by the Treaty of Maastricht, even exceeds the independence of the German central bank (Majone 2005:38–39).

Another characteristic of EU politics is that the EU takes an "opportunistic" approach to substantial matters. In the case of the SEA, the fiercest resistance came from the UK government and accordingly its liberalist preferences were incorporated to the extent necessary to overcome UK resistance at the same time as the "hidden" re-regulation agenda was played down. Today, with integration increasingly encroaching on the welfare and labor market regimes of the MS, the strongest resistance seems to be from France. Accordingly the liberalist approach, which emerged in order to overcome UK resistance, is slowly being substituted with a "flex-security" approach, seeking to combine the advantages of a free market with the upholding of national welfare systems, that has been specifically invented to overcome French resistance.[12] Viewed from the Brussels perspective, continued integration remained the primary objective in both cases however and the choice of actual policy therefore remains of secondary importance. On the other hand, this does not mean that economic concerns (e.g. efficiency and competitiveness), political concerns (e.g. in terms of influence on and the popularity of specific measures) or ethical concerns (e.g. in relation to risk regulation) does not play a role. It only indicates that such concerns are not primary and that they remain subordinated to the integration imperative. Moreover, such subordination is not necessarily problematic since most problems can be addressed in a multitude of ways, and often in a way which will enable the objective of integration and other objectives to be achieved simultaneously. As pointed out by Majone (2005) the primacy of integration does, however, create a structural bias which over time tends to systematically produce sub-optimal outcomes, for example when viewed from an economic perspective.[13]

---

[12] For a very informative critical analysis of this turn see the contribution of Christian Joerges in this volume.

[13] Not surprisingly the EU has therefore been faced with continued public criticism. An anecdotic but illuminating example of such criticism can be found in a critical comment on an European Commission discussion paper on mortgage credit in the European Union entitled 'Integration is not necessarily the right concept to guide integration' where the Chief Economist from Morgan Stanley, made the following

More concretely, the integration overlay is reproduced through the institutional balance (IB) which serves as the skeleton of the EU's governing dimension.[14] In the literature, this concept is often considered to fulfill an identical function to that of a functional separation of powers (Leanaerts and Verhoeven 2002). This view is however, based on a superficial understanding of the concepts. In the EU, legislative power is divided between the Commission, the Council and the EP; executive power is divided between the Commission, the Council and the MS; and juridical power is divided between the European Court of Justice (ECJ), the Court of First Instance (CFI) and the MS courts. Thus "it simply appears impossible to characterize the several Community institutions as holders of one or the other power since a close analysis of their prerogatives does not indicate a clear-cut line between legislative and the executive branches of the Community government" (Lenaerts 1990:13). Hence, it is futile to claim that the EU is characterized by a functional separation of powers, since none of the institutions monopolizes a single function.[15] On the other hand, this does not mean that the functional features of the legislative, executive and juridical forms of communication cannot be identified in relation to the EU. But the functional features are not attached to specific institutions, and it is exactly this lack of attachment of different forms of communication to corresponding organizational structures which makes the existing order different from the vision embodied in the modern concept of a functional separation of powers.

As pointed out by Majone (2002), the EU's governing dimension rather resembles an early modern mixed constitution since the main political-administrative institutions *jointly* share decisional and executive powers.[16] Moreover, the principle of institutional autonomy, which resembles the autonomy of the "estates" in the early-modern period, is a fundamental principle of the Union – just as the principle of loyal cooperation was an important feature of early-modern mixed polities as well as of the EU today (Ibid.).

---

illuminating statement: 'The Commission needs to keep in mind that what matters is efficiency, rather than integration as an end in itself' (Miles 2005).

[14] In the *Köster* case the European Court of Justice (ECJ) explicitly recognized the concept of IB as a central constitutional feature of the Community (Case 1970).

[15] That the Community is not based on a concept of functional separation of powers has also been recognized by the ECJ (Case 1982; Haibach 1997:1).

[16] For an overview over the evolution of the concept of mixed constitution see Riklin (2005).

The understanding of the EU as largely characterized by an "early-modern" form of power-sharing, where the Commission, the Council and the EP respectively seem to fulfill the role of the King, the Lords and the Commons, helps explain the integrationist bias of EU policies. This results from the fact that power sharing gives the EU an organic character which is oriented towards establishing unity through the suppression of centrifugal tendencies.[17] In principle, the IB ensures that all stakeholders have a say in the decision-making processes. Hence, the quest for increased integration is not just a regulatory principle guiding the EU's policy programs: integration is rather a meta-norm through which the internal unity of the EU is established, given that the logic of integration is the mechanism through which cohesion between the legal, political and administrative dimensions of the EU structure is created and continuously reaffirmed.

The price paid for such unity is substantial however, as power sharing implies that several institutional actors possess the ability to block decision-making. Not surprisingly, this has led to the development of a complex system of pay-offs, which have been introduced in order to get priorities approved. For example, the common agricultural policy was developed as a pay-off to France to guarantee it would accept liberalization of the market for industrial goods as advocated by Germany (Moravcsik 1998:159). The introduction of the SEA was, moreover, conditioned by the increased introduction of regional and social funds, which served as a system of pay-offs to economically less advanced countries such as Greece, Ireland, Portugal and Spain in the 1980s and 1990s and the Central and Eastern European countries today. This also explains why the EU has never confined its role to that of a "regulatory state", as advocated by Majone (1996).[18] The reason being that the EU's institutional setting creates a structural frame within which the exercise of regulatory functions is conditioned by the ability, using re-distributive policies, to "bribe" institutional actors who are able to block decision-making, and who will most likely, witness a sub-optimal outcome from common regulatory approaches

[17] The organic character of the Community was also acknowledged by the former president of the Commission Jacques Santer: "L'efficacité de la méthode communautaire,...repose sur la bonne coopération, sur une complémentarité organique, entre les institutions" (Santer 1995; Haibach 2000:215).

[18] For a critique of Majone in relation to the issue of regulatory and distributive policies see Follesdal and Hix (2005).

(Lenaerts 1990; Yataganas 2001a). In terms of policy outcome, strong reliance on mixed government features, which are merely oriented towards the establishment of negative limitations on the exercise of power, also explains the strong orientation towards "conservation" which characterizes policies such as the common agricultural and the common fisheries policy. Not only have these policies proved inherently difficult to reform, but they also seem to be defended by the Commission for the sole reason that they embody the idea of almost complete integration.[19]

In contrast to the above perspective, gradual expansion of the co-decision procedure and the rise of the EP could be interpreted as a tentative move towards the establishment of a federal dual system with the Council and the EP as the central players. Such a development can, moreover, be interpreted as a first step towards a clearer functional differentiation of powers (Yataganas 2001b). But the rise of the EP, increasingly acting on an equal footing with the Commission and the Council, has also augmented the complexity of the institutional setting and reinforced the character of the EU as a structure where all representative institutions have a say in all decisions. This development is, moreover, strengthened by the rise of the European Council which today shares *de facto* the right to initiate legislation with the Commission. Consequently, the Community Method and especially the co-decision variant, featuring as the central and most mature element of the EU's legislative structure, might increasingly resemble the constitutional structures of the political system in its nation-state form.

Meanwhile, new institutional forms and procedures, which reinforce the characteristics of the EU as an integrationist structure based upon shared powers, continue to emerge, through the continued expansion of the integration process. Hence, the EU's institutional development seems to be characterized by a contradictory dual movement whereby the characteristics of power sharing expand continuously while, at the same time, tentative moves towards a clearer functional separation of powers can be observed within the most developed areas of the institutional setting. With these contradictory developments in mind, it is therefore not surprising that the "expanding universe" of the EU seems to be "stumbling along", as its contradictory "early-modern"

[19] These policy areas are probably the only ones where it is possible to apply a concept of "integrated administrations" in the sense of Hofmann and Turk (2007).

and "modern" features are simultaneously strengthened, thereby creating a setting characterized by constant internal tensions between the two forms.

Partial Constitutionalism

Since Rasmussen (1985; Weiler 1987) broke the taboo and pointed out what everyone already knew concerning the "legal activism" of the ECJ, it has become acceptable to claim in public that the ECJ has been subject to a different kind of rationality than a purely legal one. Rasmussen views this as an unfortunate "politicization" of the ECJ. Bearing in mind the subordination of the EU political dimension to the logic of integration, one might be able to consider legal activism as reflecting a similar situation whereby the legal/non-legal (*Recht/Unrecht*) distinction of the ECJ, acting as an organization within the realm of the legal system, is also subordinated to the integrationist logic. Such subordination does not imply a complete exclusion of legal rationality, but merely indicates that the operations of the ECJ are subject to a "double binary coding". To the extent that social systems, in the form of interaction, organizational or functional systems, are understood as *Sinn* (meaning) producing systems,[20] such limitations can also be understood as a form of "under-differentiation" which produces "over-reductions" of *Sinn*. Not surprisingly, the occurrence of such forms of over-reduction has therefore led to the development of regulatory ideas and normative models concerning the possible transformation of the ECJ, either into a European supreme court (Pernice 1998; Dehousse 1998:148f.) or into a court capable of safeguarding its autonomy through increased self-restraint(Rasmussen 1993).

However, the EU has also undergone a rapid constitutionalization process over the last decades.[21] This process contradicts the logic of integration. As already indicated, a central function of constitutions is to enable the legal system to observe the system-internal processes of the political system while the system-internal processes of the legal system are simultaneously observed by the political system

[20] We are here following Luhmann's Husserl inspired suggestion to understand meaning (*Sinn*) as the basic element of society (Luhmann 1971).

[21] The narrative of the constitutionalization process has been written several times (Joerges 2001; Weiler 1991; Stein 1981).

(Luhmann 2000:390ff.). Processes of constitutionalization therefore tend to occur within the context of increased differentiation between law and politics, arising from increased social complexity (Luhmann 1990). Accordingly, the ongoing constitutionalization process can be understood as reflecting an increased dissolution of the integration overlay. The tendencies towards dissolution should, however, not necessarily be understood as indicating a failure for the EU since the EU in praxis remain committed to the regulatory principle of establishing "an ever closer union" through increased integration, which again implies eventual transformation into some sort of state. In this sense, the regulatory principle of statehood through integration implies "self-dissolution" in that the move towards modern statehood implies that the organic unity established through the institutional balance will be replaced with the kind of metaphorical unity that characterizes modern states (Bartelson 2001). The constitutionalization of the EU is, however, not only characterized by an increased horizontal dissolution of the EU's unity, but also by vertical hierarchization. The differentiation of increasingly independent dimensions of law and politics is conditioned by a move towards a merger of the EU dimensions of law and politics with their respective counterparts at the MS level. Thus, the EU dimensions increasingly form hierarchical peaks in new European-wide subsystems of law and politics, as concretized through the legal doctrines concerning "direct effect" (Case 1963), "superiority of Community law" (Case 1964) and "pre-emption" (Case 1971). The move towards hierarchization therefore increasingly blurs the distinction between the EU and the MS legal orders.

On the other hand, the crucial question of *Kompetenz-Kompetenz*, the question of who has the competence to decide where the border between EU and MS competences lies, remains unresolved because the ECJ claim this role for itself without such claim being acknowledged by the constitutional courts of the MS. In addition, the interrelated political question of the fundamental nature of the embryonic polity remains largely unresolved. As indicated by the failure of the constitutional treaty, there are clear limitations to how constitutional the EU can be (Maduro 2004). Consequently, the EU seems to be oscillating somewhere between being a separate legal order and engaging in a merger with the MS legal orders on a permanent basis. The resistance of the MS seems, in other words, to transform the quest for "complete" statehood into an unattainable mirage even though a certain level of constitutionalization has been achieved. Instead the EU has entered into a state of "permanent dissolution", in the sense that it continues to operate on the basis of the regulatory idea of state-building through the dissolution of the unity established by the integration overlay, whilst confronting structural conditions which make the idea unachievable. The relationship between the EU legal order and the MS legal orders therefore remains fundamentally unresolved (Weiler 1999; 286ff.).

Horizontal Constitutionalism I

One of the most original attempts to re-conceptualize the relationship between the EU and the MS legal orders is the conflict of laws approach. This approach departs from a paradox in that conflict of laws methodology is oriented towards ensuring unity whilst maintaining substantial diversity. Thus, it is an approach which is particularly well suited to tackle the fundamentally unresolved character of the interaction between the different legal orders characterizing the European context in the sense that it is an approach which takes the EU's "slogan" concerning "unity in diversity" seriously.

As argued by Joerges, the EU courts have intentionally developed "meta-norms", with the objective of achieving stabilization of conflicts between the different MS legal orders without breaking down or replacing any of the involved orders. This understanding of EU law is based on a functionalist perspective. Conflicts emerge between MS because of an increasingly higher level of interdependence between them, thereby creating the functional need for conflict resolution. The key argument promoted by Joerges is however normative; increased interdependence means that the MS are increasingly characterized by a democratic deficit since the democratic decisions of the MS are generating extra-territorial effects with greater frequency. These effects are not reflected in the democratic decisions of those states, since their only point of reference is their own constituency and not those of their neighbors. EU law (and EU integration as such) should therefore be understood as compensatory measures which ensure that the extra-territorial effects of MS actions are taken into account. The European constitutionalization process should consequently be understood as complementary to nation-state constitutionalism, as its objective is to ensure a reduction in negative externalities arising from the operations of national political systems (Joerges 2006b:790; Joerges and Rödel 2008:8).

According to Joerges, the development of European "meta-norms" has provided a legal framework within which regulatory structures such as the "new approach" through mutual recognition of technical standards and the delegation of standardization activities to private actors,[22] as well as the emergence and expansion of Comitology and agencies have been made possible. It is therefore possible to observe a relationship of mutual increase between the European constitutionalization process and the emergence of GS. In addition, the incremental build-up of a European legal framework has also served as a frame for the continued expansion of the political dimension of the EU. Hence, it is possible to consider the EU as characterized by a symbiotic relationship between three dimensions: firstly, the "semi-hierarchical" legal order; secondly, the political dimension as embodied in the triangular relationship between Council, Commission and Parliament, and thirdly, a hybrid administrative infrastructure as provided for by the GS (Joerges 2005; Joerges 2006a:493f.; Joerges 2007).

Joerges' version of the conflict of laws approach encapsulates the emergence and purpose of the European project within a highly elegant construction, which provides a suitable starting point for a legal conceptualization of current developments in Europe. Moreover, its central strength lies in the fact that it does not deduct a normative vision for Europe from a purely analytical ideal model concerning how Europe ought to be. Instead it departs from an inductive functional perspective, the main focus of which is the pragmatic solution of common problems. It provides a normative justification for the processes of conflict resolution which evolves in Europe on a day-to-day basis.

Although Joerges' model in principle has a wider scope his core interest remains the curbing of the horizontal conflicts between the MS through European measures. The following sections will therefore focus on the vertical conflicts between, on the one hand Brussels and Luxembourg and, on the other hand, the MS, as well as to the second form of horizontal conflicts, namely those occurring between the functionally separated spheres of society and which are being reflected in the GS of the EU.

---

[22] The "new approach" was introduced in 1985 as a way of getting of the deadlock which the ambition of realizing the internal market through technical harmonization found itself in at that time. The solution introduced was to limit EC legislation to the definition of "essential requirements" and then leave it up to societal actors within private standardization bodies to define the details (Schepel 2005).

Vertical Constitutionalism

The question of how the instrumentialization of EC law for pro-integrationist purposes can be curbed leads directly to the question of how the balance between politics and law can be re-configured in the EU context to ensure that the operations of the legal dimension converge with those of the political dimension. Until now the central impetus for increased integration has come from the Heads of State and Governments operating within the realm of the European Council. At the same time – after the Commission has prepared the ground – the Council has played the principal role in the day-to-day making of integrative decisions. It is however exactly this form of policy-making which has proved inadequate when it comes to the development of constitutional principles and legislative acts capable of providing suitable reference points for the European courts. The reliance on power sharing means that it is immensely difficult for the EU to produce coherent legal texts since sharing power between multiple institutions with the ability to block progress means that the outcome of legislative processes typically represents the lowest denominator. Dictated by the need to make political compromises, the result is that insufficient solutions are provided for pressing functional problems. In addition, systemic deficits occur because power sharing tends to produce legislation characterized by a mismatch of contradictory objectives and deliberately vague formulations. In other words, the EU's political dimension systematically produces suboptimal outcomes thereby creating decisional vacuums, forcing the courts to define the actual scope and intentions of community legislation.[23] Hence, it is the deficiency of the EU's political dimension in the production of coherent legislative texts which has prevented the emergence of an optimal functional synthesis between law and politics. As a result, the ECJ (and the Court of First Instance) are able to engage in legal activism based on their pro-integrationist bias.

The standard solution proposed as a means of overcoming this problem has been increased politicization. In general, increased politicization is equated with increased democratization (Eriksen and Fossum

[23] A typical example is the recently adopted service directive, which essentially leaves it to the Courts to define the scope of the directive. See Directive 2006/123/EC of the European Parliament and of the Council of 12 December 2006 on services in the internal market (Schmidt 2008).

2004). The question of how or to what extent the EU can be democratized must however begin with an analysis of the structural conditions which must be in place in order for democratic structures to emerge and function. As already indicated, democracy can be understood as a particular frame through which the political system observes its environment through reference to a collective in the form of the people. This reference allows the political system to define the section of its environment which it deems relevant in its continual selection of operations. In addition, democracy can be understood as a specific mode of legally regulated collective decision making, characterized by a differentiation of roles between government and opposition, which relies on the existence of a hierarchically organized and legally framed bureaucratic structure capable of implementing such collective decisions through the (potential) invoking of negative sanctions (Luhmann 1994a:127ff.).

As illustrated earlier the EU only partially shares these characteristics of democracy and hence remains a "quasi-democracy".[24] The status as a "quasi-democracy" is further reinforced by the absence of a singular form of European people (*Staatsvolk*). A solution has emerged with the concept of "multiple demoi" (Weiler 1995). Such conceptual "arm-twisting" will however not solve the real problem, namely the limited reach of democracy. Democratic decision-making remains conditioned by the existence of legal as well as organizational hierarchies, since collectively binding decision making is conditioned by the ability to ensure implementation and the possible deployment of negative sanctions. In other words: democracy remains a "parasite" on power (Luhmann 2000:357f.) because it is conditioned by the existence of an instrument of rule and by a monopoly of power through which democratically made decisions can be channeled. Democracy is therefore intrinsically linked to the existence of strong vertical political and legal control and demand structures on the basis of a distinction between the rulers and the ruled. This structural limitation explains why "radical democracy", encompassing society as whole, has never been able to manifest itself. Democracy remains a limited concept which is unable to manifest itself beyond the boundaries of the hierarchic order of the political system.

---

[24] Accordingly, it is hardly surprisingly that the EU does not fulfill the standards of "quality" or "good" democracy outlined by Morlino in his contribution.

The insight that democracy is impossible beyond the realm of hierarchy has profound implications for the feasibility of the objective of achieving a democratization of the EU, because it remains a structure which is partly based on governing and partly on governance. Since the governance dimension is not hierarchical in nature, it cannot be a subject of democratization. Hence, the governance dimension is not an un-democratic structure which has the potential to become a subject of democratization. Rather it is an a-democratic structure which is beyond the reach of democracy. Hence, calls for a "complete" democratization of the EU through a transfer of the basic features of nation state democracy to the EU cannot be realized since only the governing dimension of the EU can be subject to democratization.

Alternatively, the attempt to grasp ongoing developments within the EU must be based on a dual approach. A pincer movement (*Zangenbewegung*) is required which on the one hand, explores the viability and consequences of increased democratization of the governing dimension, whilst on the other hand, alternative concepts are developed to frame the governance dimension. From a constitutionalization perspective, the key issue is therefore how law can contribute to the double-sided task of facilitating and curbing the exercise of power within the two dimensions whilst maintaining the carefully developed balance between the two dimensions.

Regarding the governing dimension, the central problem involves reliance on the concept of institutional balance. But the real problem here is not "under-democratization" but rather "under-differentiation". This diagnosis also contains a possible answer to the problem of developing an adequate political "partner" for the legal system. This is because the tentative move towards transforming the institutional balance into a functionally differentiated structure resembling the classical modern differentiation between the legislative, the executive and the juridical branches advocated by Seyès and Kant, would potentially rationalize the system by granting specific institutions a monopoly on specific functions. This would undermine the kind of blocking-capability which tends to reduce community legislation into a patchwork of contradictory objectives. Simultaneously, functional differentiation would ensure effective limitations on the exercise of power because specific institutions would be confined to the exercise of specific functions thereby making it possible to clearly identify the responsible (*Letztverantwortliche*) institution. A stronger reliance on functional separation is therefore likely to improve the flexibility of the system and hence increase the EU's ability to react to changes in its environment through the incorporation of new knowledge without relinquishing the "rule of law".

The Positioning of Governance Structures

For the governance dimension the task is somewhat more complicated. The key issue involves the development of a concept of constitutionalization which ensures the stabilization of GS without damaging the flexibility of these structures, whilst maintaining the balance between the governing and governance dimensions. Hence, it is necessary to develop a concept which binds structures such as the OMC, Comitology and agencies within a coherent legal structure, whilst taking seriously the functional demand for integration. Two issues are therefore at stake; i) the positioning of the three forms of governance in relation to each other and ii) the internal organization of GS.

In relation to the first problem, the proponents of the OMC have called for a constitutionalization of the OMC (Zeitlin 2005; Sabel and Zeitlin 2008). Viewed from the perspective of traditional concept of constitutionalism this objective is based on an insoluble contradiction, in that purely political processes which operate outside the realm of law cannot be constitutionalized. From this perspective constitutionalization implies a legal framing of a social structure which facilitates the exercise of power whilst the versatility of the power structures are being reduced on the basis of a reference to a people which confers restricted authoritative power to political structures for a limited period of time.[25] In the case of the EU however, it is the MS who confer power to the Union. In addition, in a strictly legal sense, the OMC does not imply that power is conferred on the EU: one of the most widely acclaimed aims of the OMC is precisely to avoid further increases in the legal competencies of the EU. Instead it is seen as a "pure" political process aimed at achieving results through "experimentation". Hence, OMC processes are directly aimed at increasing the versatility of EU policy-making by surpassing legal constraints. The OMC therefore implies

[25] Just as it does not fulfill the non-domination requirement which remains central to republican theories, as also highlighted by Palombella in his contribution to this volume.

a break with the bonds between law and politics which have traditionally been celebrated as one of the most fundamental achievements of modernity and which were directly aimed at ensuring a balance between versatility and stability. As the OMC represents an attempt to remove the law's "irritation" of the policy-making process, it is not surprising that its emergence has been greeted, mainly by the political scientists, as a welcome innovation. Nor is it surprising that legal scholars have been much more reserved.

Despite the unease of lawyers, the kind of logic guiding the OMC will not go away. The OMC fulfils a specific "pre-integrative" function within the realm of the European integration process. Moreover and as already indicated, this function is not new (Kjaer 2009b). Instead the OMC merely professionalizes and formalizes the kind of pre-integrative mutual observation between MS which has existed ever since the Community was established.[26] From a functional perspective, the OMC is therefore neither a vehicle of deliberation nor merely an intrusive instrument. Such unhelpful dichotomies can be circumvented, by focusing on the usefulness of the OMC, as long as it remains strictly a preliminary tool, applied within policy areas where legal integration, conferring legal competencies to the EU, has not taken place. Policy areas that operate on the basis of relatively unrestrained forms of political rationality because relevant juridical frames have not yet been established.

A constructive approach to the OMC would therefore be to regard it as a necessary first encounter in the integration process within a given policy area. Rather than calling for its abolition, a positive first step would therefore be to negatively delineate its areas of deployment through legal means, thus ensuring that "colonization" of more developed policy areas is avoided. A constitutional containment of the non-legal character of the OMC would establish firewalls between "pre-integrationist", and therefore "pre-legal", and inherently political operations and policy areas where power politics has already been successfully restrained via legal instruments. Such restraints could be achieved if the treaty basis of the EU limited the deployment of OMC processes to policy areas where the Union possesses complementary (or supportive), as opposed to shared or exclusive competencies. This

[26] And in fact ever since a system of European states emerged in the 17th century (Elias 2002).

would not only serve as a safeguard against colonizing tendencies but would also ensure that the current tendency towards the application of OMC processes in policy areas where the EU does not have any competencies at all is avoided. Such a safeguard would therefore increase the probability that any expansion of the OMC is based on a conscious political decision to grant the EU the possibility of initiating such processes.

A safeguard of this kind would of course merely amount to a negative limitation of the OMC and not to a substantial juridification of the method. However, since the kind of power produced within the OMC processes is inherently difficult to curb through the deployment of legal instruments because of its fluid and non-institutionalized nature (Kjaer 2008:31ff.), the resulting kind of power is therefore difficult to frame through constitutional measures because constitutional language remains tied to an "old-European" institutionalist perspective (Borch 2005). As a consequence, moves towards constitutionalization remain dependent on the existence of formalized institutions. A negative constitutional limitation would however limit the damage which the OMC already inflicts on fundamental elements of the European legal order such as the principle of IB. A principle, which, absent alternatives, remain a pivotal measure for the protection of the rule of law in the EU context. More generally, such a safeguard would moreover ensure that the balance between law and politics and thus the balance between contingency and stability in the EU is maintained.

The concept of the regulatory state contrasts with that of the OMC across virtually all dimensions. As Majone convincingly argues, for structural reasons, there are specific societal functions which are not suitable for politization (e.g. central banking, competition policy and some forms of risk regulation). Indeed, independent regulatory institutions with discretionary power are today a common feature of most, if not all, developed democracies. To the extent that such functions is being been transferred to the EU system, a case can therefore be made for the establishment of truly independent regulatory agencies within narrowly defined policy areas.

As already noted, many agencies have already been established. However, the majority are not concerned with regulatory issues as such but instead with, for example, monitoring and dissemination. Currently, there are few indications that any of these agencies will develop into regulatory agencies with fully-fledged discretionary competencies in the foreseeable future. Indeed, a central reason for the failure of Majone's policy proposal concerning the establishment of fully fledged regulatory agencies is that the Community itself only possesses exclusive competencies in few and very narrowly defined policy areas. Hence, the range of policy areas where delegation of exclusive competencies from the Community to agencies is possible remains very limited. Yet, as the unexpected emergence and evolution of Comitology and OMC illustrates, the future remains unknown. One possible way of avoiding the emergence of European agencies with full discretionary powers – where this lacks functional justification – is therefore to introduce a constitutional safeguard stressing that a complete transfer of discretionary competencies to regulatory agencies can only occur within policy areas under exclusive Community competence. Any move towards the establishment of full-blown regulatory agencies would therefore be conditioned by the prior consent of all MS, as well as the EP, to grant the Community exclusive powers in the relevant policy area.

In between the OMC and the concept of the regulatory state, Comitology retains vibrancy. Comitology is strongest in areas of specific and complex regulation, where detailed harmonization is needed. But even if Comitology is an adequate frame for producing harmonization, its uncontrolled spread across policy areas since the 1960s embodies integration by stealth. To counter this development, a constitutional safeguard could be introduced limiting the deployment of Comitology structures to policy areas falling under the CM and which are characterized by shared competencies. Such a limitation would moreover reflect the nature of Comitology as a partly MS and partly Commission dominated realm.

The move towards a clear division of competences between the three modes of governance could moreover be complemented by the adoption of a suggestion tabled several times by the Czech Republic during the two last rounds of treaty negotiations. The Czech Republic suggested that the ability of the European Council, acting under unanimity, to transfer policy areas from the category of supportive competencies to the category of shared or exclusive competencies or shared competencies to the category of exclusive competencies without a treaty amendment should be a two-way street. This mechanism has however been developed as a one-way street in the CT (as well as in the Lisbon Reform Treaty); while it is possible for the Union to increase its competencies, devolution from the Union to the MS remains blocked. The functional need for integration however remains a contingent phenomenon insofar as it reflects the general level of societal interdependence, which in turn is dependent on, for example, economic and technological developments. The need for European meta-norms, as well as the density of such norms, therefore changes over time because the nature of the specific policy areas is constantly changing. This creates functional needs for the adaptation of policies and the institutional structures which policy-making relies on through evolution or devolution of competencies. The ongoing evolution of the EU's institutional and legal structures does not however reflect the perception that a Union characterized by adaptability rather than uniformity would be a far more viable construction. Instead of pursuing a constitutionalization of the already existing permanently changing constitution (*Wandelverfassung*), the EU remains committed to the continual reinforcement of the integrationist strait-jacket on the basis of the concept of an "ever closer Union".

Horizontal Constitutionalism II

As regards the internal organization, it is important to keep the societal function of GS in mind. GS are structural couplings which serve as the means through which the EU ensures its embeddedness in society. Whereas the EU's governing dimension can be understood in the narrow sense as an (embryonic) state because it consists of a political and a legal system coupled within a constitutional framework, a broad perspective including both the governing and governance dimensions requires an understanding of the EU as a social conglomerate. This is necessary because the governance dimension, in contrast to the governing dimension, horizontally binds together a multiplicity of functional systems and hence a multiplicity of forms of rationality. Different forms of rationality, such as economic, scientific and ecological, are of course also present within the vertical governing dimension. Within the governing dimension they however remain subordinate to and framed by legal, political and bureaucratic forms of rationality. In contrast, the governance dimension is to a greater extent, characterized by horizontal (*nebengeordnete*) forms of coordination of different kinds of rationality. Hence, GS must be understood as regimes characterized by multi-rationality which act as interfaces between different functional systems.[27] This is also expressed in the partial dissolution of the public/private distinction within the governance dimension. Governance extends beyond public structures to include elements reproduced within, for example, the economic system, the scientific system, as well as ecological forms of communication. This is because the EU's political and bureaucratic structures are dependent on the kind of knowledge which can be derived from other systems and because the EU itself is faced with a need to stabilize its relations with its environment. But GS are more than merely supportive measures for the governing dimension since they embody a systematic attempt which not only aims to directly stabilize relations between the non-legal and non-political spheres of society, but also to achieve the kind of co-ordination (*Abstimmung*) between functionally differentiated spheres such as economy, health and ecology, which is the primary societal contribution (*Leistung*) of politics in a radicalized modernity (Kjaer 2010).

When compared with the period of classical modernity, GS can in other words, be understood as functional equivalents to corporatist structures. Whereas the diminishing phenomenon of corporatism relied on the distinction between employers and employees and hence indirectly on the stratified class structure of the industrial society, the emergence of GS are, on the other hand, a consequence of the move away from stratificatory and segmentary forms of differentiation towards the ever increasing relevance of functional differentiation. With the functional equivalence of corporatism and governance in mind, it is not surprising that the demands for a democratization of European GS resemble the calls for a democratization of the corporatist system through *Verbandsdemokratie* which emerged during the period of classical modernity (Teubner 1978). Such an objective was only possible however, because corporatist organizations are hierarchically ordered entities. They are "mini-states", which have adopted the basic features of the hierarchical model of organization characterizing state bureaucracies (Kjaer 2009c). In addition, corporatism only brings together two forms of rationality – the political and the economic – within the framework of economic constitutions. In contrast, GS are characterized by strong horizontal features and far more

[27] The focus on multi-rationality means that this concept of regimes differs from the one presented by Fischer-Lescano and Teubner (2004; 2006; 2007).

complex couplings of an entire range of rationalities, thereby making a transfer of the ideals of corporatist democracy to the context of GS impossible.

As GS must be understood as highly dynamic autonomous structures, a "state-centered" perspective which only focuses on the governing dimension remains inadequate. Hence, achievement of a classic separation of functions within the governance dimension is not sufficient. Instead of the limited focus on the intersection between legal and political rationalities within the traditional doctrine of a separation of powers, it is necessary to develop a special variant. This would be directly oriented towards the separation of functions within the broader range of horizontal societal settings that are characterized by a multiplicity of forms of rationality. The principle of functional separation could, in other words, be transformed into a constitutional principle which should be applied to regulatory structures as such. Hence, not only the governing dimension, but also horizontal intermediate structures operating in between the public and the private spheres, should be subject to the constitutional principle of functional separation. A move in this direction has already been made in the area of risk regulation through the introduction of the distinction between risk assessment, risk evaluation and risk management. However, a far more incisive move towards institutional separation, reflecting the reproduction of different forms of rationality within the functionally differentiated spheres of society, is required. Several of the existing GS already follows this logic. E.g. REACH, the EU system for the evaluation and authorization of chemicals operates with simultaneous but separate evaluation processes within the committee representing the environmental and health perspectives and the committee for socio-economic analysis. Within the REACH regime functional separation is moreover combined with a central complexity-reducing mechanism that provides a solution to the problem of political overload, insofar as it reduces the problems which are of political relevance to those where real conflicts between functionally different spheres occur and moves the dossiers where convergence between societal actors has been achieved to the background, thereby allowing the political system to deal only with cases of major importance (Kjaer 2007a).

The OMC process on Research and Development (R&D) serves to illustrate what contribution functional separation can make. The OMC on R&D is characterized by a bias in rationality since the process is framed by economic rather than scientific rationality. Within all forms of governing and governance such asymmetric tendencies can be detected, thereby supporting the insight presented by Kratochwil in this volume that an "illiberal" turn is a permanent danger. It is precisely to avoid such asymmetries that functional separation is needed. Hence, extending the earlier call for a purely negative delimitation of the OMC through law, one might consider whether functional separation allowing for the separate but simultaneous processing of different rationalities can be introduced within the OMC. In the specific example of the OMC within R&D, a "duplication" of the processes could be introduced, as benchmarking and other evaluation exercises could be carried out by two separate structures. Respectively, these structures would provide evaluations from a socio-economic and a scientific perspective, whilst remaining linked within a procedural framework which ensures coherency. Ideally this would provide a basis for informed political decision-making as it would allow the political system to make decisions reflecting economic as well as scientific perspectives, thereby enabling it to fulfill the function of ensuring a balance between rationalities. From this perspective, the merger of the three council configurations for internal market, industry and research into a single competitiveness configuration which was undertaken to facilitate the OMC process in R&D was a move in the wrong direction. Indeed, the merger that took place clearly illustrates the de-differentiation consequences of the OMC in its present form and the dangers that lie in de-formalized forms of governance as well as the value of a formal legal framing of such processes (Kjaer 2009b).

References

Amstutz, Marc. 2006. "In Between Worlds: Marleasing and the Emergence of Interlegality in Legal Reasoning". *European Law Journal* 12, 6:766–84.

——. and Vaios Karavas. 2006. "Rechtsmutation: Zu Genese und Evolution des Rechts im transnationalen Raum". *Rechtsgeschichte* 8:14–32.

Bach, Maurizio. 1989. Die Bürokratisierung Europas. Verwaltungseliten, Experten und politische Legitimation in Europa. Frankfurt am Main: Campus Verlag.

Bartelson, Jens. 2001. *The Critique of the State*. Cambridge: Cambridge University Press.

Borch, Christian. 2005. "Systemic Power. Luhmann, Foucault and Analytics of Power". *Acta Sociologica* 48, 2:155–67.

Borrás, Susana and Kerstin Jacobsson. 2004. "The open method of co-ordination and new governance patterns in the EU", *Journal of European Public Policy* 11, 2: 185–208.

Bourdieu, Pierre. 1994. "Rethinking the State: Genesis and Structure of the Bureaucratic Field", *Sociological Theory* 12, 1:1–18.

Bücker, Andreas and Sabine Schlacke. 2000. "Die Entstehung einer politischen Verwaltung durch EG-Ausschüsse - Rechtstatsachen und Rechtsentwicklungen" Pp. 161–256 in *Das Ausschußwesen der Europäischen Union. Die Praxis der Risikoregulierung im Binnenmarkt und ihre rechtliche Verfassung*, edited by J. Falke and C. Joerges. Baden-Baden: Nomos Verlag.

——. 1963. Case 26/62 *Van gend en Loos v Nederlandse Administratie der Belastingen ECR 1.*

——. 1964. Case 6/64 *Costa v ENEL*, ECR 585.

——. 1970. Case 25/70 *Einfuhrstelle v. Köster*, ECR 1161.

——. 1971. Case 22/70 *Commission v Council*, ECR 273.

——. 1982. Cases 188 to 190/80, *France, Italy and United Kingdom vs. Commission*, ECR 2545, 2573.

Dehousse, Renaud.1998. *The European Court of Justice*. London: Macmillan Press.

Elias, Norbert. [1969] 2002. *Die höfische Gesellschaft*. Frankfurt am Main: Suhrkamp Verlag.

Eriksen, Erik O. and John Erik Fossum. 2004. "Europe at a Crossroads: Government or Transnational Governance?" Pp. 115–146 in *Transnational Governance and Constitutionalism*, edited by C. Joerges, I-J. Sand and G. Teubner. Oxford: Hart Publishing.

Fischer-Lescano, Andreas and Gunther Teubner. 2004. "Regime-Collisions: The Vain Search for Legal Unity in the Fragmentation of Global Law", *Michigan Journal of International Law*, 25:999–1046.

——. 2006. *Regime-Kollisionen: Zur Fragmentierung des Weltrechts*. Frankfurt am Main: Suhrkamp Verlag.

——. 2007. "Fragmentierung des Weltrechts: Vernetzung globaler Regimes statt etatistischer Rechtseinheit" Pp. 37–61 in *Weltstaat und Weltstaatlichkeit. Beobachtungen globaler politischer Strukturbildung* edited by M. Albert and R. Stichweh. Wiesbaden: Vs Verlag.

Follesdal, Andreas and Simon Hix. 2005. "Why there is a Democratic Deficit in the EU: A Response to Majone and Moravcsik", *Journal of Common Market Studies* 44, 3:533–62.

Habermas, Jürgen.1992. *Faktizität und Geltung. Beiträge zur Diskurstheorie des Rechts und demokratischen Rechtsstaats*. Frankfurt am Main: Suhrkamp Verlag.

——. 1998. "Die postnationale Konstellation und die Zukunft der Demokratie" Pp. 91–169 in Id., *Die postnationale Konstellation. Politische Essays*. Frankfurt am Main: Suhrkamp Verlag.

Haibach, Georg. 1997. "Comitology after Amsterdam: A Comparative Analysis of the Delegation of Legislative Powers", *EIPASCOPE*, 3:1–7.

——. 2000. "The History of Comitology" Pp. 185–215 in *Delegated Legislation and the Role of Committees in the EC*, edited by M. Andenas and A.Türk. The Hague: Kluwer.

Hellmann, Kai-Uwe. 2002. "Gemeinwohl und Systemvertrauen. Vorschläge zur Modernisierung alteuropäische Begriffe" Pp. 77–110 in *Gemeinwohl und Gemeinsinn. Rhetoriken und Perspektiven sozial-moralischer Orientierung*, edited by H. Münkler and K. Fischer. Berlin: Akademie Verlag.

Hintze, Otto. [1910] 1981. "Der Commissarius und seine Bedeutung in der allgemeinen Verwaltungsgeschichte. Eine vergleichende Studie" Pp. 78–112 in Id., *Beamtentum und Bürokratie*. Göttingen: Vandenhoeck & Ruprecht.

Hix, Simon. 1999. *The Political System of the European Union*. Basingstoke: Macmillian Press.

Hofmann, Herwig C. H. and Alexander Türk. 2007. "The Development of Integrated Administration in the EU and its Consequences" *European Law Journal* 13, 2: 253–271.

Jachtenfuchs, Markus and Michèle Knodt (Eds.). 2002. *Regieren in internationalen Institutionen*. Opladen: Leske + Budrich.

Jarass, Hans D. 1975. *Politik und Bürokratie als Elemente der Gewaltenteilung*. München: C.H. Beck'sche Verlagsbuchhandlung.

Joerges, Christian. 2001. "Das Recht im Prozeβ des Konstitutionalisierung Europas" Florence: *EUI Working Paper Law*, 6.

——. 2005. "Rethinking European Law's Supremacy: A Plea for a Supranantional Conflict of Laws" Florence: *EUI Working Papers Law*, 12.

——. 2006a. "Constitutionalism in Postnational Constellations: Contrasting Social Regulation in the EU and in the WTO" Pp. 491–527 in *Constitutionalism, Multilevel Trade Governance and Social Regulation*, edited by C. Joerges and E.U. Petersmann. Oxford: Hart Publishing.

——. 2006b. "Deliberative Political Processes" Revisited: What Have we Learnt About the Legitimacy of Supranational Decision-Making" *Journal of Common Market Studies*, 44:779–802.

——. 2007. "Rethinking European Law's Supremacy: A Plea for a Supranational Conflict of Laws" Pp. 311–327 in *Debating the Democratic Legitimacy of the European Union*, edited by B. Kohler Koch and B. Rittberger. Lanham, MD: Rowman & Littlefield.

——. and Florian Rödl. 2008. "Von der Entformalisierung europäischer Politik und dem Formalismus europäischer Rechtssprechung im Umgang mit dem "sozialen Defizit" des Integrationsprojekts. Ein Beitrag aus Anlass der Urteile des EuGH in den Rechtssachen *Viking* und *Laval*." Bremen: ZERP-Diskussionspapier, 2.

——. and Michael Zürn (Eds.). 2005. *Law and Governance in Postnational Europe. Compliance Beyond the Nation-State*. Cambridge: Cambridge University Press.

Kjaer, Poul F. 2007a. "Rationality within REACH? On Functional Differentiation as the Structural Foundation of Legitimacy in European Chemicals Regulation". Florence: *EUI Working Papers*, Law, 18.

——. 2007b. "The Societal Function of European Integration in the Context of World Society" *Soziale Systeme. Zeitschrift für Soziologische Theorie*, 13, 1 + 2:367–378.

——. 2008. "Three Forms of Governance and Three Forms of Power" Pp. 23–43 in *Law, Democracy and Solidarity in a Post-national Union* edited by E. O. Eriksen, C. Joerges and F. Rödl. Oxford: Routledge.

——. 2009a. "Embeddedness through Networks – a Critical appraisal of the Network Concept in the *Oeuvre* of Karl-Heinz Ladeur" *German Law Journal*, 10, 4 (April): 483–499.

——. 2009b. "Formalization or De-Formalization through Governance?" Pp. 243–257 in *Conflict of Laws or Laws of Conflict*, edited by Rainer Nickel. Oslo: ARENA Report Series.

——. 2009c. "Post-Hegelian Networks: Comments on the Chapter by Simon Deakin" Pp. 75–85 in *Networks: Legal Issues of Multilateral Co-operation*, edited by M. Amstutz and G. Teubner. Oxford: Hart publishing.

——. 2010. *Between Governing and Governance. On the Emergence, Function and Form of Europe's Post-national Constellation*. Oxford: Hart Publishing 2010.

Koselleck, Reinhart 2006. "Begriffsgeschichtliche Probleme der Verfassungsgeschichtsschreibung" Pp. 365–82 in Id., *Begriffsgeschichten: Studien zur Semantik und Pragmatik der politischen und Sozialen Sprache*. Frankfurt am Main: Suhrkamp Verlag.

Ladeur, Karl-Heinz. 2002. "The Changing Role of the Private in Public Governance – The Erosion of Hierarchy and the Rise of a New Administrative Law of Cooperation. A Comparative Approach". Florence: *EUI Working Papers, Law*, 9.

Lenaerts, Koen. 1990. "Some Reflections on the Separation of Powers in the European Community", *Common Market Law Review*, 28:11–35.

——. and Amaryllis Verhoeven. 2002. "Institutional Balance as a Guarantee for Demo-

cracy in EU Governance" Pp. 35–88 in *Good Governance in Europe's Integrated Market* edited by C. Joerges and R. Dehousse. Oxford: Oxford University Press.
Luhmann, Niklas. 1971. "Sinn als Grundbegriff der Soziologie" Pp. 25–100 in *Theorie der Gesellschaft oder Sozialtechnologie?* Edited by J. Habermas and N. Luhmann. Frankfurt am Main: Suhrkamp Verlag.
——. 1989. "Theorie der Politischen Opposition", *Zeitschrift für Politik*, 36, 1: pp. 13–26.
——. 1990. "Verfassung als evolutionäre Errungenschaft", *Rechtshistorisches Journal*, 9:176–220.
——. 1994a. "Die Zukunft der Demokratie" Pp. 126–32 in Id., *Soziologische Aufklärung, Band 4. Beiträge Zur Funktionalen Differenzierung der Gesellschaft*. Opladen: Westdeutscher Verlag.
——. 1994b. "Europa als Problem der Weltgesellschaft", *Berliner Debatte*, 2:3–7.
——. 2000. *Politik der Gesellschaft*. Frankfurt am Main: Surhkamp Verlag.
MacCormick, Neil. 1993. "Beyond the Sovereign State", *Modern Law Review*. 56, 1: 1–18.
Maduro, Miguel P. 2004. "How Constitutional Can the European Union Be? The Tension Between Intergovernmentalism and Constitutionalism in the European Union". New York: *Jean Monnet Working Paper*, 5.
Majone, Giandomenico. 2005. *Dilemmas of European integration: the ambiguities and pitfalls of integration by stealth*. Oxford: Oxford University Press.
——. 2002. "Delegation of Regulatory Powers in a Mixed Polity", *European Law Journal*, 8, 3:319–39.
Miles, David. 2005. "Integration is not necessarily the right concept to guide integration", Financial Times, 16 Dec.
Moravcsik, Andrew. 1991. "Negotiating the Single European Act: national interests and conventional statecraft in the European Community", *International Organization*, winter: 19–56.
——. 1998. *The Choice for Europe: Social Purpose and State Power from Messina to Maastricht*. Ithaca: Cornell University Press.
Neyer, Jürgen. 2008. "The justice Deficit of the EU and other International Organisations" Pp. 199–222 in *Transnational Standards of Social Protection. Contrasting European and International Governance*, edited by C. Joerges and P.F. Kjaer. Oslo: ARENA Report Series, 5.
Panezi, Maria. 2007. "Sources of Law in Transition. Re-visiting General Principles of International Law", *Ancilla Iuris* (www.anci.ch): 66–79.
Pernice, Ingolf. 1993. "Maastricht, Staat und Demokratie", *Die Verwaltung*: 26, 449–488.
Rasmussen, Hjalte. 1986. *On Law and Policy in the European Court of Justice*. Dordrecht: Martinus Nijhoff.
——. 1993. *Towards a Normative Theory of Interpretation of Community Law*. Copenhagen: Political Studies Press.
Riekmann, Sonja P. 1998. *Die kommissarische Neuordnung Europas. Das Dispositiv der Integration*. Wien: Springer Verlag.
Riklin, Alois. 2005. *Machtteilung – Geschichte der Mischverfassung*. Darmstadt: Wissenschaftliche Buchgesellschaft.
Sabel, Charles and Jonathan Zeitlin. 2008. "Learning from Difference: The New Architecture of Experimentalist Governance in the EU", *European Law Journal*: 14, 3: 271–327.
Sand, Inger-Johanne. 1998. "Understanding the European Union/European Economic Area as Systems of Functionally Different Processes" Pp. 93–110 in *Europe's Other: European Law Between Modernity and Postmodernity*, edited by P. Fitzpatrick and J. H. Bergeron. Aldershot: Ashgate Publishing.

Santer, Jacques. 1995. *L'avenir de l'Europe. Quel rôle pour la Commission? Eloge de la méthode communautaire*, Jean Monnet Lecture, 20 Oct. Florence : European University Institute.
Schepel, Harm. 2005. *The Constitution of Private Governance - Product Standards in the Regulation of Integrating Markets*. Oxford: Hart Publishing.
Schmidt, Susanne K. 2008. "Competing in Markets, not Rules: The Conflict over the Single Services Market" Pp. 31–54 in *Transnational Standards of Social Protection. Contrasting European and International Governance*, edited by Christian Joerges and Poul F. Kjaer. Oslo: ARENA Report Series, 5.
Sciulli, David. 1992. *Theory of Societal Constitutionalism: Foundations of a Non-Marxist Critical Theory*. New York: Cambridge University Press.
Scott, Joanne and David M. Trubek. 2002. "Mind the Gap: Law and New Approaches to Governance in the European Union", *European Law Journal*. 8, 1:1–18.
Stein, Eric. 1981. "Lawyers, Judges, and the Making of a Transnational Constitution", *American Journal of International Law*. 75:1–27.
Stichweh, Rudolf. 2007. "Dimensionen des Weltstaats im System der Weltpolitik" Pp. 25–36 in *Weltstaat und Weltstaatlichkeit. Beobachtungen globaler politischer Strukturbildung* edited by M. Albert and R. Stichweh. Wiesbaden: VS Verlag.
Teubner, Gunther. 1978. *Organisationsdemokratie und Verbandsverfassung: Rechtsmodelle für politisch relevante Verbände. Tübinger Rechtswissenschaftliche Abhandlungen, Band 47*. Tübingen: Mohr Siebeck.
——. 2004. "Societal Constitutionalism: Alternatives to State-Centred Constitutional Theory?" Pp. 3–28 in *Transnational Governance and Constitutionalism*, edited by C. Joerges, I-J. Sand and G. Teubner. Oxford: Hart Publishing.
Trubek, David M., Patrick Cottrell and Mark Nance. 2006. "'Hard Law' and EU Integration" Pp. 65–94 in *Law and New Governance in the EU and the US* edited by G. de Burca & J. Scott. Oxford: Hart Publishing.
Verhofstadt, Guy. 2006. *Les etats-unis d'Europe*. Bruxelles: Luc Pire.
Walker, Neil. 2007. "Post-Constituent Constitutionalism", Pp. 247–268 in *The Paradox of Constitutionalism*, edited by M. Loughlin and N. Walker. Oxford: Oxford University Press.
Weiler, Joseph H. H. 1987. "The Court of Justice on Trial", *Common Market Law Review*, 24:555–589.
——. "The Transformation of Europe". 1991. *Yale Law Journal*. 100:2402–2483.
——. 1995. "Does Europe Need a Constitution? Reflections on Demos, Telos and the German Maastricht Decision", *European Law Journal*, 1:219–258.
——. 1999. *The Constitution of Europe. "Do the New Clothes Have an Emperor?"And other Essays on European Integration*. Cambridge: Cambridge University Press.
Yataganas, Xénophon A. 2001a. "The Treaty of Nice. The Sharing Power and Institutional Balance in the European Union - A Continental Perspective". New York: *Jean Monnet Working Papers*, 1.
——. 2001b. "Delegation of Regulatory Authority in the European Union. The Relevance of the American Model of Independent Agencies". New York: *Jean Monnet Working Papers*, 3.
Zeitlin, Jonathan. 2005. "Social Europe and Experimentalist Governance: Towards a New Constitutional Compromise?" *European Governance Papers* (EUROGOV), 4.

CHAPTER SIX

THE *RECHTSSTAAT* AND SOCIAL EUROPE: HOW A CLASSICAL TENSION RESURFACES IN THE EUROPEAN INTEGRATION PROCESS

Christian Joerges

This chapter focuses on just one dimension of the rule of law *problématique*, namely, its unsettled relationship with the welfare state. It does this against the background of a specific context, namely, the German constitutional tradition. Furthermore, it reconstructs this tradition one-sidedly, in the framework of Jürgen Habermas' discourse theory of law (Habermas 1998), and it is also methodologically indebted to this author (in particular, Habermas 2001; see Joerges 2009). Although it does acknowledge the broader horizons sketched by Morlino and Palombella in this volume, as relating to the conceptual and empirical intertwinings between democracy and the rule of law, it does not further their theoretical and methodological premises systematically. Its purpose is to show the relevance – in this theoretical context – of the ultimate evolution and debate in European law, and to present – as clearly and emphatically as possible – the theses and messages, which are, in my view, of threatening topicality. In the post-national constellation – this is the sociological basis of the argument – we are witnessing a fragmentation and de-formalisation of law. These tendencies are by no means of merely academic importance, but concern the social integration of democratic societies. The present critical phase of the European project reflects these concerns. It is, however, simply impossible to find a common theoretical denominator. "The social" is an essential feature of all Western democracies. But its institutionalisation differs markedly and its constitutional importance remains an unsettled issue.

The one-sidedness of the present essay should be considered in this light. This focus does not depart from the reflections on the multi-faceted and "dual" meaning of the "rule of law", which Gianluigi Palombella proposes and examines. Quite to the contrary, it is the contextual dependency of the reconstruction of the German tradition, which makes one aware of the importance of comparative constitutionalism and of the challenging issues that European constitutionalism has to address. Similarly, the search for a transdisciplinary perspective which seeks to respond to the schisms between legal discourses and the perception of law in political science does not depart from the efforts undertaken by Leonardo Molino to identify empirical dimensions of democratic norms and to define inter-subjectively valid yardsticks for the evaluation of democratic systems. Quite to the contrary, his deliberations respond in an illuminating way to Habermas' plea for communications across disciplinary borders.

I. The *Sozialstaats* Controversy

Is the idea of the rule of law compatible with a commitment to social justice? This query was at the core of the first great constitutional debate in the newly constituted Federal Republic of Germany. The famous opponents were Ernst Forsthoff, one of the most respected disciples of Carl Schmitt, on the one hand, and Wolfgang Abendroth, defending the legacy of Hermann Ignaz Heller, on the other. The former had a *Lehrstuhl* in the prestigious Heidelberg Faculty of Law, the latter, although a lawyer by education, was a Professor in the political science department of Marburg. As if the differences in these affiliations were not telling enough: The text of Forsthoff's seminal analyses was published in the *Veröffentlichungen der Vereinigung der deutschen Staatsrechtslehrer (Forsthoff 1954a)*, the prestigious organ of Germany's public law professors, whereas Abendroth was present only as a discussant (Fischer-Lescano and Eberl 2006); he published the elaborated version of his argument in the *Festschrift* for the political scientist Ludwig Bergsträsser (Abendroth 1954). The argument was about Article 20 (1) of the German Basic Law, which states: "The Federal Republic of Germany is a democratic and social federal state". According to Forsthoff's interpretation, this social state clause was to be understood as a commitment outside constitutional law because any striving for social justice would have to resort to techniques that were incompatible with the formal structure of the rule of law. Abendroth, in his counter-argument, restated what Herman Heller had argued in his reading of Germany's first democratic constitution, the Weimar *Reichsverfassung*, namely, that the promise of social justice is inherent in the very idea of democratic rule (Dyzenhaus 1997; Maus

1984; Schluchter 1983; Stolleis 1999). Social justice and the rule of law were, to borrow a Habermasian category, co-original concepts, social justice a truly constitutional commitment. The legendary *Sozialstaats* controversy of the early 1950s, which had its roots in the laboratory of Weimar, was to persist not only in all major constitutional controversies, but also at more abstract theoretical levels, in particular, in Niklas Luhmann's distinction between "conditional" and "purposive" programming (Luhmann 1968; Luhmann 1972), Jürgen Habermas' proceduralisation of the category of law (Habermas 1996; Wiethölter 1982; Wiethölter 1989) and Gunther Teubner's early efforts to mediate between the two master thinkers through "reflexive law" (Teubner 1983). These debates are clearly not just *querelles allemandes* and it would – in view of their often noted (Caldwell 2000; Harvey 2004) paradigmatic importance – be surprising if they did not re-surface in the European integration process. This re-appearance was to be expected but is still, nevertheless, disquieting. This is because the topicality of the classical *Sozialstaats* controversy in the European arena is due to the unruly dimension of "the social", which no one other than Max Weber had underlined when he observed that the quest for social justice was an agenda of populist movements which threatened the achievement of modern law and occidental rationalism, namely, its formal qualities (Weber 1978; Weber 1994). It is precisely this threat which motivated Friedrich A. von Hayek's warnings against "The road to serfdom" (Hayek 1944), and which was invoked in important analyses of the perversion of anti-formalism in the era of national socialism (Kennedy 2004).

European integration was an explicit reaction to the disaster which, in particular, Germany's National Socialism had caused in Europe. One element of constitutive importance of this response was the commitment of the integration project to the rule of law. This answer was indispensable, but was it meant to be sufficient? Was Europe to listen to von Hayek, or was its integration project bound to be complemented by the establishment of a European *Sozialstaatlichkeit*, some kind of European social model?

II. Europe's Social Deficit

Ever since the French referendum of 2005, "Social Europe" has become a nightmare for the proponents of a European Constitution, rather than a noble complement of their project. The perceived dismantling of welfare state accomplishments was of decisive importance in France, and remained important in the later campaigns, even in Ireland. This importance was not a comforting experience for the proponents of a European social model. They found themselves in very irritating alliances with populist movements, which presented precisely the kind of irrationalism which Max Weber and von Hayek had been concerned about. The century old tensions between the rule of law and the *Sozialstaat* have apparently again come to the fore – and they seem to exhibit the same kind of destructive potential that has characterised their history. History, however, does not repeat itself. It is important to understand the impact of Europe's post-national constellation on the patterns of the controversies which all European societies have experienced – particularly because Europe is in such troubled waters. We will start our analysis with a brief historical account. However, this analysis will not attempt to explain "what really happened in the past", but will, instead, reconstruct the institutional *locus* of "the social" in the various stages of the integration project.

II.1. *The "De-coupling" of "the Social" from the Economic Constitution in the Formative Period*

The project of European integration was launched not as an experiment in supranational democracy. This observation is not meant to downplay its historical importance or dignity. The apparent political modesty of the economic objective documented a break with the previous nationalist striving for power. After the "bitter experiences" of the Second World War and its devastating effects, the prospect of economic integration was intended as a means of ensuring lasting peace and economic well-being The primarily economic and technocratic design of the project appeared, to its architects, to be a precautionary shield in a political constellation which was still unsettled. It was a choice of what seemed possible and reasonable. With hindsight, however, the implications of this choice, which were hardly foreseeable and certainly not a salient issue half a century ago, become apparent.

The choice for "economic Europe" implied a renunciation of a "European social model" which would have addressed the tensions between the rule of law and social justice. This choice has been coined by Fritz Scharpf as a de-coupling of the social sphere from the economic sphere (Scharpf 2002). This is an analytical observation, not a normative statement on the *finalité* of the European project. The normative evaluation is of course controversial. The exclusion of the social sphere from the integration project has the potential for failure which is of constitutional significance for those who assume that the citizens of constitutional democracies are entitled to determine in what kind of social order they prefer to live. This is a political right of fundamental constitutional significance. This is supported by the fact that in the course of the negotiations, France had tried to consolidate the competences of the Community in the field of social policy (Milward 1999; Scharpf 2002). Are we to interpret its failure and the neglect of "the social" in the formative era as a definite decision on a constitutional issue of the utmost political sensitivity and practical importance? "Social Europe" was not yet on the agenda and there was simply no need to engage in pertinent debates (Leibfried and Zürn 2005; Ruggie 1982). Only in the course of the intensifying impact of the Europeanisation process was Europe's "social deficit" to become apparent.

Contemporary theories of legal integration, however, had to conceptualise the European Community as it was institutionalised. Two such efforts stand out and remain of lasting importance: Germany's ordo-liberalism and Joseph Weiler's theory of supranationalism (Weiler 1981; Weiler 1991).

Ordo-liberalism is not only an important theoretical tradition in Germany, but also a powerful contributor to German ideational politics. The ordo-liberal school reconstructed the legal essence of the European project as an "economic constitution", which was not in need of democratic legitimacy. The freedoms guaranteed in the EEC Treaty, the opening up of national economies and the anti-discrimination rules, and the commitment to a system of undistorted competition were interpreted as a quasi-Schmittian "decision" that supported an economic constitution, and which also conformed with the ordo-liberal conceptions of the framework conditions for a market economic system. The fact that Europe had started out on its integrationist path as a mere economic community lent plausibility to ordo-liberal arguments – and even required them: in the ordo-liberal account, the Community acquired a legitimacy of its own by interpreting its pertinent provisions as prescribing a law-based order committed to guaranteeing economic freedoms and protecting competition at supranational level. This legitimacy was independent of the democratic constitutional institutions of the state. By the same token, it imposed limits upon the

Community: thus, discretionary economic policies seemed illegitimate and unlawful. The ordo-liberal European polity consists of a twofold structure: at supranational level, it is committed to economic rationales and a system of undistorted competition, while, at national level, re-distributive (social) policies may be pursued and developed further (Joerges 2005; Joerges and Rödl 2005).

"Integration through law" is the legal paradigm commonly associated with the formative era of the European Community outside the German borders (Weiler 1981). It is not by chance that generations of scholars have built upon it or tried to decipher its sociological basis (Vauchez 2008). The strength of the paradigm may well rest (in part) on assumptions that become apparent only when social and economic policies are viewed through its lenses. Then, we become aware of a *Wahlverwandtschaft* with German ordo-liberalism, in that only the European market-building project was juridified through supranational law, whereas social policy at European level could, at best, be said to have been handled through intergovernmental bargaining processes. This affinity has its limits, however. It was not intended that Joseph Weiler's legal supranationalism would overrule and outlaw "the political" in the same way as ordo-liberalism. It is nevertheless true that in Weiler's analysis "social Europe" was an unlikely option, simply because its advent was dependent on unanimous intergovernmental voting.

To summarise: Europe was conceived according to principles of a dual polity. Its "economic constitution" was non-political in the sense that it was not subject to political interventions. This was its constitutional-supranational *raison d'être*. Social policy was treated as a categorically-distinct subject. It belonged to the domain of political legislation, and, as such, had to remain national. Fritz Scharpf's decoupling thesis captures this constellation well, without, however, providing a basis for a definite normative theory on the constitutionalisation of Europe. It is nevertheless possible to interpret his thesis as a theory with normative implications. Scharpf's analysis rests upon the assumption that the social integration of capitalist societies will require a balance between social and economic rationality. This is not only a sociological theory (Habermas 1979; Habermas 1989), but also an assumption that summarises a political preference rooted in the histories of European societies (Judt 2005). Hence, it seems unsurprising that it should become imperative for European politics to address the social dimensions and implications of the integration project (Eucken

1952; Wegmann 2002), and it seems adequate to interpret the "decoupling" of the social sphere from the economic order, not as a kind of Schmittian decision against a European social model, but as a temporary compromise, which was to pass the debate on the institutional design of Europe's social dimension on to future generations.

II.2. *The Completion of the Internal Market, the Erosion of the Economic Constitution and the Advent of Social Europe*

What seemed originally like a sustainable equilibrium was not, however, to remain stable. One important reason for its instability was the progress of the integration project. The Delors Commission's 1985 *White Paper on Completion of the Internal Market (1985)* is widely perceived not only as a turning point, but also a breakthrough in the integration process. Jacques Delors' initiative provided the hope of overcoming a long phase of stagnation; the means to this end was the strengthening of Europe's competitiveness. Economic rationality, rather than "law", was, from now on, to be understood as Europe's orienting maxim, its first commitment and its regulative idea. In this sense, it seems justified to characterise Delors' programme as a deliberate move towards an institutionalisation of economic rationality. This seems even more plausible when we consider two complementary institutional innovations accomplished through, and subsequent to, the Maastricht Treaty, namely, the Monetary Union and the Stability Pact. Europe resembled a market-embedded polity governed by an economic constitution, rather than by political rule.

This characterisation, however, soon proved to be too simplistic (Bercusson 1995; Joerges 1994; Nörr 2007). What had started out as an effort to strengthen Europe's competitiveness and to accomplish this objective through new (de-regulatory) strategies, soon led to the entanglement of the EU in ever increasing policy fields and the development of sophisticated regulatory machinery. It was, in particular, the concern of European legislation and the Commission with "social regulation" (the health and safety of consumers and workers, and environmental protection) which served as irrefutable proof of this. The weight and dynamics of these policy fields had been thoroughly under-estimated by the proponents of the "economic constitution". Equally important and equally unsurprising was the fact that the integration process intensified with the completion of the Internal Market and affected ever increasing policy fields. This was significant not so much in terms of its factual weight, but in view of Europe's "social deficit", in terms of the new efforts to strengthen Europe's presence in the spheres of labour and social policy.

These tendencies became truly significant during the bargaining over the Maastricht Treaty, which was adopted in 1992. This is why this Amendment of the Treaty, officially presented as both an intensification and a consolidation of the integration project, met with fierce criticism. The most outspoken critique came not from the political left, but from the proponents of the new "economic turn" in powerful political quarters, and, in particular, from Germany's second generation ordo-liberals (Streit 1998; Streit and Mussler 1995). Following the explicit recognition and strengthening of new policy competences, which was accomplished in Maastricht, it seemed simply no longer plausible to assign a constitutive function and normative dominance to the "system of undistorted competition" because this competition policy had now been downgraded to one among many commitments. In addition, the expansion of competences in labour law by the Social Protocol and the Agreement on Social Policy of the Treaty blurred the formerly clear lines between Europe's (apolitical) economic constitution and the political responsibility assumed by its Member States in relation to social and labour policies.

II.3. *The Three Pillars of Social Europe and their Fragility*

The quest for social Europe has gained ever-increasing momentum since the Maastricht Treaty of 1992 (Bercusson, Deakin, Koistinen, Kravaritou, Mückenberger, Supiot, and Veneziani 1997). Three recent events nurtured the hope that progress, albeit slow, would be a matter of course. One was to have its birth with the promotion of the Open Method of Co-ordination at the Lisbon Council of 2000. This Council had primarily been dedicated to knowledge society issues and to setting very ambitious goals for Europe in pertinent industries. However, the Council felt that the agenda of "social Europe" should simultaneously be renewed. This was a daring exercise and promise. What, until then, had been perceived as an obstacle to the strengthening of Europe's social dimension, namely, the lack of genuine European competences and the unavailability of the traditional "Community method", was now re-interpreted as having both virtue and potential. The OMC was presented by its proponents as an appraising non-coercive form of policy co-ordination which emphasised mutual learning and exchange of good practices, which could be applied to politically sensitive fields, such of social protection, where harmonisation was considered by many to be neither practicable nor desirable (Sabel and Zeitlin 2008).

The second event was the inclusion of "Social Europe" in the proceedings of the European Convention. This was by not envisaged at the outset of the proceedings. "Social Europe", was not part of the original Convention agenda. With hindsight, this proved to be an untenable, even incomprehensible design in a project aiming at a "Constitution for Europe". The Working Group on "Economic Governance" was hence complemented by an additional Working Group on "Social Europe".

"Social Europe" is once again, and without any significant changes, present in the Treaty on the Functioning of the European Union, signed at Lisbon on 13 December 2007. Hence, we can observe a remarkable continuity in the discussion on the three constitutive elements of "Social Europe". All of the three elements can be understood as resulting from long-term developments. Their validity and impact would be strengthened by an adoption of the Lisbon Treaty (LT), but would not be dependent on what is now (October 2008) a rather unlikely event.

In view of its generality and status in both the Draft Constitutional Treaty (DCT) and the Lisbon Treaty, the commitment to a "competitive social market economy" is the first element to be mentioned here. The formula owes its quasi-constitutional dignity to an initiative by the then Foreign Ministers Joschka Fischer and Dominique de Villepin in the deliberations of the European Convention. It was then understood as a political signal and has retained this status (Mayer 2008). The positive connotations of its signal certainly stem from its historical origin (Ebner 2006; Joerges and Rödl 2005; Manow 2001). The notion of the "social market economy" was coined in the early Federal Republic. It represented a social model that was distinct from Hermann Heller's "social *Rechtsstaat*", but nevertheless symbolised a "third way" between *laissez-faire* capitalism on the one hand, and socialism on the other. This third way was a quite well-defined agenda which Alfred Müller-Armack had developed in numerous publications (Müller-Armack 1956; Müller-Armack 1998). This agenda envisaged re-distributive policies through taxation and subsidies, minimum wages, welfare aid, tenant subsidies, investments in higher education, and the objective of a high rate of employment. "The social" was hence relying upon a host of competences which were not available at European level. For this simple reason, "the competitive social market economy" cannot be equated with its historical model. As a former judge of the German Constitutional Court, Ernst-Wolfgang Böckenförde (Böckenförde 1997), commented more than a decade ago: "European law cannot but realize a pure market economy because it does not have the means of establishing a social market economy". Böckenförde referred to the law as it stood in 1979, which still stands today.

The recognition of "social rights" (138 DCT; 151 LT) encounters similar problems. Here one has to differentiate. Collective rights, such as the right to strike, do not have a fixed prescriptive content, but are an empowerment to promote social objectives. As the judgment in *Viking* uniquely demonstrates, the recognition of such a collective right at European level does not imply that European law should respect its transnational exercise. With regard to this position, which is by no means in line with the opinion prevailing among European labour lawyers (Orlandini 2007), social rights which grant entitlements, have to cope with a twofold difficulty. Such rights need to be substantiated by special legislation and supported by financial means (Böckenförde 1991). This is, in many cases, a serious obstacle to their establishment at European level. This is not to suggest that social rights do not "deserve recognition". However, as, for example, Jürgen Habermas underlines (Habermas 1996), it is the political quality of social rights which requires an engagement of the various branches of the political system. At European level, the judiciary will have to assume all of these functions.

The Third Pillar of "Social Europe", namely, the new "soft law" mechanisms for the co-ordination of social and labour market policies, is the most delicate of all three. Many proponents of this mode of governance suggest that its legitimacy may result from its potentially beneficial effects. Others underline and seek to promote its procedural qualities. However, this complex debate cannot be taken up in the present context in any detail. Suffice it to note that in my own view, both defences of the "Open Method of Co-ordination" fail to take the very idea of constitutionalism, namely, the idea of law mediated, and rule-of-law bound governance sufficiently seriously (Joerges 2008).

Can "Social Europe" be established on those three Pillars? While debates on each pillar continue intensively, we observe the European Court of Justice passing a series of judgments in the light of which these debates seem purely academic. According to these judgments, the EU is committed not to a social, but to a strictly neo-liberal, market economy; the exercise of "social rights" in such an economy has to respect the economic freedoms guaranteed by the Treaty, and the soft law Method of Co-ordination needs to operate in the shadow of the hard law of negative integration. This is why we do not pursue our queries regarding the stability or fragility of the three Pillars any further here, and turn, instead, to the jurisprudence of the ECJ.

III. "Authoritarian Liberalism"[1] in the Recent Jurisprudence of the ECJ?[2]

In a series of four judgments that have been handed down since December 2007 (2007a; 2007b; 2008a; 2008b), the ECJ has dealt with the impact of European law on national labour law in a way which amounts to a re-chartering of the European Union. This characterisation may seem all too dramatic in view of the doctrinal continuity of these judgments with firmly established principles and rules. Whether there is continuity or change depends, however, upon the conceptual framework in which one observes and evaluates these judgments. There is continuity if one restricts their analysis to the invocation of the direct effect of the economic freedoms in conjunction with the supremacy doctrine, a tandem, which is widely and for good reasons understood as the core of the European charter ever since the ECJ's early judgments in *Van Gend & Loos (1963)* and *Costa* v. *ENEL (1964)*. Continuity is much less apparent when one considers the subtlety of the ECJ's delineation of economic freedoms and regulatory concerns in such numerous cases, which have established the reputation of a jurisprudence which combines its insistence on Community concerns and objectives with the acceptance of considerable political autonomy of the Member States (Scharpf 1994). Continuity seems even more questionable in the light of Europe's "unfinished agenda", namely the tensions arising from its "social deficit" and its socio-economic diversity which has deepened since 2004.

III.1. *Three Background Problems*

It is submitted here that both mechanical applications of inherited doctrines fail to resolve this threefold *problématique*. This reserve is

---

[1] The phrase in quotations if from Heller 1933.

[2] The following section draws on Ch. Joerges & F. Rödl 2009a.

not meant to indicate a generalising disrespect of these doctrines. It is instead a plea to consider their legitimate scope in the light of equally fundamental constitutional principles, in particular the principle of enumerated competences, the commitment of the EU to democratic values and their importance for the functions of the European Court.

The importance of the order of competences has been addressed implicitly in the section on the decoupling of the social from the economic constitution (Section II 1 above). The limitation of European competences in the areas of social policy and labour law cannot be interpreted as an empowerment of European institutions to subject these fields to the discipline of Community principles and to overrule conflicting national legal traditions. As Antoine Lyon-Caen has recently put it (2008:2)

> Dans les sociétés d'Europe de l'Ouest, le droit du travail s'est constitué par émancipation du droit du marché, dénommé moyennant les variations terminologiques qu'il importe de ne pas oublier : liberté du commerce ici, freedom of trade ailleurs... Ce n'est pas que des règles sur le travail n'existaient pas avant cette émancipation, mais elles relevaient d'avantage d'une police du travail, partie plus ou moins autonome d'une police du ou des marchés.[3]

The uniqueness of labour law, the social and economic constitution, is an indispensable dimension of democratic orders, a feature that Heller's social *Rechtsstaat* shares with the social market economy and the ensemble of Europe's democratic tradition.

Interventions in constitutional accomplishments of such dimensions cannot be based upon the supremacy which European law grants to economic freedoms. The very same objection militates against an invocation of these freedoms as the arbiter over distributional conflicts in the enlarged European Union. The commitment to equal living conditions is constitutional principle in federations such as Germany. The implementation of this principle is certainly far from perfect. It is also true that the means at the disposal of the Union are by no means equivalent to those of the nation states. It remains, nevertheless, problematical to interpret economic freedoms and market processes as

[3] "In West European societies labour law constituted itself as an alternative to the law of the market. It developed terminological distinctions which one must not forget: *liberté de commerce* here, freedom of trade there.... To be sure, labour had been a concern for law before that emancipation occurred, but the rules converning labour operated in the framework of a law which was meant to the market or the markets."

per se legitimate alternatives to political decisions over distributional issues.

Last, but not least, one has to consider the proper function of the ECJ in the handling of these issues. The ECJ is not a constitutional court with comprehensive competences. Is this Court authorised to re-organise the interdependence of Europe's social and economic constitutions? Is its proper task to "weigh" the values of *Sozialstaatlichkeit* against the value of free market access, of the values of political democracy against the rationality of socially disembedded economies?

These three issues can only be outlined here. It is important, however, to remain aware of this background in an evaluation of the Court's recent jurisprudence. We will restrict our analysis to the first two of the four cases mentioned. In the first, *Viking*, we will focus on the Court's interpretation of the impact of primary law whereas in the second, *Laval*, we will pay particular attention to the Courts' interpretation of secondary European law (Joerges and Rödl 2005; Joerges and Rödl 2009a and 2009b).

III.2. *Economic Liberties v. Social Rights: The Viking Case*

It seems nothing but economically sound, at least in the short run, for a Finnish shipping company (Viking) to try to replace its predominantly Finnish seafarers with cheaper labour from Estonia. It seems equally understandable for the Finnish crew to seek protection against unemployment. This provided the background to the Finnish (Seamen) Union's threats to go on strike. Viking argued, *inter alia*, that the threat of collective action by the Finnish Union was incompatible with Viking's right of free establishment as guaranteed by Article 43 EC.

The ECJ quite solemnly recognised the "right to take collective action, including the right to strike... as a fundamental right which forms an integral part of the general principles of Community law the observance of which the Court ensures [...]" (Case C-438/05, *Viking* 2007:§44). With the following argumentative step however, the Court fundamentally reconfigures the traditional balance between economic freedoms at European level and social rights at national level. This reconfiguration is hardly visible at first sight. All the Court requires is that when exercising their competence in the field of collective labour law, the Member States must comply with Community law (Case C-438/05, *Viking* 2007:§40). The delicate nature of this request stems from the fact that the Community has no competence to regulate national industrial relations. The fundamental rights concerned are not within the competence of the Community, as Article 137 (5) EC explicitly provides that "pay, the right of association, the right to strike or the right to impose lock-outs" are matters to be regulated by the Member States. The Court nevertheless feels authorised to insist upon a "proportionate" exercise of the right to strike (Case C-438/05, *Viking* 2007:§46). With this asymmetrical (diagonal) interlinking of the fundamental rights of the European economic constitution with the fundamental rights of national labour constitutions, the very autonomy of the Member States' labour and social constitutions is *de facto* eroded. This move is all the more remarkable as it also directly concerns the unions even though their threat to go on strike cannot be equated with one-sided regulations via state legislation (Case C-438/05, *Viking* 2007:§57).

The separation of powers in the field of the economic and the social spheres are not clear-cut and rigid. The ECJ accordingly underlines that under Article 3(1)(c) and (j) EC, the activities of the Community are to include not only an "internal market characterised by the abolition, as between Member States, of obstacles to the free movement of goods, persons, services and capital", but also "a policy in the social sphere", and Article 2 EC states that the Community is to have as its task, *inter alia*, the promotion of "a harmonious, balanced and sustainable development of economic activities" and "a high level of employment and of social protection".

What conclusion can be drawn from all this? In principle, the "social purpose" of national labour law would legitimise collective action that is aimed at "protecting the jobs and conditions of employment". The pre-conditions, however, are that the "jobs or conditions of employment at issue…are in fact jeopardised or under serious threat", and that any actions taken "do not go beyond what is necessary to attain that objective" (Case C-438/05, *Viking* 2007:§81,84). The Court leaves such evaluation to the national courts which have jurisdiction – in *Viking* ironically an English court – and indicates only vaguely what yardstick is available for the assessment of the "necessity" of union actions (Case C-438/05, *Viking* 2007:§81–83). The incompatibility of the Court's requirements with the very nature of collective labour law is, nevertheless, striking:

> …the Court expects trade unions to espouse stated objectives and to pursue them in a suitable and non-excessive way. Remarkably, the Court

> even suggested that 'less restrictive' means need to be exhausted first. This is an incredible expectation, for it seeks to submit collective acts that are part of a struggle to a normative precept that has been developed for a context where those wielding sovereign rights are supposed to attain objectives in an unruffled and instrumentally fine-tuned way. Trade union action needs to be far cruder than bureaucratic rationality. In fact, necessarily it has to be excessive in order to attain its objective. It may well need to threaten to bring bankruptcy on an undertaking. Confronting trade union action with proportionality requirements makes it destined, from the outset, to lose out against business interests (Somek forthcoming 2009).

III.3. *Secondary Law in New Territories: The Laval Case*

The conflict constellation in the *Laval* case (Case C-341/05, Laval 2007) again related to the wage differences in Old and New Europe. Laval, a company incorporated under Latvian law, whose registered office is in Riga, had won the tender for a school building on the outskirts of Stockholm. In obtaining the tender, it took advantage of its ability to post workers with considerably lower wages from Latvia to Sweden. In May 2004, when work was to commence, and after Laval had posted several dozens of its workers to work on the Swedish building sites, the Swedish trade unions resorted to hostile actions against *Laval* with determination and intensity. Particularly effective was the blockade of the building sites, causing Laval to cede.

In the Court's judgment, secondary law, namely, that of Directive 96/71/EC concerning the posting of workers within the framework of the provision of services, is of decisive importance. According to Recital 22 of this Directive, the Community legislator did not aim at a harmonisation of the substantial-legal provisions concerning the employment of posted workers. The Member States were, instead, asked to ensure that the working conditions of those workers posted to their territory were, in a number of essential working conditions (Article 3 (1)) in compliance with their own legal provisions and minimum wage requirements (Rödl 2008).

Sweden adopted the Posted Workers Directive in 1999. Its implementing legislation included some legally prescribed minimum working conditions, in particular working hours, but failed to provide for a specific level in relation to minimum wages or any system which ensured universal applicability. "Universal applicability" is, however, required by Article 3 (1) of the Directive. Sweden intended, instead, to make use of the special ruling in Article 3 (8) (2) of the Directive, which accepts, as an alternative, wage standards which are *de facto* generally binding. Moreover, Sweden left the determination of these minimum standards to employers and employees, and there were no requirements for authoritative approval, *i.e.*, it empowered its unions to defend the wage levels for which they had bargained.

The ECJ, however, declared all the activities of the Swedish unions which aimed at this objective to be illegal. According to its interpretation, the objective of the Directive was not merely the restriction of wage cost competition, but the determination of the legality of collective actions. The Court found that the Directive prohibited all union activities beyond those essential to working conditions enumerated in Article 3 (1), that it prohibited, in particular, union activities for essential working conditions that are better than those already legally provided for (Case C-341/05, *Laval* 2007:§99), as well as union activities for all wages with the exception of the lowest wage group (Case C-341/05, Laval 2007:§70).

We are faced again with an extremely extensive interpretation of the impact of European law. Directive 96/71, which was adopted after lengthy discussions and bargaining processes, is only concerned with a conflict situation within the Internal Market. In the Court's daring interpretation, this Directive is transformed into a cornerstone of a European labour and social constitution, which outlaws important elements of the Swedish social model (Case C-341/05, *Laval* 2007:§10,92). The Court is, again, going a step too far.

Concluding Remarks

The Court's recent jurisprudence has met with harsh critique from many quarters all over Europe, in particular, the Union movement. "The only way is not to follow the Court", to exercise principled disobedience, was the answer of Fritz Scharpf, Germany's most respected political scientist, in an interview with a union periodical (Scharpf 2008). This type of critique indicates that the ECJ risks being perceived as a partisan body. Critics such as Fritz Scharpf are certainly aware of the constraint under which the Court operates. After the failure of the Draft Constitutional Treaty, at the time of its judgments still prevailing, the uncertainty about the future of the Lisbon Treaty, the Court could be perceived the one and only institution which could keep the integration project alive. This, however, is a delicate task. There is, in view of the indeterminacies of European law, considerable room for judicial manoeuvre. A more moderate and restrained interpretation suggesting procedural, rather than substantive, answers to politically highly-sensitive conflicts would be conceivable. Such a restraint seems all the more appropriate, since even the parties to these proceedings from Eastern Europe, who were all insisting on economic freedoms, should not be so sure that the dismantling of Western welfarism is in their own long-term interests.

Post scriptum

The debate of Europe's post-national constellation, has much in common with the re-building of a ship on the open sea. Our target is moving ahead and does not await the outcome of our discussions. The latest move was undertaken by the German Constitutional Court in its judgment of 30 June 2009 on the compatibility of the Act approving the Treaty of Lisbon with Germany's Basic Law. In this review, the *soziale Rechtsstaat* figures as prominently as it does in the present essay:

> The citizens' right to determine, in equality and freedom, public authority affecting them with regard to persons and subject-matters through elections and other votes is anchored in human dignity and is the fundamental element of the principle of democracy. The principle of democracy is not amenable to weighing with other legal interests. Amendments of the Basic Law affecting the principles laid down in Article 1 and Article 20 of the Basic Law shall be inadmissible (Article 79.3 of the Basic Law)...European unification on the basis of a union of sovereign states under the Treaties may, however, not be realised in such a way that the Member States do not retain sufficient room for the political formation of the economic, cultural and social circumstances of life.

The reader of such strong words may expect drastic action. Such expectations are strengthened by the passages on the authority of national courts:

> The Basic Law does not grant the German state bodies powers to transfer sovereign powers in such a way that their exercise can independently establish other competences for the European Union. It prohibits the transfer of competence to decide on its own competence (*Kompetenz-Kompetenz*)....
>
> The Federal Constitutional Court reviews whether legal instruments of the European institutions and bodies, adhering to the principle of subsidiarity under Community and Union law (Article 5.2 ECT; Article 5.1

> sentence 2 and 5.3 TEU Lisbon), keep within the boundaries of the sovereign powers accorded to them by way of conferred power (*ultra vires* review). Furthermore, the Federal Constitutional Court reviews whether the inviolable core content of the constitutional identity of the Basic Law pursuant to Article 23.1 sentence 3 in conjunction with Article 79.3 of the Basic Law is respected (identity review). The exercise of these competences of review, which are constitutionally required, safeguards the fundamental political and constitutional structures of sovereign Member States, which are recognised by Article 4.2 sentence 1 TEU Lisbon, even with progressing integration. Its application in a given case follows the principle of the Basic Law's openness towards European Law.

Strong language, indeed, but, alas, weak implications. The recent jurisprudence of the ECJ has met with harsh critique, so the *Bundesverfassungsericht* notes in para. 398 of its judgment, and then observes in the same sentence that there are also elements in the ECJ's jurisprudence which have strengthened the social dimension of the European project. This statement seems to mirror the German Court's dilemma. It is unlikely move the European project ahead. The next hurdle to be taken is the complaint against the infamous Mangold decision of the ECJ (2005), now pending before the *Bundesverfassungsgericht* – and heavily attacked by the former President of the Court, Roman Herzog (2009).

References

Cases & Official Documents

1954. "BVerfGE 4, 7, Investitionshilfe." Bundesverfassungsgericht.

1963. "Case 26/62, Van Gend en Loos." European Court of Justice.

1964. "Case 6/64, Costa v. ENEL." European Court of Justice.

2005. "Case C-144/04, Mangold v. Helm." European Court of Justice.

1985. "Commission White Paper to the European Council on Completion of the Internal Market". COM(85) 310 final: EC Commission.

2007a. "Case C-341/05, Laval un Partneri Ltd v. Svenska Byggnadsarbetareförbundet, Svenska Byggnadsarbetareförbundet, avd.1, Svenska Elektrikerförbundet." European Court of Justice.

2007b. "Case C-438/05, International Transport Workers' Federation, Finnish Seamen's Union v. Viking Line ABP, OÜ Viking Line Eesti." *11 December 2007*: European Court of Justice.

2008a. "Case C-319/06, Commission v. Luxembourg." European Court of Justice.

2008b. "Case C-346/06, Rechtsanwalt Dr. Dirk Rüffert v. Land Niedersachsen." European Court of Justice.

2009. Bundesverfassungsgericht, judgment of 30 June, Case 2 be 2/08, 2BvR 1010/08, 2 BvR 1259/08 and 2 BvR 182/09, availlable at www.Bundesverfassungsgericht.de.

Bibliography

Abendroth, Wolfgang. 1954. "Zum Begriff des demokratischen und sozialen Rechtsstaates im Grundgesetz der Bundesrepublik Deutschland." Pp. 279 et seq. in *Festschrift Ludwig Bergsträsser*, edited by A. Herrmann. Düsseldorf: Droste.

Bercusson, Brian. 1995. "The Collective Labour Law of the European Union." *European Law Journal* 1:157–179.

——, Simon Deakin, Pertti Koistinen, Yota Kravaritou, Ulrich Mückenberger, Alain Supiot, and Bruno Veneziani. 1997. "A Manifesto for Social Europe." *European Law Journal* 3:189–205.

Böckenförde, Ernst-Wolfgang. 1991. "Die sozialen Grundrechte im Verfassungsgefüge." Pp. 146–158 in *Staat, Verfassung, Demokratie. Studien zur verfassungstheorie und zum Verfassungsrecht*. Frankfurt a.M.: Suhrkamp.

——. 1997. *Welchen Weg geht Europa?* München: Carl-Friedrich-von-Siemens-Stiftung.

Caldwell, Peter C. 2000. "Is a 'Social Rechtsstaat' Possible? The Weimar Roots of a Bonn Controversy." Pp. 136–153 in *From Liberal Democracy to Fascism: Legal and Political Thought in the Weimar Republic*, edited by P. C. Caldwell and W. E. Scheuerman. Boston-Leiden-Cologne: Humanities Press.

Dyzenhaus, David. 1997. Legality and Legitimacy: Carl Schmitt, Hans Kelsen and Herrmann Heller in Weimar. Oxford: Oxford University Press.

Ebner, Alexander. 2006. "The Intellectual Foundations of the Social market Economy. Theory, Policy and Implications for European Integration." *Journal of Economic Studies* 33:206–223.

Eucken, Walter. 1952. *Grundzüge der Wirtschaftspolitik*. Tübingen: Mohr/Siebeck.

Fischer-Lescano, Andreas and Oliver Eberl. 2006. "Der Kampf um ein soziales und demokratisches Recht. Zum 100. Geburtstag von Wolfgang Abendroth." *Blätter für deutsche und internationale Politik* 51:577–585.

Forsthoff, Ernst. 1954a. "Begriff und Wesen des sozialen Rechtstaates." *Veröffentlichungen der Vereinigung der Deutschen Staatsrechtslehrer* 12:8–35.

Habermas, Jürgen. 1979. *Legitimation Crisis*. Boston: Beacon Press.

——. 1989. "Towards a Reconstruction of Historical Materialism." Pp. 114–141 in *Jürgen Habermas on Society and Politics*, edited by S. Seidman. Boston: Beacon Press.

——. 1996. *Between Facts and Norms*. Cambridge, MA: MIT Press.

——. 2001. "Constitutional Democracy: A Paradoxical Union of Contradictory Principles?", in *Political Theory* 29:766–781.

Harvey, Colin. 2004 "Special Issue on Social Democracy." in *Canadian Journal of Law and Jurisprudence* 17:1.

Hayek, Friedrich A. von. 1944. *The Road to Serfdom*. London: Routledge.

Heller, Hermann. 1933. "Autoritärer Liberalismus." *Die Neue Rundschau* 44:289 et seq.

Herzog, Roman and Lüder Gerken. 2009. "Stoppt den EuGH" (Stop the ECJ). *Frankfurter Allgmeine Zeitung* of 8 September.

Joerges, Christian. 1994. "Economic Law, the Nation-State and the Maastricht Treaty." Pp. 29–62 in *Europe after Maastricht: an Ever Closer Union?*, edited by R. Dehousse. Munich: C. H. Beck.

——. 2005. "What is left of the European Economic Constitution? A Melancholic Eulogy." *European Law Review* 30:461–489.

——. 2008. "Integration through de-legislation?" *European Law Review* 30:291–312.

——. 2009. "Europäische Konstitutionalisierung"; "Europäische Staatsbürgerschaft" in *Habermas-Handbuch - Leben - Werk - Wirkung*, edited by H. Brunkhorst, R. Kreide and C. Lafont, Stuttgart: J. B. Metzler 2009. 94–99, 312–315.

—— and Florian Rödl. 2005. "The 'Social Market Economy' as Europe's Social Model?" Pp. 125–158 in *A European Social Citizenship? Preconditions for Future Policies in Historical Light*, edited by L. Magnusson and B. Stråth. Brussels: Lang.

——. 2009a. "Informal Politics, Formalised Law and the 'Social Deficit' of European Integration: Reflections after the Judgments of the ECJ in Viking and Laval." *European Law Journal* 15:1–19.

——. 2009b. "Zum Funktionswandel des Kollisionsrechts II. Die kollisionsrechtliche Form einer legitimen Verfassung der post-nationalen Konstellation." in *"Soziologische Jurisprudenz". Festschrift für Gunther Teubner*, edited by G.-P. Calliess, A. Fischer-Lescano, D. Wielsch and P. Zumbansen. Berlin: Walter de Gruyter, 765–778.

Judt, Tony. 2005. Postwar. A History of Europe Since 1945. New York: Penguin.

Kennedy, Duncan. 2004. "The Disenchantment of Logically Formal Legal Rationality, or Max Weber's Sociology in the Genealogy of the Contemporary Mode of Western Legal Thought." *Hastings Law Journal* 55:1031 et seq.

Leibfried, Stephan and Michael Zürn. 2005. "Reconfiguring the National Constellation." Pp. 93–117 in *Transformation of the State*, edited by S. Leibfried and M. Zürn. Cambridge: Cambridge University Press.

Luhmann, Niklas. 1968. *Zweckbegriff und Systenrationalität.* Frankfurt a.M.: Suhrkamp.

——. 1972. *Rechtssoziologie*, vol. II. Reinbek Rowohlt.

Lyon-Caen, Antoine. 2008. "Droit communautaire du marché v.s. Europe sociale." in *Contribution to the Symposium on "The Impact of the Case Law of the ECJ upon the Labour law of the member States"* Berlin 26 June 2008 organised by the Federal Ministry of Labour and Social Affairs.

Manow, Philip. 2001. "Modell Deutschland as an Interdenominational Compromise." Minda De Gunzburg Centre for European Studies, Working Paper 003/2001.

Maus, Ingeborg. 1984. "Hermann Heller und die Staatsrechtslehre der Bundesrepublik." Pp. 196–220 in *Staatslehre in der Weimarer Republik. Hermann Heller zu Ehren*, edited by C. Müller and I. Staff. Frankfurt a. M.: Suhrkamp.

Mayer, Franz C. 2008. "Die Rückkehr der Europäischen Verfassung? Ein Leitfaden zum Vertrag von Lissabon." *Zeitschrift für öffentliches Recht und Völkerrecht*: 1141–1217.

Milward, Alan. 1999. *The European Rescue of the Nation-State.* London-New York: Routledge.

Müller-Armack, Alfred. 1956. "Soziale Marktwirtschaft." Pp. 390–392 in *Handwörterbuch der Sozialwissenschaften Bd IX*, edited by E. v. Beckerath, H. Bente, and C. Brinkmann. Stuttgart-Tübingen-Göttingen: Vandenhoeck & Ruprecht.

——. 1998. "The Principles of the Social Market Economy." *The German Economic Review* 3:89–104.

Nörr, Knut W. 2007. Die Republik der Wirtschaft: Recht, Wirtschaft und Staat in der Geschichte Westdeutschlands. (Teil II: Von der sozial-liberalen Koalition bis zur Wiedervereinigung). Tübingen: Mohr/Siebeck.

Orlandini, Giovanni. 2007. "Right to Strike, Transnational Collective Action and European Law: Time to Move On?" New York University School of law, Jean Monnet Working paper Series 08/07.

Rödl, Florian. 2008. "Weltbürgerliches Kollisionsrecht." Ph.D. Thesis EUI Florence.

Ruggie, John. 1982. "International Regimes, Transactions, and Change: Embedded Liberalism in the Postwar Economic Order." *International Organization* 36: 379–415.

Sabel, Charles and Jonathan Zeitlin. 2008. "Learning from Difference: The New Architecture of Experimentalist Governance in the European Union." *European Law Journal* 14:271–327.

Scharpf, Fritz W. 1994. "Community and Autonomy. Multilevel Policy-making in the European Union." *Journal of European Public Policy* 1/2:219–242.

——. 2002. "The European Social Model: Coping with the Challenges of Diversity." *Journal of Common Market Studies* 40: 645–670.
——. 2008. "The only solution is to refuse to comply with ECJ rulings." *Social Europe* 4:16–21.
Schluchter, Wolfgang. 1983. Entscheidung für den sozialen Rechtsstaat: Herrmann Heller und die staatstheoretische Diskussion in der Weimarer Republik Baden-Baden: Nomos.
Somek, Alexander. forthcoming 2009. "Idealisation, De-politicization and Economic Due Process: System Transition in the European Union." in *The Law/Politics Distinction in Contemporary Public Law Adjudication*, edited by B. Iancu. Utrecht: Eleven Publishing.
Stolleis, Michael. 1999. Geschichte des öffentlichen Rechts in Deutschland. Band 3: Staats- und Verwaltungsrechtswissenschaft in Republik und Diktatur 1914–1945. München: C. H. Beck.
Streit, Manfred. 1998. "Soziale Marktwirtschaft im europäischen Integrationsprozeß: Befund und Perspektiven." Pp. 177–198 in *50 Jahre Soziale Marktwirtschaft.*, edited by B. Cassel. Stuttgart: Lucius & Lucius.
—— and Werner Mussler. 1995. "The Economic Constitution of the European Community. From 'Rome' to 'Maastricht'." *European Law Journal* 1:5–30.
Teubner, Gunther. 1983. "Substantive and Reflexive Elements in Modern Law." *Law and Society Review* 17:239–285.
Vauchez, Antoine. 2008. "'Integration-through-Law'. Contribution to a Socio-history of EU Political Common sense." *EUI Working Paper* RSCAS 2008/10.
Weber, Max. 1978. *Economy and Society*. Berkeley University of California Press.
——. 1994. *Political Writings*. Cambridge: Cambridge University Press.
Wegmann, Milene. 2002. Früher Neoliberalismus und europäische Integration: Interdependenz der nationalen, supranationalen und internationalen Ordnung von Wirtschaft und Gesellschaft (1932–1965). Baden-Baden: Nomos.
Weiler, Joseph H. H. 1981. "The Community System: the Dual Character of Supranationalism." *Yearbook of European Law* 1:257–306.
——. 1991. "Transformation of Europe." *Yale Law Journal* 100:2 et seq.
——. 1999. The Constitution of Europe: "Do the New Clothes Have an Emperor?" and other Essays on European Integration. Cambridge: Cambridge University Press.
Wiethölter, Rudolf. 1982. "Entwicklung des Rechtsbegriffs (am Beispiel des BVG-Urteils zum Mitbestimmungsgesetz und - allgemeiner - an Beispielen des sog. Sonderprivatrechts)." Pp. 38–59 in *Rechtsformen der Verflechtung von Staat und Wirtschaft*, edited by V. Gessner and G. Winter. Opladen: Westdeutscher Verlag.
——. 1989. "Proceduralisation of the Category of Law." Pp. 501–510 in *Critical Legal Thought: An American-German Debate*, edited by Ch. Joerges and D. M. Trubek. Baden-Baden: Nomos.

PART THREE

THE INTERNATIONAL SPHERE

CHAPTER SEVEN

HOW (IL)LIBERAL IS THE LIBERAL THEORY OF LAW? SOME CRITICAL REMARKS ON SLAUGHTER'S APPROACH

Friedrich Kratochwil

As of late, the intersection of international law and international politics has become a major focal point for theoretical discussions (Abbott, Keohane, Moravcsik, Slaughter, and Snidal 2000; Goldsmith and Posner 2006). The reasons for this are not difficult to fathom. In view of the transformative changes brought about by globalization, both disciplines seem to be in a kind of a disciplinary crisis. Their respective traditional lexicons are rather deficient in coping with the transformative changes we are witnessing.

In the case of international politics we see this for example, first, in discussions about the role of new non-state actors that seem to undermine the exclusive representative character of the state. We also witness it, second, in the failure of many of the traditional multilateral regimes intended to take care of the externalities brought on by the ever-increasing interdependencies (Newman, Thakur, and Tirman 2006) and most recently by the global reverberations of the financial crisis. It is also evident, third, in the emergence of new security "threats" that range from terrorism and "asymmetric" conflicts to migration.

In international law we notice similar developments. Perhaps the most obvious is the change from a traditional preoccupation with "sources" and black letter law to "processes" (see e.g. Koh 1996; O'Connell 1999). This shift focuses the attention to transnational networks (Keck and Sikkink 1999; Slaughter 1997, 2004) of both governmental and non-governmental bodies and their occasional symbiotic relationships in solving particular problems. Here one thinks of the cooperation of the "disaggregated state" (namely the vast cooperative efforts of state agencies across boundaries), the emergence of "private authority" (Hall and Biersteker 2002), and the delivery of aid programs through NGO's.

An equally important shift has occurred with the demise of exclusive "sovereignty," which however has always provided a quite problematic interpretation of international reality. This reorientation turned attention from the state and its nation or people as the main source of legitimacy to "human dignity," which leads to proliferating catalogues of subjective rights (Kratochwil forthcoming).

Given these puzzling developments, re-visiting the boundary between "inside" and "outside," and examining the way in which present political practice draws these boundaries by means of law and institutional arrangements is doubly justified. For one, when the existing roadmaps seem woefully out of place with ongoing practices, revisions are unavoidable if the maps are to provide orientation instead of degenerating into some ossified remnants of the past.

Second, examining these new efforts at drawing boundaries has deep implications for our disciplinary understandings. Of course, we do not have to buy into the argument that now "functional differentiation" has displaced for good all other means of drawing boundaries, such as territoriality or membership, as Luhmann (1983) seems to suggest. He thereby dissolves both the "state" as the "ontological primitive" of political science as well as the supremacy of "constitutional law" that gives coherence to legal ordering. Curiously enough, these topics re-emerge, however, in the attempts to bring "the state back in" – especially after the disasters of large-scale deregulation of the global financial system – and in the "fragmentation" and constitutionalization debates in international law (Dupuy 1997; Fassbender 2005; International Law Commission and Koskenniemi 2006; Petersmann 2002).

To that extent we should not dismiss these conceptual issues too hastily by attributing them to an agenda long overtaken by events. In addition, it becomes clear that assessing these changes will be fruitful only from an interdisciplinary vantage point. Such a perspective, however, must not simply substitute detailed analysis for some overall scheme of social development – which draws its persuasive force from a simple periodization scheme of a "before" and "after", so familiar from speculations about "progress."

Interdisciplinarity, however, has its own pitfalls. After all, if our knowledge is dependent upon disciplinary boundaries both in terms of the methods used and of the questions that "make sense" – most clearly evidenced by the "just price" question which is a red herring to economists. Consequently, the transgression of these boundaries is problematic. If one erases "Consequently" prima facie, such a step does not guarantee new insights that can be integrated easily into existing frameworks. Therefore, it is not surprising that interdisciplinary work suffers frequently from the "Chinese menu approach," most clearly seen in "studies" programs at various universities. Students are to take courses in different fields, often with little concern about how the whole program is supposed to fit together.

An equally problematic approach is a "colonization" strategy. Here, one discipline offers its approach or method as a universal tool for generating knowledge. It assumes that "one size fits all," thereby downplaying the constitutive importance of disciplinary boundaries. It also maintains that actual "progress" can be made by simply applying the toolkit to a different field that until now had been afraid to ask the "right" questions – never mind that thereby some central puzzles of a field might be passed over as "non-problems."

Finally, there is a third way in which interdisciplinary work can be done. It is, however, the most difficult to pursue as it presupposes familiarity with the respective disciplines and an ability to "translate" the respective insights. It also requires an ability to examine critically the blind spots of each discipline by looking at them from the perspective(s) of the other(s).

This is where Anne-Marie Slaughter has done important work over the years (Slaughter 1993, 1995, 2000; Slaughter and Burke-White 2002). Having been trained in both international relations and in international law, she has contributed to the interdisciplinary dialogue by focusing on the implications of transnational phenomena and on anti-formalist tendencies in international law and by calling attention to global networks. In addition, Slaughter has been active in formulating a "liberal approach" to world order that draws upon the work of Andrew Moravcsik (1997) (also her husband), on the problem-solving approaches to law as pioneered by Chayes, Ehrlich, and Lowefeld (1968), on the bourgeoning field of transnational law, and on the institutional analysis that followed in IR the regime debate.

With an uncanny eye for changing practices in international life, Slaughter has been a forceful critic of simpleminded schemes purportedly explaining politics, as in the case of structural realism. Further, she has had a healthy dose of skepticism towards all attempts of conceptualizing "law" as a pure system of norms, by abstracting from both context and actual practice.

Together, Moravcsik and Slaughter have pioneered an approach to liberal politics and the rule of law that is well-articulated and able to draw upon interdisciplinary insights in developing a research program of considerable interest. Not only does it systematically integrate the social dynamics of groups in selecting policies, instead of leaving this task to structures or to autonomous governments, it also embeds "law" at the center of society.

To a large extent the merits of this type of analysis for law, and for international law in particular, are obvious, and most of Slaughter's arguments are persuasive. Her analysis is not limited to the "inter" (Kratochwil 2007b) or to the "in-between", where traditionally only an act of "will" could create an island of order in an otherwise "anarchical society." Rather, Slaughter's approach recognizes that law provides a nearly seamless web by specifying enabling and regulative conditions for social interaction and conflict resolution ranging from "domestic" constitutional and administrative law (Kingsbury, Krisch, and Stewart 2005; Krisch 2006) to international law, transnational law, and, as of late, to human rights law (Fredman 2008; Haas 2008; Tomuschat 2008). It seems that this is by all means a major achievement, since it meshes the legal and political projects of liberalism. That is, it demonstrates that autonomy, choice, and consent of the governed are interdependent with the rule of law in general (Palombella and Walker 2009).

Before I am charged with being part of a mutual admiration society, I want to interject some critical remarks which articulate points of uneasiness with some general aspects of the "liberal approach." Here Slaughter's work serves as my foil. To that extent, I want to draw out some implications of the liberal approach rather than focus my criticism merely on particular pieces of Slaughter's academic writing.

I shall make three interconnected points. The first and theoretically most salient is the technocratic bias that underlines much of Slaughter's "liberal" analysis. Despite her anti-formalist bent, I claim that her espoused approach leads to a new form of legalism disguised as "professionalism" (Kennedy 2003). The latter might be unable to sustain the weight placed upon it even though it appears to be only a logical outcome of the "rule of law" principle it purports to instantiate.

My other two points are elaborations on this theme that flesh out the implications of this objection for both politics and law. I claim that attempts to make "best practices" and "professional standards" uncontroversial by embedding them in some universalist rhetoric reduces the problem of practice to one of technique. It is also likely to engage in an "imperial" political project that mistakes in a "Right-Hegelian" fashion the existing (with which one is familiar) with the universal (which commands assent because of its "real" status).

In order to elaborate on these points, I take up the issue of the technocratic bias in the next section and show its implications for law and politics. In the section after that, I examine the problem of "universality" and the potential of these claims for imperial political projects.

The Citizen as "Client"

Anyone familiar with Slaughter's work notices that unlike traditional theories of law her approach is largely pragmatic and focuses on dispute resolution. She does not explicitly examine the sociological embeddedness of the project of law that links it to larger projects in the production of meaning (a problem of constitutional law), to epistemological issues, such as norms in general (pure theory of law), or even to some philosophical questions (law as the *ars boni at aequi* as in the older jurisprudential literature).

In her writings she rather moves in a world of "practitioners," in which adjudication, dispute settlement, and "administration of justice" take center stage. This conceptual move comes at a price. Since a focus on courts is already somewhat restrictive – given the important symbolic functions of law as a carrier of meaning and as a constituent of social life – the emphasis on the administration of justice narrows the focus even further to the managerial aspects of law in and around courts, clients, and disputes. Now, emphasis is placed on questions of efficiency and effectiveness rather than of validity, and on problems of the "how to" of litigation rather than on the "what."

In this context, one could object that such choices are inevitable and that by necessity certain themes have to stay in the background. After all, neither in economics nor in law is the assigning of original property rights directly addressed since both disciplines conventionally start only after this question has been settled. Nevertheless, as recent discussions about intellectual property rights,[1] about the knowledge commons, and about the resource management of common access property regimes (Hess and Ostrom 2007) demonstrate, leaving these issues unattended, because normal litigation and statutory law seem

[1] See for example the 2003 special issue of "Law and Contemporary Problems" and particularly Boyle 2003.

to answer these issues, might be problematic. Not only might such a stance lead to entirely mistaken legal solutions for the identified problems, as Hardin's (1968) famous "tragedy of the commons" suggested upon which advocates of "privatization" based their arguments (for criticism, see e.g. Ostrom, Gardner, and Walker 1994). It might also fail to alert us to the fact that property regimes and the law's effectiveness are ultimately not neatly separable from notions of justice and fairness that prevail in a society.

In short, when we limit ourselves to the "administration of justice," we move in the spheres of modern "professionals" and of "lawyering" instead of being concerned with traditional notions, such as sovereignty, immunity, sources, domestic jurisdiction, and their conceptual elaborations that have dominated international law treatises until recently.

This emphasis on "professionalism" might calm the often highly charged atmosphere of international legal arguments by making analyses more down to earth. It might also facilitate the resolution of certain puzzling conceptual impasses by looking at the solutions of the brethren of the bench all over the world. Thus, law seems to become increasingly a seamless web through the accrual of judicial decisions from various jurisdictions. These decisions are recognized by domestic courts despite originating from institutions that are not part of the court's own hierarchy. This means that law is no longer seen as a result of the quasi-legislative activities of international organizations or, perhaps even more importantly, of multilateral treaties by states, or even of the activities of international courts – as the emergence of "world law" has often been imagined (Grenville and Sohn 1966).

In a way, this sort of approach is not entirely novel, but it does mix and reassemble the previous theories in an entirely new fashion so that a new *Gestalt* emerges. A reader familiar with the literature in international law will recognize in Slaughter's "community of courts" reminiscences of Scelle's famous argument of the "*dedoublement fonctionelle*" of courts as both domestic institutions and institutions of the international legal order (Scelle 1932–1934). Slaughter's pragmatic emphasis and de-emphasis of formalism are also characteristic of functionalism. Yet, contrary to the latter, neither the optima of engineering or linear programming nor a purely technical logic can prevail in law. Rather, the "functionalists" (or perhaps better "neo-functionalists") are now judges and administrative lawyers who have to make defensible value choices, not simply find more efficient solutions to technical problems. Finally, an emphasis on process and on the various authoritative statements reopens the discussion about "sources" of law (for a fundamental discussion, see Kennedy 1986). That is, it encompasses a more extensive treatment than the traditional canon admits both domestically and internationally.

The focus on adjudication carried out by domestic courts is a result of the dis-aggregation of the state which Slaughter (2004) herself has described so aptly. It is also a consequence of the growth of administrative law that has already given rise to speculations concerning a world administrative law being in the making (Kingsbury, Krisch, and Stewart 2005). Finally, we should also remember the increasing importance of individuals as new "subjects" who claim rights on the basis of new international legal instruments.

For a "liberal" theory it is then in a way rather surprising that all politics seems to have disappeared, at least at first sight. Thus, "politics," conceived as the agreement among free members of a society, has been overshadowed, if not replaced, by a form of third-party authoritative decision-making "bound" by law. In other words, we see a notion of law that is closer to Judaic and Muslim traditions than to Greek or republican notions of politics.

In the democratic discourse, this very problem is addressed in the constitutional separation of legislative and adjudicative functions. It might thus be that the focus on adjudication can explain the above noted silence on the consent of the governed. After all, the writings of Slaughter and other liberals are full of appeals for establishing democratic institutions throughout the world. Similarly, the call for a new "Concert of Democracies" (Slaughter and Ikenberry 2006) (which is apparently entrusted with awarding an ISO-like seal of approval) could be interpreted in this way. Be that as it may.

On second thought it seems, however, that the initial silence might hide a wider problem inherent in this version of liberal theory. For one and most obviously, here we are dealing with an "instrumentalization" of law, which is a problem in many process-oriented approaches, as McDougal so aptly demonstrated (see for example the self-serving argument in McDougal 1955). As in the case of the former New Haven school (out of its voluminous writings, see especially McDougal and Laswell 1966), international law is no longer mainly an instrument of mediating between various social orders and their different political projects. Rather, quite contrary to the liberal notion of the primacy of the "right" over the "good", international law has become an element in the political project to establish *a particular political order*: a Western style (liberal) democracy.

Second, such a gambit is not surprising since similar allegedly "depoliticizing" strategies are familiar from domestic law. Here, controversial political choices that are unable to muster majority support are often phrased as an issue of "subjective rights" and thereby taken out of the political process in order to be decided by a court. But despite the judicial trappings and the semblance of a non-political, impartial, and objective "decision" which underlies all such moves toward judicialization and constitutionalization, we all know that here we deal with a different form of politics (see the critical analysis in Klabbers 2004; also Michelman 2003). As constitutional lawyers have pointed out, hopes to depoliticize issues through their subsumption under an abstract norm or principle cannot deliver on their promises. The expectation of arriving via formal principles at substantively "correct" solutions is unjustified, even if such a belief might have a pacifying function when it is wide-spread.

Whatever merits this latter argument might have, it is clear that the "politics" that emerges from such strategies is no longer one in which individual citizens argue for a solution to a common problem, and in which they commit themselves freely to abide by the decision when it has been made. Rather, it is one in which the individual as a "client" needs a professional advocate to plead his case before some authorities. S/he has become voiceless and lacks the power of initiative since practically nothing can be done without the help of an "expert."

This means that the political project of the "rule of law" (for a fundamental discussion, see Pocock 1957), as exemplified by the Glorious Revolution where the parliament resisted Stewarts' centralization efforts by insisting on "consent," has now transformed itself. It has become a curious mixture of clientilistic politics and international mobilization through advocacy networks. After having encountered the sophisticated plaintiff of yesteryear, who, on the advice of his lawyer, had learned that "forum shopping" might provide considerable advantages, we now meet also the judge who is increasingly looking for (and thereby picking and choosing) decisions of foreign courts which could support her decision in the case at hand.

We need not decide here whether such trends, observable in all democratic countries, are "progressive," or whether in international politics the existence of "advocacy" networks has become an important force. The point I want to raise is simply that there seem to be significant negative "externalities" for a democracy to such a narrow concept of the rule of law. A "liberal" theory of law in particular ought to pay a bit more attention to these, domestically as well as internationally.

The Bane of Best Practices

The cautionary remarks above become ever more relevant when we consider that allegedly "best" and universally applicable practices amount virtually to a capillary control of a society in the name of stabilizing "democracy" (on the difficulties, see Carothers 2006). While formerly the exercise of governmental powers was supposed to be controlled by representative institutions, such as parliament, and by a vibrant civil society that understood itself as an autonomous sphere, now the politics of "tutelage" penetrates all social structures. The "people" as the source of legitimacy for politics has degenerated into a "population" which is subjected to the management of "risks" by "professionals," be it through measures of enhancing "transparency" or through getting the "incentives" right. Foucault provided us with a description of this kind of "dystopia" in the form of a new mode of "governmentality" he calls "bio-politics" (Dillon and Lobo-Guerrero 2008).

Not only are best practices touted as "solutions" to our problems, ranging from book-keeping to peace-keeping, they are also connected to life-styles and regimes for "healthy" living. Thus, joggers and slim people might get better insurance rates but, as it was proposed *mirabile dictu* in Great Britain, overweight persons are supposed to be barred from adoption since they represent a too high "risk." From this, there is only a small step to the near-fascist disciplining of smokers going far beyond any reasonable guarantee of a smoke-free environment.

In general, the aim seems more the stigmatization of a certain group than finding a solution to a problem. Forcing people in an open railway station to go to a narrow place marked in yellow(!) or to descend at the work place (for example, at BMW headquarters) to be on display in a small glass cage that, besides being uncomfortable, lacks both seats and proper ventilation (probably in order to ensure that a sufficient dose of secondary smoke is guaranteed at all times) is hardly conducive to public health.

One might be inclined to make light of these derailments and treat them as regrettable missteps of American and European bureaucracies, and I certainly do not want to imply or intimate that Slaughter would excuse or look favorably upon such excesses. Nevertheless, dealing with them as exceptions misses the point. They are a (predictable) outcome of a politics of control that is fundamentally suspicious of personal responsibility and autonomy and of solving problems politically.

This politics of control substitutes the "coercive" dimension of law – "enforcing" public order only in cases of clear break-downs – with a "disciplinary" but more insidious measure of constant, general control. Thus, there seems to be only a small step to a perverse change of the classical presumption of social order based on the rule of law: now "nothing is innocent until proven otherwise." That there might be indeed a much closer elective affinity between liberalism and control – an affinity also antedating the present "terrorism" anxieties and the visceral responses it engenders – can be gathered from Bentham's fascination with the "Panopticon" as a means of social control.

It is one of the bitter ironies that with the demise of the Soviet empire and its obsessions with planning and control, "working by the rulebook" seems to enjoy increasing popularity in the West. It is doubly ironic that much of this obsession with control is the legacy of a British conservative prime minister, who had caught the liberal bug and became a staunch advocate of "liberalization" not only of the market but also of other social areas, such as the educational system. Strangely enough (or, on second thought, not strange at all), it did not lead to greater freedom or to a demise of the "state," but only to shifts in regulatory policy, since the new "freedoms" had to be enforced. The old bureaucracies were quick to catch on and propagated a new "public management" ideology, issuing orders after orders – no longer in the name of public welfare or the common good – but in order to ensure greater "efficiency."

The lessons of the Soviet failure were soon all but forgotten, in particular the lesson that innovation and new developments can flourish only if there exists diversity rather than uniformity of organizational forms (requisite variety). This criterion contradicts clearly the idea of one "best" solution. Another lesson is that the downfall of the Soviet empire was certainly not due to a lack of surveillance, statistics, and control. Instead, it was due to the inevitable misdiagnosis of problems by the "one size fits all" ideology (allegedly insuring objectivity and comparability) which, in addition, creates perverse incentives to falsify information. Two informative and contemporary examples come from peace-keeping and from the periodic assessment exercise of university programs in Great Britain.[2]

The first example concerns the "best practices" of policing that is part of the UN's effort to create conditions conducive to the rule of law and democracy. It is certainly true that in Weber's ideal type of a functioning bureaucracy (1972, see also the discussion on bureaucracy in Marx's *Kapital* Volume III) part and parcel of a modern state is the separation of home and office, the keeping of written records, and the special status of a cadre of administrators both in terms of their professional training and self-conception. Translated to the problem of law enforcement it means that the police (recognizable by a uniform) is bound by law (which must be inculcated into the cadets), has to keep records of arrests, must handle misdemeanors, and is charged with investigating crimes. Only in this way are courts enabled to do their job.

In the case of a breakdown of civil order, the necessary measures are then easily identified. The police must be distinguishable from self-appointed thugs who pretend to uphold public order. The staff must be instructed in its duties, and it must receive some "practical" training by experienced policemen. Because there must be the wherewithal for keeping reliable records, computers must be supplied (together with the uniforms). When the computers and uniforms arrive the training in policing can begin, all of which seem to represent the necessary steps of getting the "best practices" adopted.

However, usually soon difficulties arise due to "local" resistance. Thus, the usual way of "helping" the truth to come to light at an interrogation might not be in accordance with the new rule book, and such "customary" practices must, of course, be rectified regardless of their "success." But since this is a general problem of policing – vide the interrogation of "terrorists" – one wonders whether it can be "fixed" with some eighty or even two hundred hours of instruction on "proper methods."

More difficult is the task of keeping records, since half of the police force is illiterate (as in Afghanistan), or because it becomes simply

[2] For such proliferation within the UN framework, see e.g. UN-Habitat 2006. Supposedly, this database catalogues 2,650 proven solutions.

pointless in a country which has neither residency registration nor a national identity card (as in Haiti, see Zanotti 2006). Who an alleged perpetrator actually is becomes frequently virtually impossible to ascertain, as this would necessitate a visit to his village in order to ask the people there (who are possibly under the "protection" of another perpetrator). In any case, locals have little incentive to cooperate with "strangers" who leave soon anyway.

In short, the uniforms do their job, but the computers less so and thus they are soon "diverted" to more productive activities in the "private" sector. The security service contracted for instructing the local police writes a positive report about training buttressing it with the necessary statistics, test scores, and charts. The mission is declared a "success," thereby legitimizing not only the intervention itself but also the universal applicability of the "best practices.". Soon, however, we are back to normal, in other words in the conditions before the intervention. The only difference is now that the journalists have departed and some of the competitors in the local security game have received new resources.

The other example comes from the recurrent evaluations Margaret Thatcher bestowed on the British university system. True, there was something rotten in the state of academe, and separating the goats from the sheep, or rather identifying the shirkers, seemed like a good idea. Of course, in order to avoid the predictable bloodletting at the various departments, the assessment had to be based on "objective" criteria, such as publications and the keeping of formal records (syllabi, posted office hours, and so on). These were certainly not capricious criteria, but they assumed heroically that a high score on each of these "variables" equaled "quality" in education.

The result was a system of evaluation in which the entire British academia is for one entire year nearly exclusively occupied with preparing the reports for "making the score" which determine – very much like the IMF country score – the future resource flows to the universities. In the IMF case, the problem of "development" was soon lost from sight as every country might have different problems. Recognizing this, however, presupposes "local knowledge" and necessitates a complicated diagnostics. In both cases, it was simply assumed that "education" or "development" can be measured with a set of variables and a calculated score. After all, the measures were at least "objective" no matter whether development or education actually occurred.

Predictably, this "short-cut" gave rise to crass cases of rent-seeking behavior. Academics with a long publication list could suddenly, if not name their price, nevertheless enhance considerably their salaries if they were moving just before the assessment exercise began. Also, it made universities much better at book-keeping operations. Office hours are now posted everywhere, formal syllabi are collected, publication submissions have increased significantly, and journals proliferate to cash in on this development. "Success" was therefore insured. Meanwhile, more than half of the programs are "excellent" and thus stand out but find themselves, again, surrounded by most of their usual competitors.

The most significant change, though, might be one we would do better without. The "human capital" in the pipeline, that is those preparing for academic jobs, has been properly socialized. As a member of an evaluation panel, I interviewed at least sixty doctoral students from twelve programs in the UK. Only one named "teaching" as one of her interests when embarking on graduate studies. Significantly, she was also the only one who had by now definitively decided against a university career in favor of teaching at a secondary school. All other candidates were well aware that teaching had to be avoided at all costs, and that the mark of a successful academic is to get grants, do research, and eschew teaching obligations. Several of the interviewees even mentioned that deans used "teaching" quite effectively as a punishment for "non-productive" scholars.

What this type of adherence to a "best practice" will do to our future academic teaching, and to our capacity to innovate and to provide the necessary attention and support for our students, will become clear all too soon. I doubt that we will be able to judge the result as a resounding "success," or that the outcome has very much to do with the expectations we had *ex ante*, even though we have followed "best practices." As in the case of development, the goal is quickly lost from sight when one is busy with benchmarks and standards which allegedly get you there. As Weber suggested, in the absence of the second coming we are busy building organizations.

The last critical remark comes from a common experience that should make us suspicious of embracing simple rule-following. After all, we know that the surest way to bring "normal" life to a screeching halt is when for example air traffic controllers, who are not allowed to strike, go strictly "by the book" when they want to press their demands.

Thus, a lot more seems to be required than codifying experiences that may have worked once somewhere. Equally mistaken is to distill some lessons from cases while being oblivious to the framing conditions of the problems we face and to the "local" knowledge required in making the (general) rules work.

Instead of simply subsuming a problem under a set of prescriptions or elaborating through abstractions that successively eliminate the particularities of the cases at hand, we need to make practical judgments that do not follow any of these procedures. We need to reason from case to case: we have to judge similarities and dissimilarities of features that are not susceptible to generalization. Instead, they establish at best an analogy whose *tertium comparationis* might be helpful in recognizing some specific configurations (for a more extensive discussion, see Davis 2005).

All of this is quite at odds with the traditional procedures of social science and legal theory that try to buttress validity claims via a generalization or the universality of an invoked norm. Here we encounter a "false friend" of interdisciplinary undertakings, since universality seems to provide the key in both disciplines for the warrants ensuring the non-idiosyncratic character of our claims. The next section will subject these assumptions to scrutiny and show their problematic character.

The Problem of "Universality"

As hopefully has become evident, relying on "best practices" is usually justified on technical as well as on normative grounds. *Technically*, best practices seem to embody lessons learned and to provide the best available knowledge for solving a problem. *Normatively*, best practices are to be adopted because they go beyond local idiosyncracies.

Unfortunately, both grounds overstate their case and both are subject to rebuttals. Technically, the question remains whether a problem is well-diagnosed so that practices can work the way they are supposed to. The examples given above suggest that even if we want to rely on such support, extreme care has to be taken in framing the problem. Normatively, the strategy of privileging norms of higher universality in order to achieve success is also far from providing a conclusive proof. Admittedly, norms of higher universality are less tainted with the particulars. Yet, this makes the problem of interpretation all the more important when we are trying to "apply" these norms to concrete cases. Here Carl Schmitt's argument that the *quis judicabit* question becomes the decisive criterion (rather than the norm's universal character) is apt and to the point.

It is therefore not surprising that "practices" become quickly imperial projects. The particular practices and interpretations of the most powerful player become by sheer frequency and weight the "model" that is then to be imposed on the rest of the world, never mind its value or technical superiority. Who does not remember the insistence of the United States on its allegedly "transparent" accounting standards, while some of the greatest frauds like Enron and World Inc. were perpetrated right before our eyes? Similarly, when practitioners gave the first warnings of a global financial crisis, due to the massive abuse of reckless lending practices in which banks, regulators, and rating agencies blissfully participated, the economist Ben Bernanke, Chairman of the Federal Reserve, countered such "speculations" by maintaining that high real estate prices in the US "reflected only the strength of the US economy" (see the interview in Grantham 2009). It is indeed cold comfort that such assessments could be buttressed by "hard data" and "laws" of economics.

Normatively, similar fall-back positions can be noticed. The essentially contested concept "democracy" (Connolly 1983) is "operationalized" according to some "variables" familiar from the domestic system and prepared for export. Further questions are reduced to some instrumental scrutiny, such as whether a particular measure is conducive to the larger goal. The question degenerates quickly into one of appraising technical niceties – whether e.g. elections in State X were really multi-party ones as specified by the "operational definition" of democracy – or of ascertaining whether a move was at least "progressive" (read: compatible with "our side"). In the latter case universalism and American particularism seem to fit like hand in glove. As Jean Bethke Elshtain (2003:73f.) so aptly put it:

> The United States is itself premised on a set of universal propositions concerning human dignity and equality. There is no conflict in principle between our national identity and universal claims and commitments.

In Slaughter's defense, her arguments and rhetoric are less triumphant and universal. She hopes that the universality of chauvinism might be tempered by ongoing conversations in the community of courts, and by a judicious use of persuasive arguments irrespective of their origins.

Disturbing in this context is only a Freudian slip. Suddenly a "community" is invoked although all along we have been treated to the new organizational form of "networks," into which the old hard shell of the state has been transformed. Is this an instinctive recognition that "networks," which form and dissolve according to the whims of the participants wanting to get (dis)-connected, cannot do justice to the problems raised? After all, fulfilling legal obligations is something different from casual encounters particularly when "ongoing" and generation-transcending concerns are at issue.

Even more importantly, law cannot be stripped of its constitutive nature and of the dimension of meaning it embodies. This is so even if the focus on dispute resolution does not foreground those elements but, instead, emphasizes "technique." While the latter, as a neutral tool, is easily compatible with notions of networks, and the essential arbitrariness of contacts and connections, the concept of a community speaks more clearly to the former concerns, namely to the architecture of the legal enterprise and its connection with a "society" as an ongoing and trans-generational concern.

While the law as a technique is compatible with the image of a legal professional as a "hired gun," we have different expectations of a judge. She is not to carry the brief of a client but to adjudicate according to laws and standards that reflect the values and historical experiences of a specific group that has "authorized" them.

This does not mean that the laws so authorized have to be principally at odds with similar rules adopted by other societies, or that the specific laws cannot be brought in closer logical relationship with higher order norms or principles, as natural law adherents are always pointing out. But it does mean that it is a futile endeavor to dream of simply ascending the ladder of abstraction by using formal criteria in the hope of thereby circumventing historical contingencies or the particularities of "politics" (which is always about the particular as both Aristotle and Machiavelli remind us). Political differences arise because they point to genuine dilemmas that can no longer be simply resolved by the traditional logical means of giving precedence to the more general norm due to its more "universal" nature (Kristeva 1993 notwithstanding).

After all, this is precisely the point underlying the tragedy of Antigone (Sophocles 1991). Contrary to the usual interpretation that her appeal to a "universal law," in which human rights advocates see the first inkling of the cosmopolitan law of the future, Antigone's appeal concerns the respect of the particular duties she as a sister has to her brother. These ought not to be overridden by the "general" laws of the state.

This problem of particular duties lies at the heart of political obligations. Perhaps it also explains why even such universalists as Kant ([1795] 2005) wanted to see "cosmopolitan law" restricted only to a "right of visit." He did not conceive of it as a legislative program or as an ever-expanding list of "human rights" (Held 1995), such as an alleged "right to free trade" (for a daring expansion of this cosmopolitan law, see Petersmann 2002).

After a moment's reflection, such a proliferation of rights turns out to be only a cheap rhetorical gambit to support the desiderata of a particular life-style at the turn of the century. The artificiality of these constructions becomes clear when suddenly problems of collective life have to be translated into a catalogue of individual subjective rights. Thus, the understandable preference for a democratic form of government mutates suddenly into a subjective "right to democracy" (Franck 1992) committing thereby a category mistake of the first order.

Naturally, this error is not corrected by being repeated in endless re-recitations of the "dominant opinion." After all, democracy is only one way to politically organize a concrete community (see e.g. Cohen 2004) in order to procure the collective goods necessary for a common life and cope with historical contingencies. Thus "democracy" does not pertain to the individual in his status as a free agent, which is the domain of "human rights." Hence, there are many important questions and many worthwhile goals that are, despite their desirability, not individual rights at all. For an analogy, consider that the individual shareholders' rights are not those of the corporation.

Usually, liberal theorists have a problem with particularity. They either ignore the problem in a rather cavalier fashion or try to "solve" it by resorting to some form of transcendental foundationalist argument (for the former, see Rawls 1971; for the latter, Rawls 1993). Neither strategy is convincing.

In the first case, the problem is often part of the initial assumptions. One focuses on an existing functioning community, and in a modern version of the *interpretatio Romana* one's own society then provides more or less the material for idealizations of "best practices." Then, other forms of governance and systems of law can be seen easily as predecessors overtaken by historical events, as exemplified by Locke's (1952) famous dictum in the *Second Treatise* or by Rawls's category of "decent peoples."

As to the other "solution," i.e. the case of providing transcendental foundations, one might use the metaphor of a contract, as e.g. the early Rawls does, but which turns out to be no contract at all! The discovered principles chosen behind the "veil of ignorance" are not the result of a meeting of wills of the contracting parties. Rather, it is the cognitive status of these principles that allegedly commands assent. Therefore, they are not subject to revision in light of later experiences or to compromises characteristic of negotiations. Moreover, they need not even be chosen collectively, since any "reasonable" chooser will come to the same result (for a trenchant criticism of this conception, see e.g. Gray 1991a, 1991b).

In such constructions one has the sneaking suspicion that we are attempting to sing into existence a world in which we – against all experience – are somehow ready to treat each other as pure ends, and in which politics no longer raises its ugly head. Yet, wanting to wish the political out of existence is not the same as actually achieving a solution to the paradox that characterizes it. Namely, the existence of a multiplicity of views without a compelling algorithm to resolve these differences must be accommodated with the need to make collectively binding decisions. This dilemma shows why "rational" solutions will represent only a small part of the general choice space. This is why "will," or the capacity to commit oneself to certain courses of action (without constant updating), lies at the bottom of both politics and law, since both deal with praxis and not with universal "truths" that "theory" addresses (Kratochwil 2007a).

For this reason, norms are needed in order to stabilize expectations counterfactually, because absent such stabilization, no rational calculation is possible. Also, we need "judgment" that is no longer susceptible to generalizations or statements in universal form. True, we do need reasons buttressing such decisions (otherwise we could not distinguish between a reasoned and a capricious choice), but despite a superficial resemblance between the invoking of norms and the requirement in law to treat "like cases alike" a closer look shows that in both cases we are not dealing with logical processes of either simple "subsumption" or "generalization."

For one, under which norm a case at hand is subsumed (out of a variety of possibilities) remains hidden when we focus solely on the subsumption process. Second, what is "alike" depends on analogous reasoning and the virtually inexhaustible ways of specifying the *tertium comparationis* and not on simple inductive inferences.

Thus, the view espoused here is significantly at odds with the usual tendency, prevalent in various liberal theories of "law," to derive our political and legal obligations from universal principles of justice. Of course, universalism does prevent us from making all too self-serving arguments that neglect the interests of others affected by our choices. Similarly, the universality of basic moral principles provides a starting point for any critical reflection and deliberation. Yet, both do little in deciding particular cases or in explaining those obligations not owed to all but rather to those standing in a particular relationship to us (for further discussion of this point, see Haltern 2006). Attempts to construe our particular obligations, for example to our community or to fellow-citizens, as derivative from the justice of the regime to which we belong miss precisely this point. We, for example as Frenchmen or Italians, have special obligations to abide by French or Italian law, not by those of Australia or Switzerland, even if the latter are demonstrably also just regimes.

These special obligations are neither simply the result of the benefits we receive in pursuing our goals, nor general maxims that laws are necessary to avoid conflicts and to regulate interferences. Rather, the obligations derive from our predicament as historical beings and from the recognition that who we "are" involves us in deliberations and projects that transcend purely cognitive operations. As such we never start from "scratch" as the imagery of the "market" or even the metaphor of a "game" suggest, both of which we might enter and exit *ad libitum*. In contrast, in politics we become aware that we are always part of a "drama" in which what happens today has a long past casting its shadow and setting the stage for our actions and their success or failure.

Strangely enough, liberal theory frequently recognizes the power of the shadow of the future (discounted at different rates). Yet, it is apparently less able to integrate "historicity" into its corpus. This leaves us with the traditional veneration for forefathers or founding fathers, and for missionary political projects that promise deliverance in the future. But such an approach adds little to critical reflection and to illuminating the intersection of history, politics, and law. Placed in a transcendental realm beyond any contingency of history and politics, it is no surprise that liberal theory has little to say about synergies of law and politics that define the realm of praxis. Instead, we are thrown back to well-known puzzles that surface when treating praxis from a theoretical perspective instead of taking into account its specifically practical dimensions.

Admittedly, law can be depicted as a logically closed system so that any rule can be shown to be created by some other (secondary) rule. To assume, however, that by such logical operations one can analyze the reality of law in action, even if considered only through the narrow focus of adjudication, is to submit to legalism of the worst kind. The effectiveness of the rule of law depends crucially on extra-legal means, namely on the institutionalization of a political process contained in a constitution to which the law has to defer. In this way a "people" come to see themselves as authors of their choices, a point which in turn buttresses their readiness to make their community an ongoing and generation-transcending concern.

In this manner a "constitution" can claim "loyalty" and respect for the limiting and enabling conditions of the order that thereby takes shape (see Kahn 1997). Here "loyalty," rather than the logical criterion of "universality," provides the glue that holds things together. The rhetoric of universalism simply leaves out that duties flowing from loyalty are quite different from those resulting from universal norms or from such specific undertakings as contracts.

Loyalty is owed to those specific people and institutions that define us as historical subjects and establish who we are. Here, the interrogation by the laws in Socrates's dream shortly before his execution is one classical topos that addresses this issue (Plato 1973). One might be obliged to strangers due to promises made to them, or on the basis of their status as persons that require recognition. But one can only be loyal to friends and others that have become part of "us." Thus, loyalty connects us to particular groups and invokes specific experiences. It cannot be tailor-made as a freestanding, de-contextualized structure that can be imposed upon a group.

This seems to be the reason why loyalty becomes one of the fundamental social mechanisms that cannot be reduced to either "exit" or "voice," as Hirschman's (1970) analysis suggests. In this way, "law" becomes one of the main repositories of particular experiences and of meanings for the group. The group thereby reflects upon its practices and understands itself as the "author" of its projects, an understanding which legal "texts" alone could not produce even if they invoked universal values and satisfied criteria of justice.

The neglect of this dimension of law explains then also the contemporary controversy concerning the use of authorities. One example is citing decisions of foreign courts which in Slaughter's terms are apparently transformed thereby from a network to a "community." It seems that it is the result of obscuring the relationship between authority and authorship.

While there are good reasons to make allowances for using the best available knowledge and some unorthodox sources for certain technical aspects of resolving conflicts by adjudication, not all questions before the courts will be susceptible to such a reduction, simply because not all the reasons we accept are content-dependent. What matters most in supporting a court's decision is not what the reasons say but where they come from. At issue in cases that are resolved judicially is not the authority of reasonableness in arriving at a conclusion that all things considered a "wise man" or a philosopher could have suggested. In law, rather, the authority of the institutional standing of "source" matters. In short, we deal here with a *content-independent* form of authority such as whether an "official" can give me a ticket or incarcerate me. In this way precedents or statutes bind the judge and stabilize expectations, precisely because they have been designed to cut short content-dependent deliberations.

Thus, "authority" is not all of one cloth. There is a distinction between having authority (content-independent) and being an authority (content-dependent). There are also issues of "style" and "persuasive" authority that raise surprisingly complex questions.

Regarding style: is for example a Wikipedia citation appropriate as a source influencing a court's decision? Or do we need weightier reasons, something "more," or a "surplus of meaning," as the verbal root of the term "authority" suggests ("authority" from *augere* to increase or enhance)?[3] This is not a peripheral question.

Similarly, we can "understand" and accept that a judge invokes the "prudent man or person" argument as an ideal type in a decision. But we would most certainly object if he quoted his daughter as a source, even if all considered her to be a very sensible and prudent person. For all intents and purposes, she may have even demonstrated her good sense in a widely televised reality show!

Thus we can answer the crucial question: are decisions of foreign courts really cited because of their intellectual acumen – making them so to speak content-dependent authorities – or is it rather that they are pronouncements of "courts" and thus derive their status from a content-independent source? If the latter is the case, questions of

[3] For a fundamental discussion, see Schauer 2008.

legitimacy *do* arise and one need not be an ardent adherent of Judge Scalia's jurisprudence to see the problem with Slaughter's position. Slaughter introduces some form of "optional" authority by which one seems to be able to eat one's cake and have it too, and all is justified in terms of a "liberal" theory of law that is however increasingly located in an abstract utopia instead of being an expression of a concrete "people."

Thus, by a strange concatenation of circumstances, liberalism has mutated from a political project of the rule of law and a defense of the "old freedoms," as in the case of the Glorious Revolution, into a tutelary regime that leaves little room for meaningful choice. Instead of the citizens, we see how an international "expertocracy," allegedly "safeguarding" human dignity, informs the people what they actually ought to want.

References

Abbott, Kenneth W., Robert Keohane, Andrew Moravcsik, Anne-Marie Slaughter, and Duncan Snidal. 2000. "The Concept of Legalization." *International Organization* 54:401–419.

Boyle, James. 2003. "Foreword: The Opposite of Property?" *Law and Contemporary Problems* 66:1–32.

Carothers, Thomas (ed.). 2006. *Promoting the Rule of Law Abroad*. Washington, DC: Carnegie.

Chayes, Abram, Thomas Ehrlich, and Andreas F. Lowenfeld. 1968. *International Legal Process: Materials for an Introductory Course*. Boston: Little Brown.

Cohen, Jean L. 2004. "Whose Sovereignty? Empire Versus International Law." *Ethics and International Affairs* 18:1–24.

Connolly, William E. 1983. *The Terms of Political Discourse*. Princeton, NJ: Princeton University Press.

Davis, James W. 2005. *Terms of Inquiry: On the Theory and Practice of Political Science*. Baltimore: Johns Hopkins University Press.

Dillon, Michael and Luis Lobo-Guerrero. 2008. "Biopolitics of Security in the 21st Century: An Introduction." *Review of International Studies* 34:265–292.

Dupuy, Pierre-Marie. 1997. "The Constitutional Dimension of the Charter of the United Nations Revisited." Pp. 1–33 in *Max Planck Yearbook of United Nations Law*, vol. 1, edited by A.von Bogdandy and R. Wolfrum. Leiden: Martinus Nijhoff.

Elshtain, Jean Bethke. 2003. "International Justice as Equal Regard and the Use of Force." *Ethics and International Affairs* 17:63–75.

Fassbender, Bardo. 2005. "Sovereignty and Constitutionalism in International Law." Pp. 115–43 in *Sovereignty in Transition*, edited by N. Walker. Oxford: Hart.

Franck, Thomas M. 1992. "The Emerging Right to Democratic Governance." *The American Journal of International Law* 86:46–91.

Fredman, Sandra. 2008. *Human Rights Transformed: Positive Rights and Positive Duties*. Oxford: Oxford University Press.

Goldsmith, Jack and Eric A. Posner. 2006. *The Limits of International Law*. Oxford: Oxford University Press.

Grantham, Jeremy. 2009. "Kurzfristig Lernen Wir Enorm Viel – Aber Auf Lange Sicht Nichts." *Capital* 1:83–7.
Gray, John. 1991a. *Liberalism: Essays in Political Philosophy*. London: Routledge.
——. 1991b. "Social Contract, Community, and Ideology." Pp. 28–44 in *Liberalism: Essays in Political Philosophy*, by John Gray. London: Routledge.
Grenville, Clark and Louis B. Sohn. 1966. *World Peace through World Law: Two Alternative Plans*. Cambridge, MA: Harvard University Press.
Haas, Michael. 2008. *International Human Rights: A Comprehensive Introduction*. New York: Routledge.
Hall, Rodney Bruce and Thomas J. Biersteker (eds.). 2002. *The Emergence of Private Authority in Global Governance*. Oxford: Oxford University Press.
Haltern, Ulrich. 2006. "Tomuschats Traum: Zur Bedeutung Von Souveränität Im Völkerrecht." Pp. 867–898 in *Völkerrecht Als Wertordnung – Common Values in International Law: Festschrift Für Christian Tomuschat*, edited by P.-M. Dupuy, B. Fassbender, M. N. Shaw, and K.-P. Sommermann. Kehl am Rein: N. P. Engel.
Hardin, Garrett. 1968. "The Tragedy of the Commons." *Science* 162:1243–1248.
Held, David. 1995. *Democracy and the Global Order: From the Modern State to Cosmopolitan Governance*. Stanford: Stanford University Press.
Hess, Charlotte and Elinor Ostrom. 2007. *Understanding Knowledge as a Commons: From Theory to Practice*. Cambridge, MA: MIT Press.
Hirschman, Albert O. 1970. *Exit, Voice, and Loyalty: Responses to Decline in Firms, Organizations, and States*. Cambridge, MA: Harvard University Press.
International Law Commission and Martti Koskenniemi. 2006. "Fragmentation of International Law." UN Doc. A/CN.4/L.686.
Kahn, Paul W. 1997. *The Reign of Law*. New Haven: Yale University Press.
Kant, Immanuel. [1795] 2005. *Perpetual Peace*. New York: Cosimo Classics.
Keck, Margaret and Kathryn Sikkink. 1999. "Transnational Advocacy Networks in International and Regional Politics." *International Social Science Journal* 159:89–101.
Kennedy, David. 1986. "Primitive Legal Scholarship." *Harvard International Law Journal* 27:1–98.
——. 2003. "The Politics of the Invisible College: International Governance and the Politics of Expertise." Pp. 83–133 in *Transformative Change and Global Order*, edited by D. A. Fuchs and F. Kratochwil. Muenster: Lit.
Kingsbury, Benedict, Nico Krisch, and Richard B. Stewart. 2005. "The Emergence of Global Administrative Law." *Law and Contemporary Problems* 68:15–61.
Klabbers, Jan. 2004. "Constitutionalism Lite." *International Organizations Law Review* 1:31–58.
Koh, Harold Hongju. 1996. "Transnational Legal Process." *Nebraska Law Review* 75:181–208.
Kratochwil, Friedrich. 2007a. "Of False Promises and Good Bets: A Plea for a Pragmatic Approach to Theory Building (the Tartu Lecture)." *Journal of International Relations and Development* 10:1–15.
——. 2007b. "Rethinking the 'Inter' in International Politics." *Millennium* 35:495–511.
——. Forthcoming. "Leaving Sovereignty Behind? An Inquiry into the Politics of Post-Modernity." in [Working Title], edited by R. A. Falk and R. Thakur.
Krisch, Nico. 2006. "The Pluralism of Global Administrative Law." *The European Journal of International Law* 17:247–278.
Kristeva, Julia. 1993. *Nations without Nationalism*. New York: Columbia University Press.
Levinson, Sanford. 2004. "Looking Abroad When Interpreting the U.S. Constitution: Some Reflections." *Texas International Law Journal* 353:362–363.

Locke, John. 1952. *The Second Treatise of Government*, edited by Thomas P. Peardon. New York: Liberal Arts Press.
Luhmann, Niklas. 1983. *Rechtssoziologie*. Opladen: Westdeutscher Verlag.
McDougal, Myres. 1955. "The Hydrogen Bomb Tests and the International Law of the Sea." *The American Journal of International Law* 49:356–361.
—— and Harold Laswell. 1966. "The Identification and Appraisal of Diverse Systems of Public Order." Pp. 45–74 in *The Strategy of World Order*, vol. 2, *International Law*, edited by R. A. Falk and S.H. Mendlovitz. New York: World Law Fund.
Michelman, Frank I. 2003. "Constitutional Legitimation for Political Acts." *The Modern Law Review* 66:1–15.
Moravcsik, Andrew. 1997. "Taking Preferences Seriously: A Liberal Theory of International Politics" *International Organization* 51:513–553.
Newman, Edward, Ramesh Chandra Thakur, and John Tirman. 2006. *Multilateralism under Challenge? Power, Political Order, and Structural Change*. Tokyo: United Nations University Press.
O'Connell, Mary Ellen. 1999. "New International Legal Process." *American Journal of International Law* 93:334–351.
Ostrom, Elinor, Roy Gardner, and James Walker. 1994. *Rules, Games, and Common-Pool Resources*. Ann Arbor: University of Michigan Press.
Palombella, Gianluigi and Neil Walker. 2009. *Relocating the Rule of Law*. Oxford: Hart.
Petersmann, Ernst-Ulrich. 2002. "Constitutionalism and WTO Law: From a State-Centered Approach Towards a Human Rights Approach in International Economic Law." Pp. 32–67 in *The Political Economy of International Trade Law*, edited by D. L. M. Kennedy and J. D. Southwick. Cambridge: Cambridge University Press.
Plato. 1973. "Crito." Pp. 471–486 in *The Republic and Other Works*, by Plato, translated by B.Jowett. Garden City: Doubleday.
Pocock, John G. A. 1957. *The Ancient Constitution and the Feudal Law: A Study of English Historical Thought in the Seventeenth Century*. Cambridge: Cambridge University Press.
Rawls, John. 1971. *A Theory of Justice*. Cambridge, MA: Harvard University Press.
——. 1993. "The Law of the Peoples." Pp. 41–82 in *On Human Rights: The Oxford Amnesty Lectures*, edited by S. Hurley and S. Shute. New York: Basic Books.
Scelle, Georges. 1932–1934. *Précis De Droit Des Gens: Principes Et Systématique*. Paris: Librairie du Recueil Sirey.
Schacter, Oscar. 1977. "Twilight Existence of Nonbinding International Agreements." *American Journal of International Law* 71:296–304.
Schauer, Frederick F. 2008. "Authority and Authorities." *University of Virginia Law School*, Working Paper No. 92.
Slaughter, Anne-Marie. 1993. "Regulating the World: Multilateralism, International Law, and the Projection of the New Deal Regulatory State." Pp. 125–156 in *Multilateralism Matters: The Theory and Praxis of an Institutional Form*, edited by J. G. Ruggie. New York: Columbia University Press.
——. 1995. "International Law in a World of Liberal States." *European Journal of International Law* 6:503–538.
——. 1997. "The Real New World Order." *Foreign Affairs* 76:183–197.
——. 2000. "A Liberal Theory of International Law." American Society of International Law: Proceedings of the 94th annual meeting.
——. 2004. *A New World Order*. Princeton: Princeton University Press.
—— and William Burke-White. 2002. "An International Constitutional Moment." *Harvard International Law Journal* 43:1–22.
—— and John Ikenberry. 2006. "Forging a World of Liberty under Law: U.S. National Security in the 21st Century." Princeton Project on National Security, Woodrow Wilson School of Public and International Affairs, Princeton University.

Sophocles. 1991. *Antigone*. Translated by P.Roche. New York: Mentor.

Tomuschat, Christian. 2008. *Human Rights: Between Idealism and Realism*. Oxford: Oxford University Press.

UN-Habitat. 2006. "Best Practices: Database in Improving the Living Environment." Accessed January 18, 2008 (http://www.bestpractices.org/).

Virally, Michel. 1991. "Unilateral Acts of International Organizations." Pp. 241–263 in *International Law: Achievements and Prospects*, edited by M. Bedjaoui. Paris: UNESCO.

Weber, Max. 1972. *Wirtschaft Und Gesellschaft*, edited by J. Winckelmann. Tübingen: Mohr.

Zanotti, Laura. 2006. "Taming Chaos: A Foucauldian View of UN Peacekeeping, Democracy and Normalization." *International Peacekeeping* 13:150–167.

INDEX

INTERNATIONAL STUDIES IN SOCIOLOGY AND SOCIAL ANTHROPOLOGY

21. FUSÉ, T. (ed.). *Modernization and Stress in Japan.* 1975. ISBN 90 04 04344 6
22. SMITH, B.L. (ed.). *Religion and Social Conflict in South Asia.* 1976. ISBN 90 04 04510 4
23. MAZRUI, A.A. (ed.). *The Warrior Tradition in Modern Africa.* 1977. ISBN 90 04 05646 7
25. SMITH, B.L. (ed.). *Religion and the Legitimation of Power in South Asia.* 1978. ISBN 90 04 05674 2
31. LELE, J. (ed.). *Tradition and Modernity in* Bhakti *Movements.* 1981. ISBN 90 04 06370 6
32. ARMER, J.M. *Comparative Sociological Research in the 1960s and 1970s.* 1982. ISBN 90 04 06487 7
33. GALATY, J.G. & P.C. SALZMAN (eds.). *Change and Development in Nomadic and Pastor-al Societies.* 1981. ISBN 90 04 06587 3
34. LUPRI, E. (ed.). *The Changing Position of Women in Family and Society. A Cross-National Comparison.* 1983. ISBN 90 04 06845 7
35. IVERSON, N. (ed.). *Urbanism and Urbanization. Views, Aspects and Dimensions.* 1984. ISBN 90 04 06920 8
36. MALIK, Y.K. *Politics, Technology, and Bureaucracy in South Asia.* 1983. ISBN 90 04 07027 3
37. LENSKI, G. (ed.). *Current Issues and Research in Macrosociology.* 1984. ISBN 90 04 07052 4
39. TIRYAKIAN, E.A. (ed.). *The Global Crisis. Sociological Analyses and Responses.* 1984. ISBN 90 04 07284 5
40. LAWRENCE, B. (ed.). *Ibn Khaldun and Islamic Ideology.* 1984. ISBN 90 04 07567 4
41. HAJJAR, S.G. (ed.). *The Middle East: from Transition to Development.* 1985. ISBN 90 04 07694 8
43. CARMAN, J.B. & F.A. MARGLIN (eds.). *Purity and Auspiciousness in Indian Society.* 1985. ISBN 90 04 07789 8
46. SMITH, B.L. & H.B. REYNOLDS (eds.). *The City as a Sacred Center. Essays on Six Asian Contexts.* 1987. ISBN 90 04 08471 1
47. MALIK, Y.K. & D.K. VAJPEYI (eds.). *India. The Years of Indira Ghandi.* 1988. ISBN 90 04 08681 1
48. CLARK, C. & J. LEMCO (eds.). *State and Development.* 1988. ISBN 90 04 08833 4
49. GUTKIND, P.C.W. (ed.). *Third World Workers. Comparative International Labour Studies.* 1988. ISBN 90 04 08788 5
50. SELIGMAN, A.B. *Order and Transcendence. The Role of Utopias and the Dynamics of Civi-lization.* 1989. ISBN 90 04 08975 6
51. JABBRA, J.G. *Bureaucracy and Development in the Arab World.* 1989. ISBN 90 04 09194 7

52. KAUTSKY, J.H. (ed.). *Karl Kautsky and the Social Science of Classical Marxism.* 1989. ISBN 90 04 09193 9
53. KAPUR, A. (ed.). *The Diplomatic Ideas and Practices of Asian States.* 1990. ISBN 90 04 09289 7
54. KIM, Q.-Y. (ed.). *Revolutions in the Third World.* 1991. ISBN 90 04 09355 9
55. KENNEDY, C.H. & D. J. LOUSCHER (eds.). *Civil Military Interaction in Asia and Afri-ca.* 1991. ISBN 90 04 09359 1
56. RAGIN, C.C. (ed.). *Issues and Alternatives in Comparative Social Research.* 1991. ISBN 90 04 09360 5
57. CHOUDHRY, N.K. (ed.). *Canada and South Asian Development. Trade and Aid.* 1991. ISBN 90 04 09416 4
58. RAZIA AKTER BANU, U.A.B. (ed.). *Islam in Bangladesh.* 1992. ISBN 90 04 09497 0
61. AHMAD, A. (ed.). *Science and Technology Policy for Economic Development in Africa.* 1993. ISBN 90 04 09659 0
62. VAJPEYI, D.K. (ed.). *Modernizing China.* 1994. ISBN 90 04 10046 6
63. BRADSHAW, Y.W. (ed.). *Education in Comparative Perspective.* New Lessons from around the World. 1997. ISBN 90 04 10734 7
64. UDOGU, E.I. (ed.). *Democracy and Democratization in Africa.* Toward the 21st Century. 1997. ISBN 90 04 10733 9
65. BEHAR, J.E. & A.G. CUZÁN (eds.). *At the Crossroads of Development.* Transnational Challenges to Developed and Developing Societies. 1997. ISBN 90 04 10732 0
66. LAUDERDALE, P. & R. AMSTER (eds.). *Lives in the Balance.* Perspectives on Global Injustice and Inequality. 1997. ISBN 90 04 10875 0
67. LOVEJOY, P.E. & P.A.T. WILLIAMS (eds.). *Displacement and the Politics of Violence in Nigeria.* 1997. ISBN 90 04 10876 9
68. JABBRA, J.G. & N.W. JABBRA (eds.). *Challenging Environmental Issues.* Middle Eastern Perspectives. 1997. ISBN 90 04 10877 7
69. SASAKI, M. (ed.). *Values and Attitudes Across Nations and Time.* 1998. ISBN 90 04 11219 7
70. SPERLING, J., Y. MALIK & D. LOUSCHER (eds.). *Zones of Amity, Zones of Enmity.* The Prospects for Economic and Military Security in Asia. 1998. ISBN 90 04 11218 9
71. NANDI, P.K. & S.M. SHAHIDULLAH (eds.). *Globalization and the Evolving World Society.* 1998. ISBN 90 04 11247 2
72. ARTS, W. & L. HALMAN (eds.). *New Directions in Quantitative Comparative Sociology.* 1999. ISBN 90 04 11411 4
73. ISHWARAN, K. (ed.). *Ascetic Culture: Renunciation and Worldly Engagement.* 1999. ISBN 90 04 11412 2
74. PATTERSON, R. (ed.). *Science and Technology in Southern Africa and East and South Asia*, 1999. ISBN 90 04 11413 0
75. ARTS, W. (ed.). *Through a Glass, Darkly.* Blurred images of cultural tradition and modernity over distance and time. 2000. ISBN 90 04 11597 8
76. GERRITSEN, J.W. *The Control of Fuddle and Flash*, A Sociological History of the Regulation of Alcohol and Opiates. 2000. ISBN 90 04 11640 0
77. LEE, W.C. (ed.). *Taiwan in Perspective.* 2000. ISBN 90 04 11849 7

78. LUMUMBA-KASONGO, T. (ed.). *Dynamics and Policy Implications of the Global Reforms at the End of the Second Millennium*. 2000. ISBN 90 04 11847 0
79. HARRIS, R. & M. SEID (eds.). *Critical Perspectives on Globalization and Neoliberalism in the Developing Countries*. 2000. ISBN 90 04 11850 0
80. HOWARD, G.J. & G. NEWMAN (eds.), *Varieties of Comparative Criminology*. 2001. ISBN 90 04 12245 1
81. NDEGWA, S.N. (ed.), *A Decade of Democracy in Africa*. 2001. ISBN 90 04 12244 3
82. JREISAT, J.E. (ed.), *Governance and Developing Countries*. 2002. ISBN 90 04 12247 8
83. KEITA, M. (ed.), *Conceptualizing/Re-Conceptualizing Africa*. The construction of African Historical Identity. 2002. ISBN 90 04 12420 9
84. BERG, R. VAN DEN, *Nyoongar People of Australia*. Perspectives on Racism and Multiculturalism. 2002. ISBN 90 04 12478 0
85. DOGAN, M. (ed.), *Elite Configurations at the Apex of Power*. 2003. ISBN 90 04 12808 5
86. SENGERS, G., *Women and Demons*. Cult Healing in Islamic Egypt. 2003. ISBN 90 04 12771 2
87. WILSON, H.T. *The Vocation of Reason*. Studies in Critical Theory and Social Science in the Age of Max Weber. Edited and with a Foreword by T.M. Kemple. 2003. ISBN 90 04 13631 2
88. ZEGEYE, A. and R.L. HARRIS, *Media, Identity and the Public Sphere in Post-Apartheid South Africa*. 2003. ISBN 90 04 12633 3
89. INGLEHART, R. (ed.), *Human Values and Social Change*. Findings from the Values Surveys. 2003. ISBN 90 04 12810 7
90. BEN-RAFAEL, E. (ed.), *Sociology and Ideology*. 2003. ISBN 90 04 13104 3
91. AL-HAJ, M., *Immigration and Ethnic Formation in a Deeply Divided Society*. The Case of the 1990s Immigrants from the Former Soviet Union in Israel. 2004. ISBN 90 04 13625 8
92. AMINEH, M., *Central Eurasia in World Politics*. Conflict, Security, and Development. 2004. ISBN 90 04 12809 3
93. VINKEN, H., J. SOETERS & P. ESTER (eds.), *Comparing Cultures*. Dimensions of Culture in a Comparative Perspective. 2004. ISBN 90 04 13115 9
94. ASSIÉ-LUMUMBA, N.T., *Cyberspace, Distance Learning, and Higher Education in Develo-ping Countries*. Old and Emergent Issues of Access, Pedagogy, and Knowledge Production. 2004. ISBN 90 04 13121 3
95. HARRIS, R.L. and M. Seid, *Globalization and Health*. 2004. ISBN 90 04 14145 6
96. DOGAN, M. (ed.), *Political Mistrust and the Discrediting of Politicians*. 2005. ISBN 90 04 14530 3
97. MÉRIOT, S.-A., *Nostalgic Cooks*. Another French Paradox. 2006. ISBN 90 04 14346 7
99. EISENSTADT, S.N., *The Great Revolutions and the Civilizations of Modernity*. 2006. ISBN 90 04 14812 4
100. NIEUWENHUYS, E. (ed.), *Neo-Liberal Globalism and Social Sustainable Globalisation*. 2006. ISBN 90 04 15159 1
101. SCHRYER, F., *Farming in a Global Economy*. A Case Study of Dutch Immigrant Farmers in Canada. 2006. ISBN 90 04 15170 2

102. SHLAPENTOKH, D. (ed.), *Russia between East and West.* Scholarly Debates on Eurasianism. 2006. ISBN 90 04 15415 9
103. DAY, R.B. & J. MASCIULLI (eds.), *Globalization and Political Ethics.* 2006. ISBN 90 04 15581 3
104. ESMER, Y. & T. PETTERSSON (eds.), *Measuring and Mapping Cultures.* 25 Years of Comparative Value Surveys. 2007. ISBN 978 90 04 15820 7
105. PATTERSON, R. (ed.), *African Brain Circulation.* Beyond the Drain-Gain Debate. 2007. ISBN 978 90 04 15885 6
106. AMINEH, M.P. (ed.), *The Greater Middle East in Global Politics.* Social Science Perspec tives on the Changing Geography of the World Politics. 2007. ISBN-13: 978 90 04 15859 7, ISBN-10: 90 04 15859 6
107. SASAKI, M. (ed.), *Elites: New Comparative Perspectives.* 2007. ISBN 978 90 04 16402 4
108. RIETJENS, S.J.H. *Civil-Military Cooperation in Response to a Complex Emergency.* Just Another Drill? 2008. ISBN 978 90 04 16327 0
109. SASAKI, M. (ed.), *New Frontiers in Comparative Sociology.* 2009. ISBN 978 90 04 17034 6
110. SCIULLI, D., *Professions in Civil Society and the State.* Invariant Foundations and Consequences. 2009. ISBN 978 90 04 17831 1
111. BEST, H. & J. HIGLEY (eds.), *Democratic Elitism.* New Theoretical and Comparative Perspectives. 2010. ISBN 978 90 04 17939 4
112. BORA, A. & H. HAUSENDORF (eds.), *Democratic Transgressions of Law.* Governing Technology through Public Participation. 2010. ISBN 978 90 04 18043 7
113. HUSSAIN, I., *Afghanistan, Iraq and Post-conflict Governance.* Damoclean Democracy? 2010. ISBN 978 90 04 18033 8
114. NIEWÖHNER, J. & T. SCHEFFER (eds.), *Thick Comparison.* Reviving the Ethnographic Aspiration. 2010. ISBN 978 90 04 18113 7
115. MORLINO, L. & G. PALOMBELLA (eds.), *Rule of Law and Democracy.* Inquiries into Internal and External Issues. 2010. ISBN 978 90 04 18169 4

www.ingramcontent.com/pod-product-compliance
Lightning Source LLC
LaVergne TN
LVHW080847300926
849162LV00003B/366